Pittu D. Laungani

Understanding Cross-Cultural Psychology

Eastern and Western Perspectives

SAGE Publications

London • Thousand Oaks • New Delhi

SAGE Publications Ltd
1 Oliver's Yard
55 City Road
London EC1Y 1SP

SAGE Publications Inc.
2455 Teller Road
Thousand Oaks, California 91320

SAGE Publications India Pvt Ltd
B-42, Panchsheel Enclave
Post Box 4109
New Delhi 110 017

British Library Cataloguing in Publication data

A catalogue record for this book is available from the British Library

ISBN-10 0-7619-7153-X   ISBN-13 978-0-7619-7153-5
ISBN-10 0-7619-7154-8 (pbk)   ISBN-13 978-0-7619-7154-2

Library of Congress Control Number: 2006927823

Typeset by C&M Digitals (P) Ltd., Chennai, India
Printed and bound in Great Britain by Athenaeum Press, Gateshead
Printed on paper from sustainable resources

Contents

To my wife Ann

There are hundreds of wonderful stories in *The Mahabharata*, the great Indian Epic. There is one I believe you will appreciate. It concerns Princess Savitri who is in love with Satyavan, son of an old hermit. She is keen to marry him but the sages and the seers have prophesied that Satyavan is a doomed man, destined to die in a year. She disregards the prophecies and marries Satyavan, who is unaware of the prophecy.

On the dreaded day Savitri accompanies her husband into the woods. While chopping wood with his hatchet, he swoons and calls his wife as he falls. As she supports him she sees in the distance Lord Yama – the God of Death. He has come to collect Satyavan's soul. She pleads with Lord Yama to spare her husband's life. What is written cannot be undone, he says to her and bids her to return home and perform the funeral rites. She refuses and follows him. She is prepared to follow him to the ends of the earth. Yama, pleased with her steadfast devotion, grants her a boon, which restores her husband's life.

Seventeen years ago, the Consultants in the hospital told you that I had but a *few days to survive*. For 17 years you have fought with the Grim Reaper, propped me up, and have kept me alive. I owe these 17 years (and hopefully a few more may follow) of my life to your love and ceaseless efforts.

Pittu

To Lana Starmac, Roy Moodley, and OISE

By the time one reaches the ripe old age of eight or nine, reality replaces fantasy. One stops believing in Santa Claus. Not so in my case. Let me explain why. I have never had any connections with Toronto University, other than a friendly encounter with Professor Roy Moodley whom I met at the British Association of Counselling and Psychotherapy (BACP) Conference in London in 2004.

A month or two later he wrote to me, asking me if he could suggest my name as a nominee for the Lifetime Achievement Award, which the Ontario Institute for Studies in Education (OISE), Toronto University, offered to distinguished academics from around the world. I thought it was some kind of a joke (or a covert research project) and decided to go along with it, not unduly worried about making a fool of myself.

But I was wrong. A few months later I received a letter from Professor Moodley and Professor Lana Stermac that the University of Toronto, after due consideration by their academic committee, had decided to offer me the award. Who says Santa Claus does not exist!

It gives me great pleasure to dedicate this book to Professor Lana Stermac and Professor Roy Moodley and to OISE, Toronto University, for their kindness and generosity in electing to present me with the Lifetime Achievement Award. I shall cherish fond and endearing memories of my visit to Toronto, their kindness, care, and concern, and the lavish hospitality accorded.

Pittu Laungani
London, England
6 May 2006

Bahadur Shah 'Zafar' Last Mughal Emperor 1775–1862

The last descendent of Tamerlane to sit on the throne. The British had conquered almost all of India and in about 1857 had banished Zafar to Burma where he died remembering the motherland to his last breath. The following poem was written by Bahadur Shah Zafar as his epitaph.

Urdu

लगता नहीं है जी मेरा उजड़े दयार में
किस की बनी है आलम-ए-ना-पायेदार में ।

कह दो इन हसरतों से कहीं और जा बसें
इतनी जगह कहां है दिल-ए-दारादार में ।

उम्र-ए-दराज़ मांग के लाये थे चार दिन
दो आरज़ू में कट गये, दो इंतज़ार में ।

है कितन बदनसीब ज़फ़र दफ़्न के लिये
दो गज़ ज़मीन भी न मिली कू-ए-यार में ।

English translation

My heart is not happy,
In this barren land
Who has ever felt fulfilled
In this temporary world

Please tell my emotions
to go away somewhere else
there is not enough room for
them in my sad heart

I had requested for a long life
a life of four days
Two were spent in praying
and two were spent in waiting

How unlucky Zafar is!
For his burial
he couldn't get even two yards
of earth in his beloved country.

Foreword: Understanding Cross-Cultural Psychology

Professor Uwe P. Gielen

Why does a Chinese patient complain about her liver when she is trying to cope with a difficult family situation? (For the Chinese, the liver is the traditional seat of anger and the patient may be somatizing her psychological tensions.) Why do some English women and men feel uncomfortable in an Indian railway station? (Nobody is queuing up, and too many locals are invading their invisible but psychologically powerful personal spaces.) What does a Japanese businessman really mean when he says that he 'will try his best'? (He may merely wish to consult with his group to find out how seriously your business proposal should be taken.)

In the olden days one probably would have consulted an anthropologist to solicit scientifically plausible answers to such queries. But during the last 35 years a newcomer has emerged on the map of scientific disciplines ready to entertain these and similar questions: cross-cultural psychology. And my friend, Professor Pittu Laungani, is just the right person to introduce you to this cocky but fascinating scientific interloper.

It may be useful to trace briefly the history of psychology in order to understand better why cross-cultural psychology is so much needed in this age of globalization. The birth of academic psychology is traditionally dated back to 1879 when German scholar, Wilhelm Wundt, established the world's first fully fledged psychological laboratory in Leipzig. Although Wundt's laboratory and his conception of experimental psychology soon exerted a worldwide influence, he did insist that there are two quite distinct strands of psychology: physiological-experimental psychology and *völkerpsychologie* [psychology of peoples]. The latter meant to him a kind of cultural psychology that focuses on language, myth, cultural customs, and the ethos of various peoples.

But alas, whereas Wundt's experimental psychology was instrumental in creating modern academic psychology, his cultural psychology soon sank from view and left few traces in the world of science. The long-term outcome of this one-sided historical development has been the emergence of a scientific psychology that, while aiming at universal generalizations, in truth incorporates deeply entrenched (though often invisible) Western biases. Our developmental, personality, social, clinical, and counselling psychologies, for instance, are suffused with individualistic assumptions and values that feel natural and right to most liberal Americans and Western Europeans but that would be experienced as odd, off-center, and even immoral by the more collectivistic inhabitants of traditional sub-Saharan African villages. In this context, the Canadian psychiatrist Raymond Prince has described with charming modesty how his earlier attempts in the late 1950s to psychoanalyse African patients or to practise open-ended Rogerian interview methods with them frequently met with failure (Prince, 2004). From a cross-cultural point of view, however, such failures should not occasion surprise since both Freudian psychoanalysis and Rogerian theories of self-actualization are deeply rooted in modern secular and individualistic conceptions of human nature that diverge sharply from traditional African spiritual values, cosmologies, and self-conceptions.

Psychology, it appears, must become a much more *culture-inclusive* science if it is to be of value to those that have been socialized outside the confines of the Western world – and that means the large majority of humankind. As our author makes crystal clear in the following pages, the quest for a more culture-inclusive and culture-comparative psychology readily leads to both scientific and moral questions that can cut deeply. A science can only be valid if its theories and methods are appropriate for the topics and populations under investigation. For the cross-cultural psychologist that means an increased emphasis upon indigenous conceptions of human nature, spirituality, motivation, and human or supernatural causation, new methods suited to the investigation of illiterate and semi-literate populations, a concern for non-verbal, often barely noticeable and cross-culturally confusing signals, a special focus on groups such as immigrants, refugees, bilingual persons, culture-brokers living between several worlds, and many other new issues, topics, and populations that until now have tended to remain at the margins of mainstream psychology. In addition, cross-cultural psychologists have found it necessary to introduce new moral considerations into the field of psychology, in part because comparisons between culture-specific behavioural patterns, thoughts, and feelings are so easily distorted by a researcher's ethnocentric preconceptions and biases. If nothing else the cross-cultural psychologist must be possessed of a special sensitivity for cultural nuances and underlying values that may well be at variance with his or her own preferences and understandings. Also needed is an ability to put one's self into the shoes of others while knowing fully well that such attempts are always constrained by human limitations and non-conscious but pervasive cultural assumptions.

As will soon become clear, Professor Pittu Laungani makes an excellent guide for introducing the non-specialist reader to some of the main perspectives and questions prevailing in the field of cross-cultural psychology. Born into a large well-off family in Bombay (now Mumbai), he immigrated to England as a young man. There he received his doctoral degree under the watchful eyes of his highly productive if controversial mentor, Hans Juergen Eysenck. Subsequently he became a counselling psychologist and expert on death and bereavement as well as a playwright who playfully put Hamlet on the Freudian couch (Laungani, 1997a) and also had him treated by Carl Rogers for his 'psychological problems'. As a playwright, he has a special eye for telling detail, irony, trenchant juxtaposition and dramatic cadence that make his book a joy to read. His bicultural experiences can be felt throughout this volume since they provide him with a special vantage point from which to arrive at cross-cultural comparisons between East and West. And should you wish to gain a more personal perspective on his background and become familiar with his reflections on being an immigrant, consult Dr William West's interview with him in the August 2004 issue of the *British Journal of Guidance and Counselling*. This interview can also be found in my web-based book, *Conversations with International Psychologists*.

Let me add a few words about the author's position in the realm of cross-cultural psychology. This form of psychology, although barely 35 years old as an established discipline with a definite identity, can already boast of a considerable variety of theoretical approaches and methodologies. For instance, among the members of the International Association of Cross-Cultural Psychology, one frequently encounters a positivistic conception of science emphasizing the value of socio-cultural analysis in terms of specific variables and quantifiable responses, together with some attempts to order cultures on various dimensions such as Hofstede's (1991, 2001) 'famous five'. Our author, however, is travelling down a different scientific path by introducing his own conceptual scheme to elucidate his trans-cultural comparisons. Furthermore, he tends to favour detailed or 'thick' comparisons of various cultural patterns, an approach that makes the field come alive to the novice seeking a vivid introduction to some of its intricacies. Throughout, his concern is with the intertwining of cultural meanings and feelings, thoughts and behaviours. His approach is at times closer the qualitative, emic (culture-specific) concerns of cultural psychology than the outlook of traditional, quantitative, etic (universalizing) cross-cultural psychology. This is also evident in his latest book, *Asian Perspectives in Counselling and Psychotherapy* (2004a).

In this context, one may wonder what Wundt would have said about the resurrection of cultural psychology after its long sleep. To be sure, Laungani's cultural psychology is dressed up in much more modern and well-cut clothes than Wundt's old-fashioned, long-winded, and rather poorly dressed version. After all, cultural psychology has come a long way since the early 1900s!

During the last few decades, academic psychologists have increasingly left their ivory towers in order to apply their insights to problems of practical importance. This is certainly true for cross-cultural counselling psychologist such as Laungani, who knows that in today's 'global village' cultural misunderstandings and tensions can have serious and even deadly consequences. Immigrant patients may feel misunderstood by their doctors and nurses and consequently withhold vital information from them, Spanish air traffic controllers encounter difficulties when trying to understand Japanese pilots attempting to provide crucial flight path information in English, Chinese and other Asian immigrant college students frequently outperform European-origin students in the United States, Navaho medicine men and African 'witch doctors' are asked to work together with modern allopathic doctors to better serve indigenous clients, English spectators to a soccer game make monkey noises whenever a black player touches the ball, President Bush is ordering American troops to occupy Iraq in order to fight what he conveniently labels 'evil', and a thousand other, sometimes positive, sometimes troublesome, and sometimes deadly cross-cultural encounters are taking place daily around the globe. We all need to understand such situations better in order to make the world a more liveable place for ourselves, our children, and our grandchildren. Professor Laungani's lively book is certain to make a valuable contribution towards achieving this difficult yet fundamental goal!

Uwe P. Gielen
Institute for International and Cross-Cultural Psychology
St Francis College, New York City

Acknowlegements

It is to my ancestors that I must first offer my worship. To worship one's ancestors is a hallowed custom in most non-Western cultures: India, Malaysia, China, Japan, and several other African, Caribbean, and South American countries. I would be failing in my moral duty were I to ignore my ancestors. As the very term implies, my ancestors are all dead; several have been dead for over three, if not four thousand years. But that is immaterial. In fact I find it easier to converse with the dead than with the living.

The dead have more time at their disposal – in fact an eternity – than the living. Besides, the dead have transcended all their personal, private concerns. But their thoughts, their words, their philosophies, their poetry, their discourses, and their wisdom remain. They await us and are ever ready to guide us and offer us the comfort of their knowledge, their nobility, and their wisdom. It is to the dead that one often turns and from whom one learns – as I have done in the process of writing this book.

Sadly, the contributions of the dead are hardly ever formally acknowledged in print – other than a quote here and a quote there, followed by references at the end of the book. To mention the names of all those wise sages from whose words and ideas I have benefited would involve compiling an extensive bibliography! But that could turn out to be a dangerous ploy; one could easily miss an important name or add an unintended one. What matters is not that one refers to Buddha or Plato, Homer or Herodotus, Socrates or Gandhi, Aristotle or Aquinas, Confucius or Mahavira, Aurelius or Ashoka, Seneca or Cicero, Jesus or Krishna, Dante or Milton, Shakespeare or Sophocles, Mohammad or Moses, Galileo or Newton, Kant or Hume, Freud or William James, Tolstoy or Tagore, Darwin or Russell – what matters is their individual and combined wisdom, which all these and many, many such persons have left behind for posterity. They may not, in the modern sense of the word, be referred to as psychologists; their vision, their concerns, and their depth of understanding transcended the narrow boundaries into which modern disciplines have to a certain extent been straitjacketed. They have left behind a legacy whose value we have still not been able to assess accurately; perhaps we never will.

It is to all those people that I humbly acknowledge my irredeemable debts. They have taught me to think, to feel, and to experience a sense of wonder – even awe. They have taught me to perceive the world from perspectives which I had never dreamed possible. Such people never die. They are always available when one's soul yearns for them.

It is fitting that Seneca in his essay, *On the Shortness of Life,* has the last word on this subject: '*Since nature allows us to enter into a partnership with every age, why not turn from this brief and transient spell of time and give ourselves whole-heartedly to the past, which is limitless and eternal and can be shared with better men than we?*'

It is to the living that I must now turn. I have been extremely fortunate in having friends, colleagues, and associates who each in their own ways have helped me with the writing of the book – clarifying my ideas, separating wheat from chaff, offering invaluable suggestions, restructuring the text where relevant – not a stone has been left unturned. Even Job – the epitome of patience – would have envied them their patience! I feel humbled and over-awed by their care, concern, and their kindness. If from time to time they did resent my intrusions into their own busy lives, they kept their displeasures to themselves. All I can do is to acknowledge with deep gratitude and humility their unstinting help and their best wishes. Although the book is mine, all the following persons have played a dominant role in its production. They are:

Dr Waseem Alladin, UK

Professor Amnon Carmi, Israel

Mr Michael Carmichael, UK

Professor Richard deZoysa, UK

Professor Juris Draguns, USA

Dr Ulhas Fuat, USA

Professor Uwe P. Gielen, USA

Dr Colin Lago, UK

Dr Roy Moodley, Canada

Professor (late) John Morgan, Canada

Dr Sandra Neil, Australia

Dr Ann O'Roark, USA

Professor Stephen Palmer, UK

Professor Danai Papadatou, Greece

Professor Durga Parikh, India

Mr Mike Pawson, UK

Dr Nicolo' Piptone, Italy

Professor Mujeeb Rahman, Canada
Ms Claire Reeve, UK
Dr Alan Roland, USA
Dr Sabar Runsromjee, Australia
Professor Rupa Shah, India
Dr Greesh Sharma, USA
Professor Charles D. Spielberger, USA
Professor Lana Stermac, Canada
Dr Antoinette Thomas, Canada
Dr Dennis Trent, USA/UK
Dr William West, UK

Introduction

A book with a difference! That is what Michael Carmichael, Editor at Sage Publications, calls it. After reading the first four chapters he was convinced that this book was going to be *very, very* different from several other books in cross-cultural psychology whose publications he has been involved with over the years. Some differences can be embarrassing and painful and are best avoided. Others can be exhilarating and pleasurable – that was how Michael chose to see it.

Convinced that it would 'break new ground', Michael encouraged me to continue to express myself in what he regarded was a free-flowing, personalized, conversational, critical, confrontational style, sprinkled with literary metaphors, quotes, and 'emotionally charged' vignettes.

The question that you might ask here – and you would be well within your rights to do so – is *why* I have elected to steer away from the conventional 'third-person-singular-style' and write an *academic* book in a personalized manner. After all, you will be investing several hours of your busy and precious time, not counting the money you (might) have spent on it, and you would wish to ensure that your time was well spent. An explanation is in order.

In the past it was not uncommon for academics of most disciplines to write in the first person singular. Some of the world's greatest books in philosophy, religion, medicine, cosmology, politics – right from the ancient Greeks and the Romans to the present day – have been written in the first person singular. Imagine the impact those books have had on the growth and development of Western civilization and on the minds of people over the centuries. Consider the writings of Pythagoras, Cicero, Seneca, Aristotle, Marcus Aurelius, St Augustine, St Aquinas, Epicures, Descartes, Hume, Kant, Bacon, Locke, Berkeley, Spinoza – to name a few chosen at random – and one is as though mesmerized by the profound wisdom accompanying their brilliantly crafted words. Plato of course went a step further, scaling Olympian heights! He wrote his great philosophical works in the form of plays. Reading Plato is like seeing a great drama unfold before one's eyes. His philosophical works, as we know, are still read and reread and argued over even today. One may question Plato's formulations, as indeed many have done, including Popper (1966); one may take serious issue with his *Republic,* or any of his other plays, but it is difficult not to be moved by the radiant beauty of his words and ideas. Many of the great works in science too during the Enlightenment period were written in the first person singular. Even the most abstract issues – ontological, teleological, cosmological, epistemological – were articulated in the first person singular.

Books are human creations. And like human beings each book has a life of its own. Unlike human birth, the gestation period for creating a book may vary from just a few months, or even a few weeks in some cases (for example, B. F. Skinner's *Walden Two,* Upton Sinclair's *The Jungle)* to several long, untiring years (for example, Tolstoy's *War and Peace;* Dostoevsky's *The Brothers Karamazov,* Dante's *Divine Comedy).* But despite one's attachment to one's own creation, there are no guarantees how long one's creation will survive. Sadly, most books die a premature death, on occasions even *before* the author's death, leaving hardly a trace of their very existence. Others may survive for a few years, but it is only the really exceptional ones that outlive their creators by several centuries, even attaining a state of immortality. But regardless of how long a book lives, it is not unusual for their authors to form deep attachments to what they have brought into the world.

Within the field of psychology too, until about the beginning of the twentieth century, and even later, many scholarly works were written in the first person singular. Freud, one of the most prolific writers, wrote most if not all his books in the first person singular. So did Carl Jung, William James, Charles Darwin, and several other American and European scholars. If for instance, you were to browse through William James's *Varieties of Religious Experiences*, you would be amazed not only by its scholarship but also by its incredibly beautiful, lucid, and powerful style of expression. Admirers of William James, for instance will tell you that he wrote with the dash and panache of a novelist, with dialogues, conversation pieces, reminisces sprinkled lavishly throughout the book. (His brother Henry James, on the other hand, one is told, wrote his novels with the staid dullness of many a modern day cross-cultural psychologist!)

In choosing to write in the first person singular, I have tried to follow in the footsteps of the older and wiser writers of past generations and centuries. And I shall continue to do so. Luckily, we live in an age where I am unlikely to be found guilty of heresy. My editor friend Michael and his associate Claire assure me that neither the dark instruments of torture nor the fiery stake awaits me – a cold shoulder perhaps, a vitriolic review, a hastily withdrawn invitation to an international conference, a rejection slip for a submitted research paper, is the worst I can expect from the academic fraternity after the book's publication. Since there is nothing heretical (or salacious) in my book, I shall of course never enjoy the notoriety of seeing my book go up into flames. It was, you might recall, Girolamo Savonarola, a vicious, infamous Dominican dictator and reformer, during the Medici era in Florence, who ordered the burning of all books that were considered immoral, his actions being referred to as 'The Bonfire of Vanities'. But you might recall that Savonarola himself met with the same fate, and in so doing achieved the martyrdom that was his due. Divine justice, one might choose to call it.

I have found that the use of the first person singular makes it easier to establish a relationship with the reader. I find it comforting to write in the first person singular, and have always done so. It allows me to express my own observations and ideas, my own feelings and emotions, my doubts and misgivings and my own confusions and conundrums with greater freedom and naturalness. And since I write as I would talk, say to a friend, a colleague, an associate, or a student, I feel that the reader comes to see it in a similar way, too. It is of course possible – even likely – that you may disagree, dislike or take exception to what I say, and *how* I say it. But that is a risk I am not afraid to take.

But old order, as Tennyson pointed out several years ago, changeth, yielding place to new. Not many academics, particularly in the field of psychology, choose to express themselves in the first person singular. From time to time some do use the occasional 'I', but that 'I' is merely a convenient form of expression, not the internal 'I' which William James referred to in his writings.

Let us consider the reasons for such a change. Why have psychologists given up the practice (if not the art) of writing in the first person singular? There is among contemporary psychologists and other social scientists an unvoiced belief more honoured in its observance than in its breach that rational, objective, and (seemingly) scientific writing needs to be distant, dispassionate, impersonal, and even rather dull. Not surprisingly, most academics working in this field tend to adopt a third-person singular style of writing.

Second, in writing as they do, they are keen to ensure that each important statement is corroborated with relevant empirically derived research references. Empiricism is the god to which Western psychologists in particular pay obeisance. But empiricism has its own shortcomings. If you consider a telephone directory you will note that it is a precise, faultless, empirical product. It is perfect. Yet sadly, other than listing names and addresses of subscribers, it tells us nothing of any great value. (In any case, you'd never be able to locate the number of a person whose name and address you could not remember!)

Third, the psychologists seem reluctant, even rather coy to express their own doubts and dilemmas, their own confusions and uncertainties in their writings. It would seem that they are unwilling to 'stick their neck out' by making unverified and uncorroborated statements. One cannot but feel that the authors of such books choose to hide behind an iron curtain, disseminating their 'sanitized' views in a monotonous voice, booming out of a pre-recorded hi-fi system! This form of writing to me seems soulless. (Given that the concept of 'soul' has been ruthlessly excised from the vocabulary of contemporary Western psychology, it is not inappropriate to refer to their writings as soulless.)

Apart from a brief biographical sketch of the author (and perhaps his or her picture) printed on the dustcover of the book, the reader does not get to see the author as a real person but as a disembodied voice transposed into words and sentences. The reader learns little of the author – in terms of what he or she *really* believes, thinks and feels about the subject matter.

To venture into the area of cross-cultural psychology is like sailing through uncharted oceans. It requires the courage and the single-minded determination and tenacity of Christopher Columbus. One can never predict what one might encounter! Imagine the problems: ethical, social, religious, economic, familial, gender-related, health-related, linguistic, and so on, that one is bound to encounter. Even the hardiest, the most learned and erudite scholar could fall into unseen traps. The field of cross-cultural psychology (including, to a large extent, counselling and psychotherapy) is by no means as clear or as precise as, say, Euclid's geometry, or the theorems of Pythagoras. Theories formulated in the West – like cheap wine – *do not* always travel well into non-Western cultures. In fact, there is hardly a theory in cross-cultural psychology – notwithstanding the grandiose claims of their proponents – that is cast in stone.

Let us take one illustrative example. Western psychologists, in their attempts to distinguish between Western and Eastern cultures in terms of their major value systems, have formulated several bi-polar concepts, such as *individualism* and *collectivism*, the first of which (individualism) applies to Western cultures, and the latter (collectivism) to Eastern cultures (Triandis, 1994). I am wary of the manner in which Western psychologists use the terms 'individualism' and 'collectivism' when referring to people from Western and Eastern cultures respectively. There are other terms too, such as 'horizontality' and 'verticality', 'closed' and 'open', 'rigid' and 'flexible', which are used. I tend to be sceptical at best and disbelieving at worst at the use of such terms when describing differences between Western and Eastern cultures. The labels are by no means value-free; they are refined versions of old stereotypes: Western societies are individualistic, Western societies are horizontal, western societies are open, Western societies are flexible, Western societies are rational and Western societies are secular. None of these attributes apply to non-Western societies, which are communalistic, vertical, hierarchical, rigid, religious and superstitious.

So much has been written by so many on the ideas surrounding individualism and collectivism that it has virtually been elevated to the status of an inviolable law – almost akin to Einstein's $E=mc^2$. No doubt there is some truth in the above formulations; empirical evidence supports the idea that Westerners to a large measure operate on an individualistic model, and people from Eastern cultures, particularly from the Middle East, Pakistan, India, Bangladesh, Sri Lanka, Indonesia, Thailand, on a communalistic (but not necessarily on a collectivist) basis in their day-to-day lives. A careful analysis of the philosophical and religious value systems related to the law of karma among the Hindus in India demonstrates very clearly and succinctly the notion of individualism. *Collectivism (or communalism) has no part whatever to play in the law of karma, which is fiercely individualistic in its orientation.* Each individual is responsible for his or her own karma, and is fully aware that whether the fruits of his actions in his next birth turn out to be sweet, sour, or poisonous is directly related to the nature of his or her moral actions. Since the very psyche of Indians (Hindus and Buddhists) is built around the law of karma (and of the Muslims around the will of Allah), it is astonishing, not to say naïve, that Western psychologists should have failed to consider its importance. For Western psychologists to admit to the *individualistic* nature related to the law of karma (of which no Hindu is unaware) would bring into serious question the validity of their formulated theories. Such embarrassments are best ignored. And the theory will remain intact for a while – but only for a while.

At any rate, most if not all theories, particularly in the human sciences, sooner or later come under the hammer. To use consumer jargon, all theories have a 'sell-by date'. Like living organisms, theories are born, survive (or thrive) for a while, and then die, and as Popper (1972), Thomas Kuhn (1970), Lakatos and Musgrave (1970), and several other eminent philosophers of science and epistemologists have pointed out, are replaced by other theories of increasing truth content, but none ever reaching a state of eternal, timeless perfection. Given the impermanent nature of theories, it is incumbent upon the author(s) – *they have an indisputable moral obligation to their readers* – to come clean about the confusions and contradictions surrounding their work lest the readers take away an unwarranted, if not false impression.

To take the reader into one's confidence, to come clean, to spell out the uncertain nature of their formulations, is not easy. Academic reputations are hardly ever built upon premises of doubt; Descartes perhaps with his famous dictum *(cogito ergo sum)* was the only exception. An author might not wish to be seen as a person who doubts, who is uncertain, who is undecided on certain important issues in the book. Would a reader trust an author who doubts? Isn't the author supposed to know best? But these are species arguments, false rationalizations, which protect the author from criticisms and condemnations. And writing in the third person singular keeps the author even further away from the reader. Should the author wish to establish a 'relationship' with the reader, the use of the first person singular is perhaps a good way to forge such a relationship. But the modern convention of writing in the third person singular remains.

The vast majority of books on cross-cultural psychology and other closely related areas, such as cultural diversity, multiculturalism, counselling, psychotherapy, racism, and so on, are written by Westerners from America, Canada, and several other European countries, including England, Germany, France, Holland, Italy, Greece, and a few Eastern European countries. Most of them are written in the third person singular. It is not hard to understand why. Cross-cultural psychology, to a large extent, is the handmaiden of mainstream Western psychology (Boring, 1929/1950; Leahey, 1997). In the later part of the nineteenth century, many psychologists were keen to turn psychology into a scientific discipline. There were exciting discoveries being made in evolutionary theory, physiology, biology, statistics, and neuro-physiology. Psychologists in the West, and particularly in America and in Britain, and to a certain extent in Europe, undertook precise, quantifiable, scientific research, and by so doing, hoped to discover laws of human behaviour, which would have universal applicability and would be used in promoting human welfare (Miller, 1969).

In their eagerness to turn psychology into a science, they espoused the natural science paradigm (Barnes, 1979), and Western psychology came to be defined as the science of human and animal behaviour. They were convinced that the laws of the natural sciences would apply not only to the American people but also to the rest of the world. Concepts such as purpose, consciousness, awareness, mind, self, identity, morality – concepts which give meaning and substance to our lives – were seen as being redundant. They were abandoned. Metaphysical abstractions were thrown overboard. They also discarded fundamental religious, existential, spiritual, and such other human concerns from their scientific vocabularies. These terms were replaced by concepts such as positivism, operationism, empiricism, environmentalism, materialism, secularism, radicalism (a la Skinner) behaviourism, scientism, and a few other-isms, such as humanism, individualism, and cognitivism.

Barring a few exceptions, the general trend was toward constructing sophisticated experimental, psychometric research designs, which were then subjected to complex multivariate statistical analyses. Several eminent psychologists have argued stridently against such a rigid scientific approach and have even shown that the use of the natural science model in psychological research often lacks 'ecological validity'. Their criticisms have fallen on deaf ears. Sigmund Koch, the great American psychologist, remarked that he would 'prefer a defective understanding of something of value over a safely defended description of something trite' (in Robinson, 2001: 420). William James too, refused to accept a psychology that won 'system' at the price of reality itself (Robinson, 2001).

The proper study of human beings and human nature necessitates our having a wider, a more comprehensive view of what one means by humanity and what it means to be human. This involves our accepting the premise that we all live our lives at two inter-related levels – the outer level (that is the overt, behavioural level) and the inner level. In other words, there is the 'outer' self, or the social self, and the 'inner' self, or the private self. To concentrate on only the outer level – the social self – is to study human beings in one dimension, referred to by Herbert Marcuse as the 'one-dimensional man'. It would therefore be essential to take the 'inner' person – the metaphysical and spiritual, the private and non-observable– and the 'outer', or 'observable' person as a whole and *not separate them as appears to be the case at present*. The two – the inner and the outer – enjoy a symbiotic relationship, an issue which we shall discuss in the book.

In historical terms, cross-cultural psychology is a fledgling discipline. Until about the 1950s, Western psychologists, particularly in America and to a lesser extent in other European countries, were 'culturally myopic'. The acquired cultural myopia was due largely to the fact that Western psychologists in general, and American psychologists in particular, chose not to see the vital role that each culture in its own unique way played in the development of the human psyche. Not just on the development of the human psyche, but equally importantly on the economic productivity, political, social, artistic, aesthetic, and moral development of the culture.

The impression that still lingers is that cross-cultural psychology is as is defined by Western psychologists. The world is as *they* see it. They believe too that the rest of the people in the world also see the world as they see it – through Western spectacles. In other words, they propose what Berry, Poortinga, Segall, & Dasen (1992) refer to as 'an absolutist position', which assumes that 'human phenomena are basically the same [qualitatively] in all cultures: honesty is honesty, and depression is depression, no matter where one observes it' (p. 1103). That, as many contemporary cultural anthropologists – particularly those espousing a cultural relativistic stance – would point out, is utter nonsense (Shweder, 1991b, 2000; Grondona, 2000).

Until about 20 years ago, cross-cultural psychology in the Third-world countries (which, incidentally were referred to as *Turd World Countries* by some executives in the United Nations, as Shiva Naipaul pointed out to his brother, V. S. Naipaul) was a misconceived 'clone' of American psychology. But luckily, the situation has begun to change. Indigenous psychologies have made an appearance. Problems that seem relevant to Eastern cultures, problems with which people can identify – problems of poverty, caste, education, literacy, health and illness, family patterns, marriage, dowry, death and after-life, and so on, are taken on board. Even the methods of investigation do not always follow the natural science model, as is the case with American psychology. However, there is a danger in the Eastern cultures wanting to go it alone. The research methods used by Western psychologists are robust and are capable of displaying trends and probabilistic relationships; they ought to be used, modified certainly, but not abandoned.

Before we have a brief look at the chapters and the manner in which they are organized in the book, there four points that need to be made:

1 The book, it needs to be stressed, is not an applied text or a training manual, or a DIY kit. It offers little guidance as to what you might do, how you might behave in a given situation, how you might relate to people in different cultures, under different conditions should you at some stage decide on an extended trip to another culture. The book allows you to 'enter' into the world of peoples of other cultures and see it from *their* own unique perspectives. It offers you an understanding, an insight into the lifestyles of people of cultures different from yours: the manner in which they think, make choices, informed judgements – concerning religion, morality, ethics, social and familial life, and marital, sexual, intellectual, financial, and other matters.

2 The title, *Cross-Cultural Psychology,* would suggest that the book delves into a variety of cultures, dotted around the world. That is not entirely the case. The book focuses largely on India and on Western societies, England, and America. Although other Eastern cultures are brought into the book from time to time, the main emphasis is on India. The reason for this is not hard to follow. India, if it needs to be stressed, is a truly multi-cultural society. On the one hand India has a formal, written Constitution, a common politico-legal system and the rule of law. India is also the largest democratic country in the world, with the present population hovering at around 1.1 billion, which is more than 16 times the population of Britain, and around 4 times the population of the United States. The fact that 1.1 billion people live within the physical geographical boundaries of India is its greatest unifying force. On the other hand, the country consists of different religious groups that have lived in India for centuries; they consist of Hindus, Muslims, Sikhs, Christians, Catholics, Parsees, Jews, Bahai's, Buddhists, Jains, Europeans, and a multiplicity of tribal and other minority groups (Nepalese, Tibetans) dotted around the country. India is by no means a monolingual country; over 35 languages, not counting the hundreds of dialects, are spoken in India. People from the far northerly

states of India are fair-skinned, whereas those from the southern states, such as Tamilnadu, Andhra Pradesh, and Kerala, tend to be dark-skinned. Despite the fact that about 78 per cent of the population in India consists of Hindus, they are divided not only by their caste structure, but also by their linguistic, culinary, dietary, social, familial, religious beliefs, and other traditional customs and practices. Even the levels of education and literacy, poverty and affluence, patterns of childrearing, health and illness, position of women, patterns of worship, vary from one region to another, even from one village to another.

Given the heterogeneity of India in terms of its people, languages, climate, religious practices, dietary practices, patterns of socialization, occupations, and so on, India is best seen as a gargantuan multicultural society.

3 I believe that for cross-cultural psychology to become a strong, robust, and vibrant discipline it is important to find bi-cultural psychologists for such collaborative work. Roland (1988) regards bi-cultural psychologists as those who are born and brought up in one culture (Western or non-Western) and at a later stage in their life have emigrated to another culture. Bi-cultural psychologists, because of their familiarity and intimacy with Western and non-Western cultures and their ability to speak and understand different languages and customs, are in an ideal position to undertake collaborative work. They are better able to understand and evaluate different patterns of beliefs and behaviours than those cross-cultural psychologists who have had little or no experience of having lived in different cultures. The case of Sir James Fraser, who wrote the 12 volumes of *The Golden Bough* (1932/1954), comes to mind. *The Golden Bough* was a study in magic, superstitions, rites and rituals, and religious practices across all societies in the world. When asked if he had visited all the societies about which he had written the twelve volumes, he shrugged his shoulders and was reported to have boasted with undisguised arrogance, *'Good God, no!'* He had never met nor indeed visited any of the lands of the people of whom he wrote (Beattie, 1964). It is clear that his analyses of societies were based largely on the available writings of colonial administrators, missionaries, historians, and the like, which of course were based on their own preconceptions and stereotypes.

One might see this as an exceptional case of prejudice. However, one finds a similar theme in James Mill's (a great utilitarian philosopher) writings in his book, *History of British India* (1817), which ran into 10 volumes. In one of the volumes he mentions that a person 'may obtain more knowledge of India in one year in his closet in England, than he could obtain during the course of the longest life, by the use of his eyes and ears in India' (quoted in Khilnani, 1997: 158).

In this context it would be fascinating, not to say extremely informative, to find out how many of the Western cross-cultural psychologists from America,

England, and other European countries make it their business to stay for extensive periods in the counties in which they are interested. How many of them feel it necessary to learn their languages, their customs, their rites and the rituals, their belief patterns, their social behaviours, their arts, music, and literature in the course of their work? My own guess is that most Western cross-cultural psychologists come to depend upon the local collaborators for their research enterprizes. The local collaborators are only too happy to oblige because of the cachet involved with working with Western academics, getting their papers published in prestigious Western journals, obtaining research grants and/or research postings. It saddens me to admit that many academics in India, despite nearly 60 years of independence, have still not been able to discard their imperialist yoke.

Yet, the situation is so different when Western academics from time to time come to non-Western cultures for conferences. About five years ago, I attended the SARC Conference (South Asia Regional Conference) held in Bombay (now Mumbai) in 2001. It attracted several well-known and prestigious cross-cultural psychologists from America, the United Kingdom, France, Australia, Hong Kong, Singapore, Malaysia, Taiwan, and other countries. It came as no surprise to me (and to other Indian delegates) to learn that hardly any one of the foreign delegates spoke or had any fluency with any of the Indian languages. There were a few cross-cultural psychologists from the West who did speak several Indian languages, but like me, they were bi-cultural psychologists who had emigrated to the West several years ago. The saving-grace for Western psychologists lies in the fact that English is the lingua franca at most international conferences and therefore it is not incumbent upon them to learn any foreign languages.

In India, conferences generally start with a prayer. After all the delegates are seated, a group of devotees appears. A silver oil lamp is lit. A hymn is sung in Sanskrit. It is an invocation to the gods, to 'bless' the conference, ensuring its success. It is a very touching and moving ceremony. The Western delegates, I noticed, were quite bemused and even rather embarrassed by the spectacle.

Sitting with a few of them at the luncheon table, the conversation became even more interesting and animated. One of the Indian delegates was expounding the story of the great Indian epic, *The Ramayana*. He explained how Rama (one of the Indian Gods) had to solicit the help of monkeys to rescue his wife Sita, who had been kidnapped by Ravana, the demon king of Sri Lanka. At this the Western delegates laughed. 'Fancy that! Monkeys helping Gods!' When the laughter subsided, the Indian delegate asked them in the gentlest possible way how they, as hard-nosed scientific psychologists, would care to explain 'immaculate conception'. Was it an immaculate conception or just an immaculate *misconception*? Lunch ended in silence.

4   This brings me to my final issue, namely, the important role of religion in the day-to-day lives of people in India and in other Eastern cultures. Most Western psychologists appear to shy away from considering the role of religion in people's lives. Paradoxically, this neglect is nowhere more evident than in cross-cultural psychology, counselling and psychotherapy. Despite the fact that several counsellors and psychotherapists, both in America and in Britain, are themselves religious-minded people, even regular churchgoers, they avoid talking about religion in their professional work with their clients. Counselling and psychotherapy have almost come to be equated with general medicine, in which religion has no part to play in the treatment of a client. To ignore the role of religion in their professional work and yet be religious in their private lives must create considerable cognitive dissonance among them. But leaving that aside, the point to remember is that the vast majority of people in non-Western cultures do not lead their lives on the basis of a secularist philosophy. Religion is ingrained into their psyche from birth. For the Muslims, life is ordained and predetermined by the will of Allah, for the Buddhists and the Hindus, life revolves round prayer, devotion, *bhakti,* renunciation and the law of karma. The ideas underlying secularism and their attendant beliefs have yet to find favour among people in non-Western cultures. To ignore or dismiss all these major religious considerations because of their lesser importance in western society is hardly likely to lead to a genuine understanding of cross-cultural psychology.

Let us now look at the chapters in the book. The book contains 10 chapters in all. The first five chapters deal with conceptual and theoretical issues, the final five chapters deal with descriptive and applied issues.

Chapter 1

Examines the multiple meanings assigned to the term 'culture'. It is not an easy word to come to terms with. To some, culture may mean referring to a person of impeccable manners and good breeding: a person who is well behaved, polite, educated, considerate, and caring – in Victorian terms, *'a gentleman'*, or *'a lady'*. Biologists, microbiologists, biochemists, medical researchers, forensic scientists, and others in allied professions entertain a completely different notion of culture. Cultures are what are collected from humans and animals and examined and analysed in laboratories. Academic disciplines, such anthropology, sociology, psychology, history, economics, political science, journalism, and so forth, on the other hand, have formulated their own conceptions of culture. At a popular level the word 'culture' is used (many would say abused) in such a way as to make it virtually incomprehensible: one hears of the culture of violence, the culture of greed, minority culture, racist culture, primitive culture, feminist culture, celebrity culture, gay and lesbian culture, underclass culture, culture of complaint, and so on. To make matters worse, a prefix is often added to the term culture, which then leads to a 'sub-culture' of violence, greed, racism, underclass, and so on. Several years ago, T. S. Eliot (1948) pointed out that this process of fragmentation is likely to lead to the disintegration of the culture. Attention is then focused on under-standing cultural stereotypes surrounding the concept. The chapter then offers meaningful explanations of the term culture from a psychological perspective.

Chapter 2

Considers the nature and the rationale of cross-cultural psychology. It argues that cross-cultural psychology is genuinely concerned with understanding human diversity in all its forms, and about discovering behaviours, which are 'universal' or culturally invariant, and those that are influenced by cultural factors. Are we the same the world over? Do we all share certain common psychological, biological, and behavioural characteristics with others? Is there a common humanity that we all share regardless of our cultural backgrounds? Or are we each a product of our own culture, and in many ways different from one another? The chapter examines many of the conflicting and complementary views on this subject. The chapter also examines two issues of great concern to psychologists, politicians, social scientists, economists and governments all over the world: globalization and multicultualism, or cultural diversity. The potential impact of globalization and multiculturalism is unpredictable at present. The chapter ends with an examination of the role that indigenous psychologies have started to play in this field and what light they might throw on the above issues.

Chapter 3

Is easily the most important chapter of the book. Each culture devises its own internally consistent sets of rules. To understand a given pattern of behaviour in another culture, it is necessary to understand the system of rules and the assump-tions which guide the private and social behaviours of people in that culture. The chapter presents a theoretical model, which explains similarities and differences between Eastern cultures and Western cultures in terms of their major values systems. Several testable hypotheses have been deduced from the proposed model.

Chapter 4

Is concerned with the role of ethics in research, particularly in cross-cultural settings. One does not need to be told that all our meaningful relationships with others have an underlying ethical basis. That is taken as being axiomatic. We all, as the German philosopher Kant pointed out a few hundred years ago, need to relate to other human beings as *ends in themselves* and not as means to an end. This imperative applies even more forcefully when undertaking cross-cultural research. This type of research is sensitive. One is dealing with groups of people from different cultures; one is in a country which one may not have been to before; one may be unaware of their social and familial customs, their traditions, their belief systems, their patterns of worship, the way in which they bring up their children, their gender relations, their behaviours towards the elderly, and so on. Although the major psychological and psychiatric organizations have provided ethical guidelines related to research, there is still the need to tread cautiously in this area lest we commit unforgivable blunders – say the wrong things, insult people without meaning to. It is important for us not to forget that as researchers working in other countries, our motives and personal behaviours need to be like those of Caesar's wife, 'beyond suspicion'. We also need to ensure that under no circumstances do we wittingly or unwittingly exploit them for our own academic gains. A few case studies have been discussed in the chapter, where the rules have been broken, leading to grief, and in one or two instances, devastation for the people of that particular culture. Although all the major psychological and psychiatric organizations offer clear ethical guidelines for undertaking research, serious mistakes can and do occur with extremely serious consequences.

Chapter 5

Is concerned with methodology, namely, how shall we go about studying other cultures? What empirical techniques shall we use which would allow us to understand rationally, objectively and explain cultural similarities and differences? To test any method one needs to have a hunch, a guess, a conjecture, or a theory in mind. In other words, one needs to know what one is testing, and why. Since chapters on methodology can sometimes seem drab and tedious, it 'kicks off' with a culture-specific vignette, which you are invited to interpret correctly. You may find that you own interpretation of the scenario played out before you does not match the interpretation that follows. The chapter examines the importance of constructing theories, however tentative the might be. But all theories if they are to acquire any substance, any validity, need to be tested rigorously. Several different strategies for testing cross-cultural theories are articulated. They include the use of experimental methods, non-experimental methods, which may include controlled observations, the use of questionnaires, and so on. What is also important to understand are the assumptions a researcher makes when testing a theory across different cultures: should the researchers start with the assumption that the particular behaviour (or concept) in which they are interested is 'universal'? Or is it 'culture-specific'? This poses a serious dilemma, which is often referred to as the 'emic-etic dilemma'. The differences between the emic and etic approaches are clearly described.

Chapter 6

Describes an imaginary journey of a young English postgraduate research student to India. It is to be a three-month stay in Bombay and in one or two neighbouring villages. The research involves undertaking a comparative analysis of personality structures between university students in England and a comparable group of university students in India. It is assumed that the research student has never before been to India. During his stay in India most of his preformed attitudes, assumptions, stereotypes, and prejudices concerning non-Western cultures come into serious question. Initially, he is intimidated and bewildered by what he encounters: lack of hygiene in villages, distressing poverty, and strange customs and traditions. But gradually, he learns to accept and cope with the strangeness and the differences and diversities that he encounters. With the assistance of the university staff members, he settles down, completes his research assignment, and returns to England.

Chapter 7

Examines the nature of family structures and childrearing practices across cultures. The manner in which the term 'family' is defined has undergone a dramatic change in recent years, particularly within Western societies where a family ranges from one-parent families, gay/lesbian families, transsexual parents, transgender parents, children living in communes, in foster homes, and so on. Such radical changes are then contrasted with families living in non-Western cultures. The impact of variations in family structures on childrearing practices, gender differences in patterns of socialization, the growth and development of children, is examined in depth and contrasted with Eastern approaches. The main features underlying contemporary Western and Eastern families are articulated. Finally, the chapter considers the future impact of globalization on family structures, and the economic growth and political development of both Western and non-Western cultures.

Chapter 8

Argues that we all perceive the world and the people in it subjectively. Even our own perception of our self tends to be subjective. What adds to the difficulty is that our perception is inconstant; it varies, and from time to time serious conflicts – psychological, relational, goal-directed – arise between our perception of our private inner self – the 'I' – and the external outer self – the 'Me', which we present to the world. The importance of resolving the 'I'–'Me' conflict cannot be overstated. A therapeutic strategy specially designed to help a person to resolve the 'I'–'Me' conflict is described in some depth. Since all meaningful interactions, to a large extent, depend on the process and the style of communication, the chapter considers the factors such as the use of metaphors, the idiosyncratic use words, which facilitate interaction. I have also argued that intercultural communication, whether it occurs at a day-to-day superficial level or at a professional level, is facilitated when both parties have a clear and objective understanding of their respective worldviews.

Chapter 9

Is concerned with understanding the nature of health, happiness and illness across cultures. Several definitions of health and illness are offered: subjective, medical, psychological, cultural, religious, ancient, and contemporary and their shortcomings are articulated. Since health is often understood as *freedom from* illness (organic and psychological), the chapter considers the arguments related to *the 'freedom from' model of health in medicine*, and *the 'freedom from' model of health in psychology*. Both these models are carefully examined and are seen as being negative in their philosophical outlook because their concern is focused more on *avoidance* of ill health, rather than on *acquiring positive health*. In contradistinction to the 'freedom from' models, two new models are offered – *'freedom to' model of health, happiness and illness in psychology and the cross-cultural model of health, happiness, and illness*. In these two sections, Western approaches are compared with non-Western approaches. The differences and similarities in terms of values, notions of faith and rationality, religious beliefs and secularism, familial and communal factors, and so on, between Western and non-Western approaches are clearly articulated.

Chapter 10

Is the final chapter of the book. The reader will have noticed that all the chapters put together form a life-span approach. Therefore it is fitting that the final chapter should deal with the universal problem – a problem which no culture was, has been, is, or ever will be exempt from – namely, death and dying. There are several common threads that run through Western and Eastern approaches to dying and death: fear, denial, terror, techniques of avoidance, desire for an afterlife, death without undue suffering, a good death, and so on. But despite the similarities, there are marked differences between Western and non-Western attitudes and approaches to death. The remarkable progress of medical science in the West has brought into question a variety of medical, ethical, social, economic and logistical problems, such as how death shall be defined, its medicalization, sanitization of death, issues related to euthanasia, resuscitation, keeping patients alive on life-support machines, transplant surgery, scientific and pseudo-scientific attempts by cryonicists to bring the dead to life, and so forth. Given the decreasing impact of religious beliefs and values, the emphasis has shifted from the performance of religious rituals to secular approaches to death, which tend to be ritual-free. In non-Western countries, such as Pakistan, India, Malaysia, the Middle East, and several others, religious beliefs and death-related rituals play an important role. There is a strong desire to ensure that persons, upon reaching the end of their life and having fulfilled all their religious, familial, communal, and charitable obligations, die 'a good death'.

Let us sit then, you and I
And read the words that, greet our eye,
Revel in the bright images
Dancing through the pages.
In silence let us pause and ponder
Over the worlds that lie beyond, and yonder.
Let us read from beginning to end
Before we condemn or commend.

Part I

Theoretical Perspectives

What Is
This Thing
Called Culture?

Imagine that you are in India. You are travelling on a train from Bombay (now known as Mumbai) to Delhi. You have a window seat in a First Class compartment, which is empty. Presently an Indian family of four – a man, a woman, and two children – enters your compartment. The coolie (porter) disgorges their luggage, haggles over his payment, and finally, with a half-hearted salute, leaves.

No sooner does the train start than the man strikes up a conversation with you. Much to your astonishment, he starts to pry you with personal questions: your name, your nationality, your age, your occupation, and a variety of other questions, including your reasons for coming to India. No stranger in England, you know from your own experience, would *dare* ask such personal and impertinent questions.

Even your close friends would tread more cautiously! What an uncultured brute, you say to yourself. You wonder how in the nicest possible way you might tell him to mind his own business.

Meanwhile, the woman accompanying him has been busy. From a wicker basket next to her she removes a few paper packets; nostrils quiver as the aroma of savoury Indian snacks wafts through the compartment. The man turns to you once again and opening each packet carefully offers you a snack. You are even more bewildered. A moment ago, he was being personal almost to the point of rudeness, a moment later, kindness itself. Why would a total stranger wish to share his food with you? Several explanations rush through your head. Is the offered hospitality a form of atonement for his initial rudeness? Is he one of those who still 'suffers' from a post-colonial 'hangover' and is trying desperately to impress you because you are white, a foreigner? Would his behaviour and his openhearted hospitality have been any different if his travelling companion had been a fellow Indian instead? Or is he just being friendly, hospitable because that is 'part of *his* nature'? Would another Indian family have behaved similarly? Is it an Indian custom, a part of Indian culture? Any one of the explanations could be the 'correct' one, or none. Or they could all be partially relevant. Although the encounter that I have described might seem exaggerated to you, it is neither idiosyncratic nor unique in any way – certainly not from an Indian point of view. As I have stated elsewhere (in conversation with West, 2004),

> People from Eastern cultures, by which I mean people from the Indian sub-continent, in general tend to relate on a personalized and emotional basis. Feelings, intuitions, and subjectivity, play a large part in their assessments of and relationships with others. This means they seldom shy away from asking personal questions – even of strangers: 'How old are you? Are you married? Do you have children? How many children do you have? Do you have a job? What kind of work do you do? What's your salary? Which caste do you come from?' These questions can be and often are asked at the very first meeting between strangers . . . These are seen as practical, matter-of-fact questions. There's no embarrassment whatever in asking such types of questions. They serve as markers, which determine whether one will continue to relate to the person concerned at a social level or ignore the person after the initial preliminaries. Thus, within the first five minutes one works out a pattern of relationships, and there's no beating about the bush. One doesn't have to wait for a long time to find out what the other person does for a living. (pp. 430–431)

Once you take these factors into account, the bizarre behaviour of your travelling companion begins to make sense. The point being made is this. Our perception of the world and the people in it is generally reflected through our cultural lenses. By perception I mean not the images that strike our retina, the sounds that vibrate through the tympanic membrane of our ears, or the smells that tickle our nostrils, but our *interpretations* of the events that unfold before our senses. It is our subjective interpretations influenced by our upbringing that allow us to revel in rapturous rhapsodies when listening to the *Pastoral Symphony*, or gnash our teeth at the sound of a road drill. One should not, however, conclude that all our perceptions are subjective and arise from our own cultural upbringing. That clearly is not the case.

As human beings we all share what might be termed 'a common humanity'. We are all born as helpless and defenceless infants. We need care, comfort, food, and shelter for our biological survival, which runs parallel with our cognitive, linguistic, and emotional development. Without human care and guidance, it would be impossible for us to acquire any human characteristics.

The nature of human nature

In the past, there was a strong belief that human nature was universal. People all over the world acted in accordance with their inherent nature. In invoking human nature as the fundamental explanatory construct one did not have to look further. If a given behaviour is part of human nature and is shared universally, then there is nothing more to be said. 'It's human nature! ' Just as there is no fighting against 'fate' – a theme enshrined in many religious philosophies – there is no point in going against human nature. Is there such a thing as a universal human nature? One has heard the phrase 'human nature' so often and in such a wide variety of situations that one has come to believe that one knows what human nature really is. How far is this belief justified? And how far do we really know and understand what human nature means? The word 'nature' suggests that *all* human beings are born with certain physical and psychological characteristics, which they share in common. The term 'human nature' is often used as an umbrella term to explain a variety of complex and even contradictory behaviours, including greed and avarice, weakness and strength, selfishness and selflessness, vice and virtue, kindness and cruelty, industriousness and indolence, willpower, or the lack of it, pursuit of pleasure, avoidance of pain, love and aggression, and so on.

The concept of human nature has fascinated philosophers over the centuries. In their search for general laws of human nature, philosophers, right down from the times of Plato to the present, assumed that there exist certain unchanging, invariant attributes, which all human beings share. Plato referred to such unchanging attributes as 'essences'. All one had to do was to discover the key to those 'essences' and one could unlock the doors of human understanding. Moreover there has never been a shortage of theories concerning human nature. Over the years, philosophers, prophets, social scientists, psychologists, sociologists, economists and biologists, have proposed a wide variety of theories of human nature.

But gradually the idea of a universal human nature came to be questioned. Machiavelli perhaps was one of the first philosophers during the Rennaissance period to question the universality of human nature. Locke, the famous British philosopher, gave it no credence. He asserted that there are no innate ideas in the human mind. He proposed the *tabula rasa* theory, in which he argued that nature was a blank slate upon which experience (nurture) etched its indentations, thus pre-empting the present-day controversies related to nature/nurture theory. Locke's formulations were of significant appeal to the early behaviourists, in particular Watson, followed by Skinner. Skinner, the radical behaviourist, even went to the extent of proposing that there were species-specific modes of learning and that all behaviour was modifiable through carefully programmed reinforcement contingencies. But the belief in human nature hasn't quite gone out of fashion and the search for universals has by no means been abandoned.

One of the goals of cross-cultural psychology is its search for 'universals', namely behaviours, which despite variations in cultures, climates, ecology, terrain, levels of affluence, can be classified as universals (Berry, Poortinga, Segall, & Dasen, 1992). We shall discuss these issues in depth throughout the book.

Nature and nurture

The main arguments related to human nature as Fukuyama (2002) points out have centred on defining the boundary line that separates nature from nurture. The controversy between nature and nurture came to a head when Charles Darwin proposed his spectacular theory of evolution. Concepts such as random selection, variations due to environmental influences, survival of the fittest, the limitations set by nature itself on growth and development led to a re-evaluation of the ideas underlying theories of human nature. In keeping with Darwinian theory, it would be more correct to say that the variance in human behaviour is likely to be far greater than for virtually any other species.

Hull (1998) points out that there are no true human universals that can be traced to a common nature. One can hardly talk about human nature without at the same time considering the important role of nurture. Human beings are cultural animals. They are capable of modifying their behaviour based on learning. They are also able to pass that learning on to future generations in non-genetic, culturally transmitted ways (Eisenberg, 1972; Fukuyama, 2002). Paul Ehrlich (2000) goes a step further. He argues that *it is in human nature not to have a single nature*. Human nature can be understood less by its uniformity and more by its variation. It was in the mid-twentieth century that psychologists, biologists and geneticists began to investigate the nature and the degrees of variations in human behaviour with respect to what we are as a result of our experiences.

Modifying the formulation of Locke, it would be fair to say that nature (which consists of our chromosomes, genes, our DNA structures) provides a template on which experience writes. This suggests that there is a continuing interactive process between nature and nurture. Since the interactive process is continuous, it makes it difficult to predict with any degree of precision the influence our genes exercise over our behaviour. Therefore our perception of others, the world around us, and even our own internal subjective world is not simply a matter of inherited biological and genetic mechanisms. It is more than that. It is influenced by our familial orientations, our processes of socialization, which include our beliefs, attitudes, and the values prevalent in our culture.

For any encounter to be meaningful, it is necessary that the persons involved are aware of the rules, which guide and foster their encounters. But for either party to misunderstand the rules, or to flaunt the rules, or to arbitrarily change the rules during the course of the encounters, is likely to lead to an impasse. The rules that guide these encounters are generally unwritten and unspecified.

The problems underlying inter-cultural communication and interaction will be discussed in depth in a later chapter. Suffice it say for the moment that to understand and interpret correctly the behaviours of persons from different cultures one needs to acquire not only a body of objective knowledge but also the sensitivity to construe the world from the perspective of the other person. Sadly one is not born with such ability; nor is it acquired overnight. The reverse is often the case. It is easier to misunderstand than to understand. This is partly because a) one is rooted in one's culture and as a result it becomes easier and safer to see the world from one's own cultural perspective, and b) one is often unwilling to admit that one does not know, or that one does not understand. Under these conditions stereotypes rush in where even common sense might fear to tread.

Stereotypes

A stereotype is a negative, unpleasant value-laden judgment that we often form of another individual or a group that we see as being 'different' from ours. Some differences are quite obvious: skin colour, age, mode of dress, physical appearance, patterns of speech, and so on; others are more subtle, such as a person's social class, education, learning, manners, and so forth. But even a brief encounter with a person may reinforce negative evaluations: the person may appear to talk too loudly, too crudely, too rudely, too coarsely, may have a conspicuous physical handicap or blemish, may smell, may seem unkempt, untidy, aggressive, or whatever. Aronson (1992), Gudykunst and Bond (1997), Matsumoto (1996a) and others have pointed out that when we resort to stereotypes we tend to divide people into 'in-groups' and 'out-groups'. It is then assumed that members of 'in-groups' (that is, the group to which we belong or aspire to belong) possess positive, desirable and praiseworthy qualities. 'Out-groups' on the other hand are seen as possessing negative qualities ranging from indolence and stupidity to cruelty and savagery. Although stereotypes have little or no basis in reality, they are widely shared. They may arise from our initial impressions and intuitions, through hearsay, through the prevalent beliefs within our own in-group, through experience, which may be imagined, baseless, or fantasized.

Persons subscribing to stereotypes can see neither any logical contradictions nor any irrationality in their evaluations of other people. They believe that all the negative characteristics attributed to an individual are also to be found in all the members of that group. Thus the entire group is tarred with the same brush – no exceptions! Thus – all Muslims are fundamentalists! All Hindus are deeply religious and superstitious! All Jews are shrewd and mercenary! All English people are tight-lipped and reserved! All blacks are lazy, and so on and so forth. Allport (1954) pointed out that one of the main functions of a stereotype 'is to justify (rationalize) our conduct in relation to that category' (p. 187). Having placed a person in a particular category, such as bad, or mad, or primitive, or stupid, or lazy, or superstitious, or evil, it becomes easier to justify our own behaviours towards them. We may despise them, avoid them, keep away from them, segregate them, discriminate against them, deny them equal rights and opportunities, banish them, imprison them, torture them, and in extreme cases, exterminate them.

The belief in the truth of stereotypes is the first step in the expression of national and racial prejudices (Allport, 1954). If unchecked, and when skilfully manipulated by political demagogues, such bigotry leads on to acts of extreme violence, which past history reveals, have often led to genocides of the most appalling kind. No country in the world, from times ancient to times present, has been free from the savagery arising out of such bigotry. *All civilizations have been awash with blood.*

Let us flavour a few national stereotypes to understand the generalized nature and their negative value-laden overtones:

- *Americans*: brash, aggressive, naïve
- *Afro-Caribbeans*: dumb, athletic, musical
- *French*: rude, arrogant, untrustworthy
- *Germans*: meticulous, boring, militaristic
- *Indians*: ignorant, religious, superstitious
- *Irish*: lazy, intemperate, alcoholic
- *Italians*: operatic, romantic, quarrelsome
- *Pakistanis*: religious, militant fundamentalist

Paxman (1998), writing about the English, lists a large number of stereotypes, which the English hold against the Welsh, the Scots, the Irish, the Indians and the Africans. He points out that even journalists and other literary figures of the past era, including Samuel Johnson, Thomas Carlyle and several others, traded in ugly and hurtful stereotypes concerning different nationalities. Daniel Defoe, the famous eighteenth-century English novelist incensed at the contempt with which the English held people of other races and nationalities, reciprocated the 'compliment' when he quoted in his poem, *The True Born Englishman* (1701/1984):

... A True Born Englishman's a contradiction!
In speech, an irony! In fact, a fiction!

Here are a few more sweeping statements:

- I know why the sun never sets on the British Empire: God wouldn't trust an Englishman in the dark. (Duncan Spaeth)
- The Irish are a fair people; they never speak well of one another. (Samuel Johnson)
- If one could only teach the English how to talk and the Irish how to listen, society would be quite civilized. (Oscar Wilde)
- A woman is only a woman, but a good cigar is a smoke. (Rudyard Kipling)
- It was wonderful to find America, but it would have been more wonderful to miss it. (Mark Twain)
- The German mind has a talent for making no mistakes but the very greatest. (Clifton Fadiman)

Slightly less well-known stereotypes related to what two foreigners of the same country do when they meet abroad:

- The Italians start an opera.
- The Indians start a family.
- The Germans start a putsch.
- The English start a club.
- The French start a romance.
- The Americans start a car park.
- The Greeks start to bicker.

One can see from the above that stereotypes are confined not just to national groups; they cover an entire range of human feelings and experiences, stigmatizing persons, countries, art, literature, drama, music, language, culinary practices, religion, patterns of worship, work patterns, and so on. There is hardly anything about which people do not form a stereotype!

It is often assumed that stereotypes generally, if not exclusively, are formed by people of limited learning, limited education, by the poorer, ill-informed sections of any society. This, as Mark Tully (1995), a renowned English journalist and broadcaster who lives and works in India, says is a mistaken assumption. He reports, 'I have never been able to understand why British journalists who are open Francophiles, overt admirers of America, or enthusiasts for some other Western country which they report are not likely to be accused of being partisan, but correspondents who identify with countries whose cultures are not European or American are regarded with the gravest suspicion' (p. viii). Furthermore, one has only to examine the writings of philosophers from Plato and Aristotle onwards, right through the middle Ages to the nineteenth and twentieth century (e.g. Ward & Lott, 2002) to realize the contempt in which several eminent philosophers held people of other races.

Sadly, even the writings of many humanist and liberal thinkers such as Locke are sprinkled with hurtful and damaging stereotypes (Parekh, 2000). Kathy Squadrito

(2002) presents a critical analysis of John Locke's writings concerning the 'native' (American Indians). Locke argued that since (American) Indians could not rise to the level of a civilized society, it was incumbent upon the English to colonize them – a sentiment not dissimilar to the one expressed by Rudyard Kipling, when he referred to the control and power exercised over the Indians (in India) as a 'white man's burden'. It has been argued that Locke's writings on the subject led to the dispossession of native Indians in America. John Stuart Mill, the great liberal thinker who is seen as the defender of the ideology of cultural diversity and self-development, found it very easy to justify colonialism and the gradual disintegration of traditional cultures and societies which, according to him, were found wanting 'in autonomy, individuality, go-ahead character, restless energy, ambition and constant progress, they were backward societies ... and had to be civilized' (quoted in Parekh, 2000: 45). He even insisted that such societies had no right to territorial integrity. Despite the dangers inherent in the use of stereotypes they remain as the main armoury of most people (Allport, 1954; Aronson, 1992; Brown, 1965; Campbell, 1965; Pettigrew, 1978). Stereotypes appear to be an integral part of humanity. Like a deadly virus, most people tend to become infected by them.

Can stereotypes be changed? Several factors, such as contact, exposure, working together, status and power, socio-political changes, legislation, are known to have a beneficial impact on certain kinds of stereotypes (Lindgren & Tebcherani, 1971; Nichols & McAndrew, 1984; Triandis & Vassiliou, 1967). In certain instances, the 'reality' of a situation contradicts the stereotype that a given individual may have formed about a particular group, as when a white person encounters a black or an Asian doctor in a hospital or in a surgery. How does the bigot in this situation deal with the contradiction? One of the easiest ways is to 'create' a separate pocket in one's mind, in which these contradictions are accommodated. But the stereotype remains intact. 'You're ok, mate, but the rest of your countrymen!' I have heard this sentence thrown at me on so many occasions that I have come to see it as an oblique apology – an iron fist in a velvet glove.

In recent years, the creation of 'positive' stereotypes has been initiated by multi-national organizations anxious to promote their technology, their consumer goods and services across the world (Aronson, 1992; Fukuyama, 2002; Taylor, 1989). In addition to multi-national organizations, The World Bank, The IMF, the United Nations and its several organs, several governmental agencies, including non-governmental organizations, are all actively involved in promoting positive stereotypes related to a variety of issues, ranging from health and illness, education, family welfare, respect for and defence of human rights, to the eradication of poverty, AIDS, and other life-threatening diseases.

A word of caution, lest one is borne aloft on clouds of misplaced optimism. Even positive stereotypes can easily get tarnished and turn into negative stereotypes. This becomes evident in international sports events, such as the Football World Cup, the

Cricket World Cup, Olympics, where the pride and 'honour' of a country appears to be at stake. Witness the 'flag-waving', the 'tribal singing', the 'tribal bonding' of each nation. Witness the passions that soar to dizzy heights of patriotism followed by fierce, ugly battles between supporters of rival teams. Such 'positive' stereotypes often lead to disastrous social, economic, and political consequences (Stiglitz, 2002).

Let me highlight the nature of stereotypes – at a milder level – by describing two casual encounters. The object is to demonstrate that even a casual encounter between two strangers can lead to a misunderstanding, which, rightly or wrongly, may appear hurtful to one of the parties in the encounter. At a later stage though, one may reflect upon the misunderstanding rationally and analytically, and although appreciating the triviality of the misunderstanding, one may yet fail to arrive at the truth or otherwise of the misunderstanding.

Box 1.1

This casual encounter occurred in London several years ago. It was a warm and glorious Sunday morning; all the summer flowers were in bloom. A benevolent sun shone out of a cloudless blue sky. I strolled down to my local newsagent to buy the Sunday papers. There was no one in the shop, except for the shopkeeper, who, I guessed, was in his mid-forties. I had not seen him before. I smiled at him and asked for the papers. We chatted briefly as I bought a few other items from the shop. Just as I was about to leave, he turned to me and said, 'Oh, you do speak posh!'

I was surprised, embarrassed and flattered by his compliment: surprised because I do not speak English with what is generally considered to be a 'plummy' accent, embarrassed because the compliment was undeserved, and flattered that he had chosen to see my accent as a posh accent. I thanked him and wandered through the park, heading home. On the way, my thoughts turned to the brief encounter, and putting the paper aside, I sat down in a bench to reflect on what had transpired.

On the face of it, it seemed such a trivial and inconsequential event that it hardly merited a second thought. Yet I felt bothered by it, and could not let it go. There was something about the compliment, which somehow did not seem right. I felt impelled to explore it further.

Interpretation of Box 1.1

Several questions come to mind. Why did the shopkeeper pay me this compliment? Had the benign weather created in him a mood of generous benevolence? Would he have paid me the same compliment had it been a cold, miserable, and rainy day? Was he seeking human companionship and had used this less-than-subtle strategy to hold me

(Continued)

a while longer in his shop? Would he have noticed my accent had the shop been crowded with other customers? There could have been any number of reasons. But the question, which struck me most forcefully, was this: would he have paid the same compliment if the customer, instead of me, had been, like him, white? I wondered and came to the conclusion that perhaps not. If that were the case, why was I singled out for such a compliment?

This line of reasoning on my part led to a series of questions, which may be stated as a set of propositions:

1 The white shopkeeper holds the belief that in general non-whites do not speak 'posh' English.
2 He encounters an Asian (Indian), who is non-white.
3 He concludes that the Asians do not speak 'posh' English.
4 The accent surprises the shopkeeper.
5 The shopkeeper pays a compliment to the Asian customer.

Let us for a moment assume that the shopkeeper would not have paid me the compliment had I been white. If this interpretation were valid, then it would follow that the shopkeeper was operating from a set of *negative* stereotypes concerning the ability of Asians to speak English in a manner that *he* considered to be 'posh'. 'Posh' English could then be spoken only by the educated middle or upper middle class white Caucasians. Such an interpretation transforms the nature of the compliment: it then becomes a back-handed compliment – such as the one which many non-white professionals, in the course of their working lives, have often heard from whites: 'You're ok; it's your fellow countrymen …' In other words, the compliment drains out the melanin from the Asian or African or whoever, turning him (or her) into a token white. Creating a small pocket in one's consciousness (or sub-consciousness) in which a few non-whites are allowed to take *temporary* abode, as 'honorary whites', is not an uncommon form of psychological defence. This is a *modern* form of racism, which is referred to as *aversive racism* (Katz and Taylor, 1988). But there is no way of establishing that the shopkeeper was in any way an aversive racist, or an old-fashioned racist. To my shame, I must confess that initially I partially believed in his being an aversive racist and felt that the shopkeeper may have acted on a set of negative stereotypes. But to arrive at such an interpretation without any shred of evidence would not only be baseless but would also be an indication of my own paranoia. It might even be construed as a form of inverted racism. In fairness to the shopkeeper, it must be recognized that the shopkeeper may in fact have been paying me genuine compliment, far, far removed from any implied negative stereotypes related to skin colour and ethnicity. Since I have no way of knowing what went through the shopkeeper's mind at that moment, the truth in this case shall never be known. Had I decided to return to the shop and confront the shopkeeper on this matter, I would have looked a far greater fool than I already was in entertaining such unfair and undignified interpretations in the first instance. One must not discount the possibility that the compliment may have been genuine, but it may have sprung from a set of negative stereotypes related to the inability of non-whites to speak English with a 'posh' accent.

Box 1.2

A few years ago, my wife and I were flying from Bombay to London. Since our flight was delayed by a few hours, we sat in one of the restaurants at the Sahar International Airport, to have some breakfast. The restaurant at that early hour of the morning was virtually deserted. The maitre d'hôtel who took our order was extremely courteous and friendly and spoke fluent English. He was dressed in a dark suit, with the badge of the hotel for which he worked pinned to his lapel. He took our order and several minutes later, a waiter in a white uniform brought our breakfast. From time to time the maitre d'hôtel come to our table and spoke to us. Nothing of any great importance was said; pleasantries were exchanged. He had time on his hands. So did we.

After we had paid the bill, I asked the maitre d'hôtel, if I might make a local telephone call. I wanted to speak with one of my family members before our flight was called. The maitre d'hôtel stood by his desk, paying hardly any attention to my telephone conversation. At some point, however, I started to speak with my cousin in Urdu, instead of in English. At this he pricked his ears, looked at me with unrestrained curiosity. The manner in which he drummed his fingers on his desk made it clear that he was anxious to talk to me once again. No sooner did I put the phone down than he looked at me with surprise, bordering on wonder.

'You speak very good Urdu, Sir. Your accent is perfect! Where did you learn to speak such good Urdu?'

Interpretation of Box 1.2

I could tell that he was complimenting me more on my accent than on my linguistic repertoire. Other than a misperception of my cultural identity, the interpretation of the second encounter is not significantly different from the first one. It was clear that he too operated on the stereotype that foreigners did not speak fluent Urdu. His surprise and eagerness to discuss it with me testified to that. Besides, it would seem reasonable to suggest that in the course of his work at a large, busy international airport, he must have waited on several foreigners from all over the world virtually every day. The fact that he was surprised at hearing what he referred to as fluent Urdu being spoken by a foreigner would suggest further that he may not have heard it before.

The lesson that I learnt from these trivial encounters was that it is necessary to confront one's own underlying motivations, including one's own stereotypes and prejudices, openly and honestly. In my eagerness to remove the mote from the other person's eye, I had overlooked the beam in my own. Such an attitude is hardly likely to foster genuine cross-cultural interactions.

First, if a serious misunderstanding or misinterpretation can occur in such casual, trivial, and impersonal encounters – regardless of the basis of the misunderstanding – what are the chances of very grave misunderstandings occurring in encounters which are serious, prolonged, and intense in situations that involve working together, living close to one another? Understanding one's stereotypes and inner prejudices is no doubt the first step in acquiring some sensitivity in one's attempts to understand and meaningfully relate to people of different cultures.

The two episodes, taken together, appear to run through a similar theme. In the first one, there was the expectation that Asians do not normally speak 'posh' English (whatever the term 'posh' might mean) and when one comes across someone who does, one is taken by surprise. In the second, too, there is a similar expectation that the English (or whites) do not normally speak Urdu (or other Indian languages) fluently. The few that do, do not speak it with a good, clear accent. The major difference, which underlies the two episodes, is the one related to the perception of identity. In the first instance there was no mistaking my 'racial', 'cultural', or 'ethnic' identity. In the second instance, the maitre d'hôtel misperceived my 'racial', 'cultural', or 'ethnic' identity. He could of course have been misled in his misperceptions by seeing me with my wife, who is English. There were similarities too. The shopkeeper in London was surprised that an Asian could speak 'posh' English. The maitre d'hôtel was equally surprised that an 'Englishman' could speak fluent Urdu.

It is now time to examine the nature of culture, which will then serve as a launching pad to understanding the nature, rationale, and scope of cross-cultural psychology.

Culture

Like most abstract words, such as intelligence, personality, goodness, virtue, the word 'culture' is also difficult to define. It is more easily misunderstood than understood, more sinned against than sinned. It is a word that is quite often misused, abused, and reviled. Sometimes, it is used with reference to a person: learned, suave, sophisticated, well mannered, therefore, cultured. At other times it is used as a mantra to explain away differences between groups of people. Thus, if any noticeable differences in attitudes, values, and behaviours are not easily understood, they are 'explained away' in terms of cultural differences. The term 'culture' may then become the wastebasket into which unexplainable, unacceptable, social and moral behaviours are often dropped. In recent years the diverse uses of the word 'culture' have proliferated within the social sciences. Diverse inputs, instead of making the meaning any clearer, have tended to cloud the concept even further. For instance, the term 'culture' has been divided and subdivided into other diverse terms. Sociologists have written about popular culture, media culture, mass culture, minority culture, ethnic culture, aborigine culture, black culture, white culture, feminist culture, gay culture, lesbian culture, drug culture, colonial culture, modernist and post-modernist culture, Marxist and post-Marxist culture, high-brow, middle-brow, low-brow culture, techno-culture, organizational culture, managerial and executive culture, culture of complaint, culture of violence, culture of the classes, the culture of the under-classes – the list is virtually endless. Further divisions have been created by adding the prefix 'sub' to the word culture, creating a sub-culture of violence, a sub-culture of drugs, and so on. If one were being pedantic, one could sub-divide a sub-culture into a sub-sub-culture, creating a meaningless fragmentation of the concept.

Popular conceptions of culture

At a popular level in our own subjective way, we all have a fairly clear idea of what we mean by culture, although we may not be able to offer a precise definition of the word. We are each born into a particular family, which has a genetic and social history of its own. A family is a microcosm, an integral part of a wider section of our community, which in turn is a microcosm of the society in which we live and grow up. Society provides us with a structure. It provides us with rules and norms of behaviour. It regulates our beliefs and practices, and as an integral, united part of society we are able to make sense of ourselves, of our own lives, of others, and of the world around us.

Yet, amidst the unity we notice wide variations in people, not just skin colour, but language, dietary practices, religious beliefs and practices, social interactions and relationships. The differences extend into religious, political, social, economic, physical, ecological, linguistic and other environmental domains. Despite the heterogeneity, we experience a sense of belongingness, a feeling of 'oneness' among the diverse groups around us. As a good example of unity within heterogeneity one might turn to the state of Kerala in Southern India, where four different religious groups – Hindus, Muslims, Catholics, and Jews – have lived for centuries in relative peace and amity. Although they worship different gods, participate in different rituals, eat different foods, they are all, to a large extent, united by a set of core values, which form an integral part of the culture. However, such feelings of 'oneness' under certain conditions are easily overturned, leading to the formation of hurtful and antagonistic feelings and stereotypes towards those who seem different from us. Yesterday's friend becomes today's sworn enemy.

Academic conceptions of culture

In the past, information concerning peoples of other cultures came from different sources – from the writings of travellers, novelists, the Crusaders, conquistadors, explorers, mariners, colonial administrators, civil servants, religious missionaries, historians, 'soldiers of fortune' and scholars who visited and stayed in foreign lands. Their writings were a curious mixture of racism and denigration, wonder and appreciation, anger and envy of the magnificent aesthetic, artistic, architectural, poetic, philosophical, religious, and literary creations of people of Eastern civilizations, whose roots were shrouded in antiquity.

Very few social scientists undertook systematic and carefully designed ethnographic field studies. Most of the early writings of social scientists, including those of anthropologists and psychologists, were derogatory and racist in their formulations (Bock, 1980; Harris, 1968). Non-European and non-white societies came to be judged as being backward, primitive, superstitious, and inferior, whereas white, Western societies as being enlightened, intelligent, moralistic, and superior. Differences between blacks and Europeans were generally explained in terms of intellectual and moral inferiority; the blacks were seen as a lazy, immoral, and primitive race. Their putative 'sexual prowess' was elevated to a myth of gigantic proportions. In America in particular, a black man was seen as a potential sexual threat to the white women. Several literary masterpieces such as those of Ralph Ellison (1952) *Invisible Man*, William Faulkner (1948/1968) *Intruder in the Dust*, Richard Wright (1940/1972) *Native Son*, James Baldwin (1964) *Nobody Knows My Name*, Harper Lee (1960) *To Kill a Mockingbird* among others, have condemned such blatant beliefs. But they had little impact on the dangerous stereotypes held by Americans, particularly in the southern states of America.

Anthropological perspectives

It was not until the early twentieth century, however, that anthropologists gradually began to undertake ethnographic field studies. But such studies were the exception rather than the rule. For even Sir James Fraser, who wrote 12 volumes of the classic *The Golden Bough* (1932/1954), which was a study in magic, superstitions, rites and rituals, and religious practices across all societies in the world, claimed with unconcealed arrogance that he had never met nor indeed visited any of the lands of the people of whom he wrote! In this context it is interesting to note that the British Empire had established vast colonies all over the world. Yet few concerted attempts were made by social scientists to undertake ethnographic field studies. Looking at it through hindsight, it is clear that a great and unique opportunity went a-begging (Jahoda & Krewer, 1997).

The study of cultures has been of interest to anthropologists (Geertz, 1973; Kroeber & Kluckhohn, 1952; Leach, 1964; Murdock, 1964; Singer, 1961; Tyler, 1969; Shweder & Sullivan, 1993) and more recently to cross-cultural psychologists (Barnlund & Araki, 1985; Berry et al., 1992; Brislin, 1990; Kakar, 1979/1992; Laungani, 1999b, 2000b, 2001c, 2002c; Roland, 1988; Segall,

Dasen, Berry & Poortinga, 1999; Smith & Bond, 1993; Triandis, 1972, 1994; White, 1947; Whiting, 1963).

Their early writings as was stated earlier were blatantly racist and derogatory. But gradually, under the charismatic leadership of Franz Boaz (1911), several anthropologists, including Margaret Mead, Ruth Benedict, and others, started to undertake ethnographic field studies – with 'unbiased', 'value-free' purity. Boaz was sensitive to criticisms of ethnocentrism and racism with which the discipline had become tainted. His object was to undertake pure, unbiased, scientific research. All personal biases, subjective predilections, educated guesses, stereotypes, and so on had to be jettisoned – before undertaking a voyage to another country.

Margaret Mead, the famous American anthropologist, undertook fascinating studies in the South Sea Islands, and among the tribes in New Guinea. Malinowski (1927) studied the Trobriand Islanders in the South Pacific. Ruth Benedict (1934/1946) studied the Japanese psyche. The anthropologists stayed among the people of the cultures they visited, immersed themselves in their lives, participated in their rites and rituals, so as to understand the structure, the beliefs, the values and the patterns of their lives. In general they were concerned about constructing a holistic 'system' that would enable them to describe and explain comprehensively the lifestyles, the attitudes, the beliefs and the values of the people they studied. They defined culture in holistic terms, as the 'total attainments and activities of any specific period and group of humans' (Triandis, 1980: 1). It incorporated within it all the distinctive human forms of adaptation and the distinctive ways in which different human populations arrange and organize their lives on earth (Levine, 1973; White, 1947). Each culture was seen as having its own unique structure and pattern. And each part of the pattern included, beliefs, attitudes, values, rules, laws, symbols, rites, rituals, taboos, patterns and networks of com-munications, which allowed them to order, organize, and regulate their lives.

However, in their concern to undertake pure, unbiased, research, uncontami-nated by their own preconceptions, they adopted a *relativistic* stance. Cultures, they argued, needed to be studied from within their own unique framework. Some relativists question the very enterprise of cross-cultural comparisons. They argue that since each culture is *unique*, it makes no sense whatever in undertaking any comparisons (Shweder & Sullivan, 1993). Therefore the only legitimate position they could adopt was one of *relativism*. Such a position, in so far as the anthro-pologists were concerned, had one significant advantage. It allowed them to 'play safe', in the sense that it allowed them to describe and explain observed differences in cultural terms, *without making any value judgements, which could lead to their being accused of ethnocentrism.* They believed that to impose their own values was not only wrong but was also unlikely to increase their understanding of other cultures. In so doing they also 'closed the door' on having to explain inter-group cultural variations in universal biological and genetic terms. Conceptually and methodologically their discipline was more allied to psychiatry and psychoanalysis than to psychology (Jahoda & Krewer, 1997; Klineberg, 1980). But with increasing collaboration the dividing lines separating disciplines have blurred and in recent years new specialist areas such as psychological anthropology, cognitive anthropology, cultural psychology, and so on, have emerged (Munroe & Munroe, 1980). Their explanations to a large extent were in keeping with Freudian theory, which by then had had a powerful impact on the Western mind. In keeping with Freudian formulations, they offered interesting insights into the psyche of the people they studied.

Psychological perspectives

How do psychologists define and construe culture? Barnlund and Araki (1985) tend to construe culture from a *behaviouristic perspective*. To them, cultures 'have no existence except as they are manifest in the behaviour of people who constitute them. A culture is only an abstraction based on common [characteristics] ... displayed in the behaviour of a given community of people' (p. 9). Clearly there is a problem with this definition. How would the authors promoting such a view of culture explain deviant, bizarre, uncommon, anomalous, and even one-off behaviours exhibited by some of the people of such a society? Valsiner (2000) on the other hand sees culture in terms of *organized psychological functions*, which may be intra-personal and also inter-personal. Culture, according to Haviland (1975), may be seen in terms 'of shared assumptions where people can predict each other's actions in a given circumstance and react accordingly' (p. 6). Geertz (1973) identified culture as a historically transmitted pattern of meanings embodied in symbols' (p. 89). Many psychologists have emphasized several factors which constitute a culture: ecology, physical geography, climate, common language, dietary practices, religious beliefs, and so on (Leach, 1964; Murdock, 1964; Whiting, 1963). Some on the other hand have focused on the value systems and the networks of communications as being the essential ingredients comprising a culture. A few have argued that a proper definition of culture would need to include geographical territory occupied by the people one referred to as belonging to a culture. Helman (1994) looks upon culture as a set of guidelines for understanding one's own behaviour, our interactions and relations with others, and one's own construction of the world.

When examined carefully, the differences in definitions and interpretations of culture are cosmetic rather than structural. What unites the cross-psychologists in their attempts to understand cultures is their belief that all human beings share several common universal behavioural and emotional characteristics – what they refer to as *absolutism,* a term generally favoured by Western psychologists. At the same time, each culture or each society has its own unique features, which vary along several important dimensions, such as ecology, climate, levels of education, technological development, political, social, economic, and environmental conditions, beliefs, attitudes, and value systems. Value systems have a significant bearing on a variety of other factors, including child-rearing techniques, patterns of socialization, development of identities, kinship networks, the social and familial relationships, work and leisure pursuits, religious beliefs and practices of people of that society (Kakar, 1979/1992; Laungani, 1998; Roland, 1988; Smith & Bond, 1993; Whiting, 1963). Thus their task, as they see it, is to investigate and highlight the processes, which are universal across cultures and can be explained in biological and genetic terms and those that are culture-specific.

It is now time to take stock. Despite the theoretical differences that separate the anthropologists from the cross-cultural psychologists there appears to be a fair degree of consensus among them concerning the nature of culture. Both groups of academics have articulated the salient features that are inherent in all cultures. The differences lie mainly in their theoretical orientations and the methodological strategies used to investigate the problems. What is indeed refreshing is the fact that the boundaries that divided one discipline from another have blurred. New inter-related disciplines, such as psychological anthropology, cognitive anthropology, comparative anthropology, forensic and medical anthropology, cultural psychology, indigenous psychology, multicultural psychology, have emerged and have led to occasional cross-fertilization of research strategies. Whether such cross-fertilizations will bear fruit or lead to cross-sterilization is a futuristic issue.

Let us now try to incorporate the diverse viewpoints, weave them together to obtain a clearer and more precise view of culture.

Culture:

- All cultures possess a set of core (primary) features.
  The core features constitute the essential requirements of any culture.
- All cultures possess and a set of *peripheral (secondary)* features.
  The peripheral features may vary from culture to culture.

Core features of a culture:

1 A past history, which may be recorded and/or oral.
2 Regulated political, legal, and social systems and communication networks.
3 A dominant, organized religion(s) within which the salient beliefs and activities (rites, rituals, taboos, and ceremonies) are given meaning, legitimacy, and a sense of continuity.
4 A set of core values and traditions, including regulatory norms of personal, familial and social conduct, patterns of socialization, kinship patterns, gender roles, to which the people of that society subscribe and attempt to perpetuate.
5 Artefacts unique to that society, such as literature, works of art, architecture paintings, music, dance, drama, religious texts, philosophical texts.

Secondary features of a culture:

1 Freedom from linguistic, religious, political, and social persecution.
2 Shared common language(s).
3 Internationally recognized common physical and geographical boundaries within which people of that particular society live.
4 Housing and other living arrangements.
5 Socially accepted dietary, health, and medical practices.

Conclusion

I should like to end this chapter on a note of caution. Although the above exposition of culture is comprehensive, there is a nagging possibility that the dramatic changes taking place in the world today may force one to re-evaluate our notions of culture and consequently our approach to cross-cultural psychology. At least two major issues are of serious concern: the problems related to the process of globalization, and those concerning multiculturalism, or cultural diversity. We shall discuss these issues in the next chapter.

Nature, Rationale and Scope of Cross-Cultural Psychology

The previous chapter was devoted to understanding the nature of culture. We saw that 'culture' is a fairly fluid term. It holds different meanings for different people. It also arouses different feelings and emotions in different people. We noticed that each of the major social science disciplines approaches the notion of culture differently. Their approaches vary in terms of (1) the kinds of problem areas they investigate, (2) the theoretical assumptions, which guide their work, and (3) the methods they use in their investigations. These points need some explanation. It is best to do it with a hypothetical example in which you play the lead role.

Imagine that you are a world-renowned anthropologist. You have been invited to study the people living in one or two of the Polynesian islands in the South Pacific. Imagine further that your academic training has been in Freudian psychology and psychoanalysis, and you hold that subject dearly to heart. Freudian theory provides you with a framework within which you undertake your detached observations. You are aware too that you cannot be completely detached since you live among the Islanders. Thus on the one hand you are a participant in their culture, and on the other a detached observer – two roles which are not always easy to play, despite your rigorous training. Your interest, let us say, is in observing young children and the manner in which they are socialized by their parents and carers. You undertake a series of careful observations of children of varying ages, keep detailed notes and records of both the children and their carers, and eventually when you have accumulated substantial data, attempt a meaningful explanation of the process of socialization. You discover that all the children go through the unconscious conflicts and traumas related to the three principal stages of psychosexual development postulated by Freud – the oral, the anal, and the phallic. These findings allow you to construct a composite picture of the patterns of socialization of children in the Polynesian islands. On the strength of your findings you argue that children not only in Western countries but also in Polynesian cultures experience similar unconscious conflicts. In other words, the psychosexual stages are universal. They affect all children all over the world. And culture, it would seem, does not make a difference.

Now this is precisely what Malinowski (1927) did when he stayed among the Trobriand Islanders in the South Pacific in the early 1920s. He found the children went through precisely the same types of conflicts that had been originally postulated by Freud – but there was a difference. While Freud 'discovered' Oedipal hostility which male children manifested towards their biological fathers, Malinowski found that the children manifested their hostility against their *uncles* and not against their biological fathers. Why was that the case? He found that it was the uncles who were largely responsible for bringing up children, not their biological fathers. From this Malinowski concluded that the Oedipus complex is a universal phenomenon, a crucial stage, which all children went through *but their unconscious hostility was a function of culture.*

All this is fine. But now let us suppose for a moment that you are not an anthropologist but a scientifically orientated psychologist, well versed in learning theories, experimental design, quantitative analyses of data and so on. Would your observations and your interpretations have been different from those of Malinowski? More to the point, would it even have occurred to you to look out for unconscious conflicts and traumas in children? The short answer is, no. The reason, as you know, is simple. Behaviourist theories have no 'truck' with Freudian theories. They are hardly, if at all, concerned with unconscious mental processes. Their focus has always been on overt, observable, measurable behaviour. Given your own attachment to a scientific model, your assumptions and methods of observations of children would have been markedly different from those of the psychoanalytically orientated anthropologist. You would see child development largely in terms of stages of learning (instead of stages of psychosexual development) where reinforcement contingencies and other behavioural techniques for the shaping and the modification of behaviour played an important role. You would even wonder if there was any 'truth' in the notion of the Oedipus and the Electra complex, and whether such vague and esoteric terms were worth considering, let alone investigating.

It now becomes clear that the problems we elect to study and the methods we choose to investigate the problems are guided by the theoretical framework to which we subscribe. Implicitly or explicitly, we carry our theoretical assumptions with us as a tortoise its shell. While the tortoise cannot discard one shell and acquire another, we can certainly shift our allegiance from one framework to another – or as Thomas Kuhn, the American philosopher, would have phrased it, abandon one paradigm and adopt another.

Nature and rationale of cross-cultural psychology

Cross-cultural psychology is concerned with understanding behaviours of people across cultures. Such a concern becomes meaningful if we assume (and are able to verify our assumptions) that our behaviour, to a large extent, is influenced by the culture in which we live. This is not to suggest that there is no uniformity of behaviours across cultures. There are behaviours which to a large extent are influenced by the cultures in which people live, and there are those that transcend cultural boundaries and might be considered to be universal. In the previous chapter we noted that the anthropologists in their pioneering field studies of cultures 'stole a march' over the cross-cultural psychologists, who in that sense were belated entries in this field of research. Moreover, since the 'approaches' and the methodologies of the cross-cultural psychologists were different, if not incompatible, each went their own way.

In general, cross-cultural psychology is concerned with the following three questions:

1 Are we all the same the world over, regardless of our cultural backgrounds?
2 Are we each a product of our own culture?
3 Do we share certain common psychological and behavioural characteristics across cultures?

These are intriguing questions. The first one, as one can see, is concerned with the idea of *universalism*, or *absolutism*, namely that human beings regardless of their cultural backgrounds, regardless of their upbringing, display the same or similar emotions and other psychological and behavioural characteristics. The second question raises issues of cultural specificity, namely the dominant impact of culture on shaping behaviours. The final question attempts to bridge the gap between universalism and culture-specificity. It suggests that a variety of behaviours transcend cultural boundaries and are common to other cultures. Let us discuss each of these viewpoints briefly and see where we stand.

Universality of human nature

In the past, 'human nature' was used as an umbrella term to explain a variety of complex behaviours, including greed, weakness, strength, avarice, selfishness, aggression, virtue, kindness, sacrifice, persistence, lust, indolence, sloth, willpower, lack of willpower, pursuit of pleasure, avoidance of pain, and so on. It was argued that all human beings are products of nature and most if not all our behaviours are also a product of nature. Philosophers over the centuries, from Parmenides, Plato, and Aristotle onwards to the present century, have speculated on the nature of human nature. Religious beliefs too have played a great part in enforcing such views. The supporters of the creationist doctrines – a vibrant voice in certain States of America – argue that we are all God's children and are thus created equal and we all share a common human nature. (However, as George Orwell and several others have pointed out, some are more equal than others.) Most Europeans subscribed to the biblical accounts of creation, described in the first chapters of Genesis; to them they were true (Simonton, 1999). Such beliefs have not gone unchallenged. Locke, the famous British philosopher, for instance, gave little credence to the notion of the universality of human nature. He proposed the *tabula rasa* theory in which he argued that what others referred to as inborn human nature was a blank slate on which experience (nurture) etched its indentations.

The controversy between nature and nurture came to a head soon after the publication of Charles Darwin's *The Origin of Species*. In it he argued that human beings, like other species, had evolved over centuries, and in that sense were no different from other species. Darwin's spectacular theory led to a re-evaluation of the ideas underlying theories of human nature. The variations observed in human beings and in animals far outweighed the assumed similarities, thus limiting the role of genetics in understanding human behaviour. Incensed at Darwin's formulation, the supporters of the creationist theory of the human race questioned and dismissed Darwin's theories. Over a hundred years of wrangling has not brought the Darwinists and the Creationists any closer. The battle between the creationists and the evolutionists hasn't quite died down. Not surprisingly, it is still very much in evidence in the United States – particularly within the Bible-belt areas, and even has the tacit support of President Bush.

In addition to Darwin's monumental work on evolutionary theory, exciting discoveries were being made in physiology, biology, statistics, and neuro-physiology.

Psychologists in America and in Britain, and to a certain extent in Europe, felt a compelling need to undertake precise, quantifiable, scientific research, and by so doing hoped to discover laws of human behaviour which would have universal applicability and would be used in promoting human welfare (Jahoda & Krewer, 1997; Miller, 1969).

In espousing the natural science paradigm (Laungani, 1996c), they were convinced that their laws and discoveries would apply not only to the American people but also to the rest of the world. In their zeal, they dispensed with meta-physical abstractions and discarded religious, existential, spiritual, and such other fundamental human concerns from their rigid scientific vocabularies. In their attempts to discover universal laws of human behaviour, every conceivable aspect of human behaviour – perception, cognition, motivation, intelligence, personality, memory, child development, socialization, identity, adolescence, psychopathology, social behaviours, prejudice, diagnosis and treatment of mental disorders – was examined from a scientific perspective.

At the beginning of the twentieth century, the American psychologists chose to ignore the impact of Darwinian theory and undertook 'context-free' research studies to determine the universality of human psychological processes (Segall, Dasen, Berry, & Poortinga, 1999). Thus the whole approach of the 'scientifically orientated' psychologists of the early twentieth century was aimed at using methods which included standard psychological tests and such other measuring devices on people of other cultures, with the underlying belief that these methods would ultimately enable them to 'discover' the lawfulness of human nature, which was unchanging and common to humanity (Klineberg, 1980). The American psychologists in their misplaced zeal chose to believe that the *world was as they saw it*. They believed too that the rest of the people in the world also perceived the world as *they* perceived it – through American spectacles. They were convinced that they would obtain findings that would be 'universally valid for all of humankind' (Segall et al., 1999: 34). In other words, they were proposing what Segall and colleagues refer to as an *absolutist* position, which assumes that 'human phenomena are basically the same (qualitatively) in all cultures: honesty is honesty, and depression is depression, no matter where one observes it' (p. 1103). I find it difficult to sympathize with this oversimplified view of human nature.

So strong was their belief in the idea of universality that they continued to deny the influence of cultural factors on human behaviour (Laungani in conversation with West, 2004). They remained culturally myopic. Luckily, cultural myopia is not a genetic abnormality and is not incurable. It is an inability, an unwillingness, or failure on the part of an individual to recognize that some of the most obvious differences in beliefs, attitudes, values, and behaviours among different groups of people are related to their own unique cultural backgrounds. If one is to make sense of their behaviours, their belief systems, the manner in which they perceive the world, it is imperative that one takes into account the impact of those cultural factors. Had the 'scientifically oriented' psychologists got off their 'high horses' and acquired a different pair of 'culture-sensitive lenses' they could hardly have failed to notice that human nature was not the same the world over. Luckily, in recent years cross-cultural psychology has finally moved away from its untenable and indefensible position and has adopted a relatively open-minded, inquiring approach to cross-cultural research. But there is no indication that this change will lead to a paradigm shift, which Thomas Khun articulated in his famous book, *The Structure of Scientific Revolutions* (1962).

Are we each a unique product of our own culture?

Does each culture produce its own inimitable template? A simple answer would be a qualified yes. In the past, cultures often remained isolated from other cultures. To a large extent they remained uninfluenced, unaffected, and unwashed by other cultures and thus were able to retain their own cultural idiosyncrasies, values, beliefs, behaviours, and their unique modes of living. The pioneering studies of anthropologists brought to our awareness the lifestyles of people living in remote and isolated parts of the world.

The anthropologists advocated a *relativistic stance*. No attempts were made to compare cultures, and consequently no attempts were made to grade cultures on a scale of values. An anthropologist could not say, would not say, that one culture was better or worse than other cultures. The *raison d'être* for their unwillingness to grade cultures was based on their belief that each culture evolved its own unique system. They believed that it would be naïve, meaningless, and in the long run pernicious to judge cultures. For judgement involves using standards. This they found impossible to do because they believed that there was no logical and objective way of deciding what and whose moral, ethical, religious, social, familial, economic standards would form the basis of cross-cultural comparisons.

Thus on the one hand there were the *cultural relativists* (the anthropologists) who placed all their emphasis on the influence of cultural factors as explanations of human behaviour, and on the other there were the *absolutists* (the scientifically oriented psychologists of the past) who sought to explain behaviours to a large extent in biological, non-cultural terms. These were the two extreme poles, which divided anthropology from psychology. It is only in recent years that both groups, to a certain extent, have shifted ground from their entrenched positions (Jahoda, 1990). This is evidenced in the sub-disciplines which have mushroomed around psychology and anthropology: psychological anthropology, comparative anthropology, indigenous psychology, cross-cultural psychology, cultural psychology, biological anthropology, and so on.

Sharing common psychological characteristics across cultures

Even a casual observation confirms the view that people are different – not just in different cultures, but even within one's own. None of us is a carbon copy of the other. We are not the alphas and betas that Aldous Huxley portrayed in his novel, *Brave New World*. Imagine if each of us were! Imagine a world in which we were all like robots. The world as we know it and see it is not like a gigantic photocopier producing the same image, creating the same person, again, and again, and again, ad infinitum. And heaven forbid if we all resembled Mary Shelley's Frankenstein! What a frightening and deadly boring world would we inhabit. How refreshing it is to be different.

Hull (1998) points out, there are no true human universals that can be traced to a common nature. One can hardly talk about human nature without at the same time considering the important role of nurture. Human beings are cultural animals. They are capable of modifying their behaviour based on learning. They are also able to pass that learning on to future generations in non-genetic, culturally transmitted ways (Eisenberg, 1972; Fukuyama, 2002).

Reason, intuition, experience, and observation tell us that despite differences we also share a variety of common emotional, behavioural, linguistic, and other psychological characteristics with others, which anthropologists refer to as *taxonomies of universals*. Several anthropologists (Goldschmidt, 1966; Lonner, 1980; Murdock, 1945; Wescott, 1970) have constructed a variety of such taxonomies of universals. The taxonomies range from simple universals, biological factors, human sexuality, human aggression, facial expressions, non-verbal behaviours, child rearing practices, and so on.

There are other commonalities too. Right through our lives we may experience moments of joy, wonder, happiness, excitement, peace, good fortune, a sense of fulfilment in our lives. On the negative side we also go through pain, suffering, fear, sorrow, depression, illness – although each of us may define and react to such experiences differently. Suffering, as the Buddha had pointed out, is part of the human condition. We are also conscious of and 'live' in an extended timescale. Through reflection, we can 'move' in and out of *our* past, live momentarily in the present, and may even acquire some awareness of what the future might hold. We know too that we have no awareness of time and life *before* we were born, and we know too that we shall have no awareness of time and life *after* we are dead. Our experiences also tell us that we all, without exception, share a common 'fate' – a fate of which we are all painfully aware. We know that at some point our life as we live it will come to an end. Despite our denials, despite our attempts to prolong it, despite our increasing faith in the powers of medical science, the curtain *will* come down over our life, never to rise again (Becker, 1973). We shall all cease to be. It will all be over. It is this extraordinary awareness that separates us from animals who live in the present, in the here and now, and have no awareness of their mortality. But we do. *We all know that death is but a breath away!*

One would have been justified in assuming that by now the debate concerning the universality and variation in humanity would have died down and been laid to rest – but apparently, not. Opinions are still divided, the controversies sharp as ever. The problem continues to be argued at several levels: religion, philosophy, ecology, environment, climate, biology, science, anthropology, psychology, politics, genetics, neuro-physiology, and so on. But our main concern, however, is to search for and examine those psychological processes which meet the criteria of universals and those which are culture-specific. To achieve this end it would be necessary to take into serious consideration some of the major factors, including religious beliefs, family structures, ecology, climate, levels of industrialization, levels of education and affluence, political structures, and so on, which have a bearing on the issue. We shall delve into these factors from time to time throughout the book, as and when it becomes relevant to raise them.

The current status of cross-cultural psychology

Cross-cultural psychology has had a chequered career. In the early part of the twentieth century, cross-cultural psychology started as a fledgling discipline, lacking direction, partly overshadowed by anthropology. Research in the area was sporadic, idiosyncratic, and empirical. Little attention was paid to theory construction. Nor were any serious attempts made to understand cultures from non-European perspectives, or the perspectives of the subjects studied. Many of the pioneering studies of Bartlett (1923, 1937), Benedict (1934/1946), Mead (1928, 1932), Rivers (1901), Woodworth (1910), and others were Eurocentric in their biases. Many of the earlier studies, as Klineberg (1980) points out, were painfully racist in their formulations. Psychological tests, purporting to measure cognitive, perceptual, and intellectual processes validated on European subjects, were administered to the 'natives' and 'primitives' from other cultures. Their low scores were taken as indicators of their inferiority to the European races. It was not until the 1960s that cross-cultural research in psychology started to have an accelerated growth (Biesheuvel, 1969; Jahoda & Krewer, 1997). This was reflected in the growth of publication outlets and the creation of journals devoted specially to cross-cultural psychology. One wonders why there was such reluctance on the part of Western psychologists to test their theories in other parts of the world. Not even Britain, which after all had its colonies spread around the globe. But as I have pointed out elsewhere (in conversation with West, 2004), conquerors do not always feel the need to understand the conquered. It is clear that exciting research opportunities went a-begging. Nonetheless, the early research studies created the groundwork for future developments. Although in the last 40 years cross-cultural psychology has 'come a long way', it has still not acquired the status of a separate discipline with its own epistemological, theoretical, or content-related features (Ratner & Hui, 2003).

Although cross-cultural psychology is genuinely concerned with understanding human diversity, about discovering behaviours which are 'universal' or culturally invariant, and those which are influenced by cultural factors, its main concern appears to be with methodology. Cross-cultural psychology, as Brislin (1983) points out, *is defined by its method.* Several other scholars working in the field also appear to share this view (Berry, 1969; Eysenck & Eysenck, 1983; Frijda & Jahoda, 1966; Vijver & Leung, 1997). Thus, the emphasis hitherto has been on the empirical testing of hypotheses *derived from mainstream psychological theories.* In recent years, serious disagreements have begun to appear among cross-cultural psychologists concerning methodological and theoretical issues. The disagreements have centred round the types and the viabilities of the methodological approaches adopted in cross-cultural investigations. Many researchers favour the use of an eclectic model in their investigations (Miller, 1997), and there are others (Ratner & Hui, 2003) who prefer a scientific methodological approach in their investigations. It has been argued that an eclectic approach has serious limitations (Laungani in conversation with West, 2004). It is not easily amenable to any rigorous testing, nor can meaningful comparisons be undertaken. On the other hand the scientific approach has its own serious limitations, for the measures used in other cultures to test specific hypotheses may turn out to be culturally irrelevant, even meaningless. We shall discuss these issues in depth in the next chapter. There are three other issues that need our attention before bringing this chapter to a close:

1 Globalization.
2 Multiculturalism and cultural diversity.
3 The growth of indigenous psychologies.

Globalization

In the last two to three decades the scope and the study of cultures has extended beyond one's wildest imagination. The study of cultures is no longer the preserve of 'ivory-tower' academics, as was the case a few decades ago.

There are several interested groups, ranging from the International Monetary Fund (IMF), The World Bank, the World Health Organization (WHO), the World Trade Organization (WTO), multi-national organizations, financial institutions in Western countries, all of who have vested financial, economic, and political interests in the poverty-stricken developing countries. The suave bureaucrats in the above organizations – 'missionaries in designer suits and crocodile leather briefcases' – profess their stated aim: the eradication of poverty and an equitable distribution of wealth in developing countries. The eradication of poverty can only be achieved by a concerted attempt at globalization.

Several other factors too have contributed to the massive push towards globalization: the extraordinary growth in telecommunication networks, extra-terrestrial satellite systems, the rise of the Internet, the push towards the use of mobile telephones around the world, transfers of currencies around the world, and such other technological and monetary innovations. All these factors have contributed significantly to the growth of the 'culture industry', which has become more than an academic issue: it is now a major political and economic 'force', which is of increasing concern to major Western governments.

The bureaucrats are aware that unlike the marauders and the conquerors of centuries past, they cannot trample their way into developing countries. They need to tread with caution, circumspection, and discretion. They need to have a deeper understanding of the lifestyles and the culture of people they visit – hence the growth of the 'culture industry'.

Evidence suggests that foreign aid, which is a major thrust in the process of globalization, has brought benefits to millions of people in the developing countries. It has conferred colossal, economic, technological, informational, social and political benefits to the developing nations (Das, 2002; Marglin & Marglin, 1993; Stiglitz, 2002). According to Das (2002), economic prosperity has brought about an upward shift in levels of poverty, a newfound confidence in people, evident in their Western style of living which includes luxurious high-rise blocks, the furnishing of their homes, membership to exclusive Western-type clubs, Western culinary preferences, modes of dress, artistic and other aesthetic preferences, increasing use of communication and information technologies, and last but not the least, foreign travel.

Globalization, it would appear, has led to modernization and Westernization of people in Eastern cultures, and it shall not be long before this leads to homogenization. Eastern cultures will soon start to imbibe and internalize Western values of *individualism, rationalism, humanism, empiricism,* and *secularism.* Over time, they will become indistinguishable from other Western countries. Since the West will set the 'gold standard', all developing countries will aspire to achieve such a standard, thus completing the process of homogenization. The idea underlying homogenization, as Parekh points out, is based on the belief that 'there is only one correct, true or normal way to understand and structure the relevant areas of life' (2000: 1). That, *of course* – as the 'experts' never tire of reminding us – is the Western way!

Stiglitz (2002), however, warns us that in the long-run, globalization will have a devastating effect on developing countries because it will result in the erosion of one's cultural traditions and heritage. A large part of the 'blame', according to Stiglitz, rests with the Western bureaucrats involved in negotiations of financial aid, technological 'know-how' and other forms of assistance to developing countries. He argues that the mismanagement, highhandedness, insolence of Western bureaucrats, create more problems than they are meant to resolve. *And this, combined with their lack of adequate understanding of the local, regional, and national problems, customs, and cultures, has a devastating effect on developing countries.* Stiglitz is of the opinion that economic prosperity in developing countries, if not exactly a myth, is a failing enterprise.

Multiculturalism and cultural diversity

Multiculturalism, like postmodernism, is a term that defies a precise definition. It is best seen as an umbrella term, which incorporates within it a variety of shades of meanings, nuances, attitudes, beliefs, and values. However, the central tenets of multiculturalism can be stated as:

- All human beings are products of their own culture.
- Multiculturalism is not a political credo.
- Each culture has its own uniquely acquired ways of construing its own world(s), which give meaning to their lives.
- Within each culture there exist a plurality of values and traditions.
- The 'plasticity' of human behaviour enables persons to transcend (within certain limitations) their own culturally embedded boundaries.
- Each culture is in some ways flawed because no culture has all the answers to the Socratic question of what constitutes the good life *and how it should be lived* (Parekh, 2000).
- Each culture has something of value to offer to another culture and, equally importantly, something of value to learn and imbibe from another culture.
- A mixture of cultures is more likely to lead to an enrichment of one's intellectual, emotional, spiritual, humanitarian, and moral visions.

From a psychological point of view, the mixture of cultures within the mainstream of Western society provides exciting opportunities to academics, scholars, clinicians, doctors, health professionals, artists, writers, poets, musicians, and a host of other interested care-providers, for learning and acquiring insights into a variety of cross-cultural issues. In addition to clear psychological insights it also becomes possible to tease out the social, economic, and political consequences which are likely to occur with people of different cultures, speaking different languages, imbibing different moral values, share and/or compete for available resources related to occupations, housing, medical care, and so on (Jahoda & Krewer, 1997).

The multiculturalism movement – or rather crusade – started in the 1970s, first in Canada and Australia, and then in America, followed by other European countries including the United Kingdom, Sweden, Denmark and Germany. The world has turned into a global village. In the last three decades there has been a steady flow of people from the EU countries, from Eastern Europe, from the new Commonwealth countries, from Africa, Hong Kong, Korea, Thailand, China, Australia, New Zealand, Japan, and from countries in South East Asia and South America to Britain, Canada, America and several other European countries. Persons coming to the West have included a vast assortment of political refugees, asylum seekers, highly educated professionals, tourists, and other types of 'settlers'.

Most Western nations are founded on the ideology of liberal democracies. The important question concerning multiculturalism in the West is one of 'how'. How shall the respective governments of each of the Western countries deal with questions of rights and duties, equities and equal opportunities, freedom of speech and worship, health and medical care, childcare, the care of the elderly and the handicapped, problems of language, learning, education, housing, parity of treatment, gender differences, sexuality, and the freedom to live their lives in accordance with their own value systems, without fear of discrimination, persecution and rejection? How will all these vital issues be dealt with in a satisfactory manner? One of the many tenets of humanitarian societies is their concern for and the care of the minorities, the underprivileged, the marginalized, *living not only within their own societies but also the recent migrants*. But despite their liberal democratic ideologies, not all Western nations are united in their views on the agendas (and of course the kinds of agendas) to create conditions that would lead to the creation of genuine multicultural societies. Opinions are divided. At one end of the political continuum, there are the liberal, humanitarian Westerners who see themselves as 'their brothers' keepers' and believe it is their moral and humanitarian duty to look after not only the newcomers who migrate into their country but also many groups who feel marginalized and alienated within the mainstream society. At the other end of the political spectrum are those who view migrants at best as potential resources for 'cheap labour' and at worst as 'free-loaders', 'spongers', and 'exploiters' of the system. The lessons of history too point out that human beings are perhaps the only species that finds it difficult to live not only with themselves, but also with one another. Human beings perhaps are the only species that kills for fun, sport, and profit. Human beings perhaps are the only species that imprisons, incarcerates, tortures, burns and executes people who hold beliefs that are different from those of their captors. A psychoanalyst following in the footsteps of Freud would point out that the human psyche, which lies concealed in the deeper layers of one's unconscious, is like a cauldron of violent, explosive, instinctual forces of unreason which, from time to time like the brew concocted by the three witches in *Macbeth*, overflows, causing havoc.

Among many politicians too there is an oft-voiced opinion that for multiculturalism to 'work' – whatever that might mean – it is incumbent upon the migrants to imbibe the norms and values of the host country. This would speed up the process of assimilation and integration within the mainstream society. Occasionally politicians go to absurd lengths in their attempts to create a unified multicultural society. Here is a recent example from Britain: a few years ago one of the Ministers (the Home Secretary) put forward the strange suggestion that all migrants – not only the ones that have been living in Britain for several decades but also the recent arrivals – would need to learn the British National Anthem, as a test of their loyalty to Britain. This was a bizarre suggestion, to say the least. One wonders how many indigenous native-born white British know the words of the National Anthem let alone having the ability to sing it! Besides, one could train a parrot to recite the National Anthem. Luckily, saner counsels prevailed. The suggestion was ignored and the politician's 'profound' pronouncements died through inertia.

When persons leave their own culture and migrate to another, they do not leave their history, their cultural norms and values behind. Nor do they jettison them at the frontiers of their chosen country. They bring with them their culturally acquired psyche, and all that they have imbibed from their own culture: their social, communal, familial, norms and values, their hopes and their aspirations, their dreams and their desires, their fears and their doubts, their art, their music, their literature, their culturally determined ways of construing the world and everything that was an integral part of their culture. Admittedly people have the ability to adapt and incorporate some changes within their cultural identities, and many over time even succeed in acquiring a fairly fluid bi-cultural persona – a beautiful term coined by Alan Roland – which allows them to switch from one to the other as demanded by a given situation. Like the proverbial beast of burden, culture is a load that is not easily discarded. One never travels light. One carries one's culture like a tortoise its shell. The shell offers safety and protection. When danger threatens, one, not unlike the tortoise, withdraws into one's shell. The shell is robust and solid. It can withstand knocks and shocks. But destroy the shell and you destroy the tortoise. One is handcuffed to one's culture by its past social history. Attempts to coerce migrants to jettison their 'cultural baggage', or discard their shell upon migration – as seems to be the stated aim of several politicians in Britain and in other Western countries – is not only naïve but dangerous.

At a personal level, I might add that although I have lived in England for more years of my life than I have in India, there is within me an 'Indian-ness', which I can no more discard than a tortoise its shell – nor would I like to! My refusal to transform myself into a compliant English 'clone' often gets me into hot water, but I'd rather the defiance than the surrender. For surrender would mean the loss of my 'birthright' and with it my moral integrity. At any rate it is virtually impossible to relinquish an identity that one has developed over the years and pull out a new one with the speed of a magician pulling a rabbit out of a hat or the great B. F. Skinner pulling a habit out of a rat! I could not predict the damage that such a change would do my psyche. I was unprepared to take the risk.

But over the years one may learn to play the 'game' of living in two cultures without consciously tilting the balance either in one direction or the other. Alan

Roland in his excellent thought-provoking book, *Cultural Pluralism and Psychoanalysis* (1996), refers to such a person as a 'bicultural' person.

Yet all is not doom and gloom. There is a noble, angelic, even god-like quality in humans, such as Hamlet points out when he says:

> What a piece of work is man,
> how noble in reason,
> how infinite in faculties,
> in form and moving how express and admirable
> in action how like an angel,
> in apprehension how like a god:
> the beauty of the world,
> the paragon of animals!

(Hamlet, Act II, Sc.2)

From a social psychological point of view, the mixture of cultures within the mainstream of British society provides exciting opportunities to academics, scholars, clinicians, doctors, health professionals, and a host of other interested care-providers, for learning and acquiring insights into a variety of cross-cultural issues. For instance, several fundamental questions can be raised. How do people from different cultures bring up their own children? What constitutes child abuse in their culture? What are the parameters that they consider important in the socialization process? What are their attitudes and values towards women, towards the sick, the infirm, and the elderly? What rules govern their family structures and kinship patterns? How do they grieve and mourn for their dead? How do they perceive members of the host culture, and vice-versa? How do they attempt to relate to one another? To what extent do they succeed or fail to succeed in forming meaningful relationships with members of the host culture? What are the factors which lead to failures and successes? What effect do the dominant values of the host culture have on their own system of values? How far do their own values impinge upon the values of the host culture? In addition to clear psychological insights, it also becomes possible to tease out the social, economic, and political consequences which are likely to occur when people of different cultures, speaking different languages, imbibing different moral values, share and/or compete for available resources: occupations, housing, medical care, and so on. What are the short-term and long-term consequences which are likely to occur in such a culturally diverse society?

In recent years, multiculturalism has become an important item on the political agenda of most European governments. In Britain, multiculturalism (and cultural diversity: the two terms are virtually indistinguishable from one another) is seen as a major issue, and various government initiatives have been put into action to achieve this end in several sectors of society (Parekh, 2000). Even in the United

States, the struggle by the blacks followed a cultural route; the black leaders were vociferous in their claims for recognition and acceptance of their ethnic identity, whose origins they traced to Africa. 'Black is beautiful' was one of the most popular and strident signature tune of the blacks in America in the 1960s and 1970s. From a psychological point of view it needs to be stressed that although all human beings share a variety of common biological, physical, and psychological characteristics and behaviours, they have uniquely different, diverse, and idiosyncratic ways of responding to their environment and to their own world. Human behaviour is neither static nor a 'finished' product. It evolves. It reconstitutes itself culturally. Human behaviour is self-reflective and diversified. Human beings, regardless of their cultural origins, have the ability to share certain common values and agree to common commitments. It does not therefore follow that such consensual agreements will necessarily lead to a corrosion of one's cultural identity, one's traditional values, leading to the acquisition of a 'universal' Western identity. Despite economic prosperity (or economic deprivation), people do not jettison their own cultural identity. Most human beings, like chameleons, have the distinct ability to adapt and incorporate the changes within their cultural identity, without wrecking their ancient structure.

Let us take India as an example. The history of foreign rule over India extends over a millennium. India was ruled by the Turks, the Moguls, the Dutch, the Germans, the French, the Portuguese, and last but by no means the least, the English. Yet, Indians managed to retain their unique caste-system, their law of karma, their glittering gallery of gods, their 35 to 40 recognized languages, their 1000-plus dialects, their extended family networks, and to a large extent, their ancient values, which bound them together and continue to do so. Even the concerted attempts initially by Muslim rulers and a few hundred years later by Christian missionaries to convert Hindus (particularly from the lowest caste) to Islam and Christianity respectively, did not meet with great success.

Herein lies an interesting paradox. On the one hand there is increasing recognition of multiculturalism and cultural diversity all around the world (the major aims of cultural diversity have been enshrined in a book published in 2002 by UNESCO, entitled *Cultural Diversity: Common Heritage, Plural Identities*, and on the other, a belief in the eventual homogenization of cultures, the world over. Despite the difficulties in reconciling these two polarized views, it would be unwise to underestimate or ignore the impact of globalization on the cultural identity, the pattern of life, and the structure of family life of people in developing countries.

It is possible that globalization in all its magnitude and economic power may transform the ancient value-systems of Eastern cultures, and lead to a process of 'cloning'. At a superficial level it might seem as though the East is beginning to become indistinguishable from the West. But the cosmetic changes taking place must not lull one into believing that the bell has already begun to toll, proclaiming the demise of ancient values in Eastern cultures. It is difficult if not impossible to predict what the long-term consequences of such a change are likely to be.

The growth of indigenous psychologies

Until about the 1960s, cross-cultural research, as stated earlier, was largely a Western enterprise. The choice of research projects, the theoretical assumptions, the methods used to investigate the problems, all had a distinctive Eurocentric orientation. *In other words, Western approaches were used to investigate Western 'problems' in Eastern cultures.* Psychology in Eastern countries itself was then a fledging discipline – a poor imitation of Western psychology. Even the psychology courses that were taught at undergraduate and graduate levels in universities in Eastern countries, including Asia, were exclusively Euro-American in their orientation. So were the books and journals – imported texts from England, America, and a few other European countries.

During my own undergraduate and postgraduate days in India, the psychology we were taught was mainly from the imported texts. For example, in social psychology, we learnt about a variety of racial, political, and social problems, about child development and social interaction, about racial prejudice and authoritarianism, group dynamics and group conflict, about social perception and social interaction, about conformity and obedience to authority, and so on, *from an exclusively Western perspective*. But we were taught little or nothing about problems at 'home', such as those related to poverty and inequality, urban and rural life, family health and welfare, population control, caste and inter-group prejudices, religious conflicts, and so on – themes that were as relevant in the 1960s as they are today. It was clear that Euro-American psychology had been exported lock, stock, and barrel – almost, one might say, as an industrial product.

Not only the teaching but also the research undertaken by psychologists in Eastern countries was largely imitative (Enriquez, 1993; Kakar, 1997; Kim & Berry, 1993; Laungani, 1996c; Nandy, 1974; Sinha, 1993; Sinha & Kdo, 1997). Their main research strategies involved investigating and replicating Western-type problems using the original and/or translated versions of Western instruments. The imitative trend needs an explanation. There was among many psychologists a belief (not entirely unjustified) that imitative research would enable them to have their research findings published in European and American journals, and in terms of their own career prospects help procure them teaching and research assignments in European and American universities. But the lack of relevance of such studies within the Eastern cultural context either went unnoticed or was ignored for reasons of expediency. A few critics, including Sinha, have looked upon researchers engaged in imitative studies – particularly the ones in India – as those who have been unable to shed the yoke of their colonialist upbringing.

The growth of indigenous psychologies has been slow, if not painful. But indigenous psychology is now becoming a vibrant force within cross-cultural psychology, and poses a challenge to the hegemony hitherto enjoyed by Western psychology.

But what is indigenous psychology, or more importantly, what are indigenous psychologies? Given the vast number of countries that constitute eastern cultures and including those in Central America, it makes sense to talk about indigenous psychologies in the plural, instead of indigenous psychology in the singular.

Durganand Sinha offers a pertinent explanation; he refers to indigenization as the 'transformations of the scientific psychology that was borrowed from the West that would allow it to take on a character suited to the socio-cultural milieu of the country' (1993: 34). The indigenous psychology approach is part of the scientific tradition. Thus, Sinha extols the virtues of the scientific methods used by Western psychologists and recommends their usage in investigating problems that are of relevance to that particular culture. Kim and Berry too offer a similar definition. According to them, indigenous psychology is 'the scientific study of human behaviour (or the mind) that is native, that is not transported from other regions, and that is designed for its people' (1993: 2).

So far so good. But the problem that arises is this: if any comparisons between cultures are to be made, how might they be accomplished? This is a serious methodological and ethical problem, which we shall discuss in the following chapter.

A Conceptual Model of Cross-Cultural Differences in Eastern and Western Cultures

A strange event unfolds before your eyes as you stand in the balcony of an old building, overlooking a narrow street in Lahore, Pakistan – a country you have never been to before. Although the sun has been up for quite a while, it is relatively cool and quiet outside. Suddenly you hear sounds of laughter, singing, and rejoicing. A large group of people, men and women, come surging into the street. Amidst the rejoicing, the singing the dancing, the giggles and the laughter, you notice several women parading a white silk sheet by holding its ends above their heads. The bed-sheet has a few red stains on it. The women stop outside a house; a door opens and they all rush inside.

Your curiosity aroused, you ask yourself, who are these women? Why are they singing and dancing? Why were they parading a bed-sheet? What do the red stains signify? From the dancing, the singing and the laughter you are certain that it is a joyous event, a festive occasion. But what does it signify? Is it some kind of a religious festivity? How do you explain it to yourself? It is obvious that it is a joyous occasion. That much is clear. It is obvious too that the bed-sheet is in some important way connected with the rejoicing. Would you have guessed (or worked out) the function of the bed-sheet and the red stains on it? Among many orthodox Muslim the parading of the bed-sheet with its red stains, through the streets, indicates the consummation of a marriage and, *more importantly,* proves the virginity of the bride. A public demonstration of the consummation of the marriage and the evidence of the bride's virginity are seen as reasons for rejoicing. The marriage is deemed to be pure. This is a popular cultural ceremony performed by many Islamic families in India, Pakistan, and several other Middle Eastern countries.

It is in situations such as these that our interpretations of events may falter. Whatever cues one may have used in the past to interpret an event may be found wanting in these instances. Even our sense of rationality and logic may fail to come to our assistance. We remain puzzled, even mystified. The more unique a given cultural experience, the more difficult it becomes to understand it and consequently explain it. To understand such experiences and explain them satisfactorily would require a shift – a gestalt switch – in one's cultural perspective. Without such a shift, one would be condemned to perceiving an event almost exclusively from one's own cultural perspective. In so doing, one might easily fall into the trap of misreading or misinterpreting the experience or the event to which one is exposed. Some events cannot be explained rationally, cogently, and coherently without taking into consideration their cultural origins. Bereft of their cultural underpinnings, the events make no sense whatever. As an extreme example of our inability to explain an event or a series of events let us turn to the writings of Primo Levi. Primo Levi managed to survive the atrocities during the period of his incarceration in the Nazi concentration camp in Auschwitz. Although he survived the horrors and returned to his home in Turin where he wrote several books on his experiences, he found it difficult to 'explain' the atrocities in a sensible, rational, and coherent way. All the 'markers', the cues, the parameters that he had used in the past to understand and thereby explain events failed him. He found it impossible to 'make sense' of the atrocities that he witnessed all around him for the entire duration of his confinement. He could not explain them because he could not understand them. This is undoubtedly an extreme example. But by no means does it alter the logic of the argument.

It needs, however, to be emphasized that not all events one experiences in another culture are unique and therefore difficult to interpret correctly. As has been made clear in the preceding chapters, human beings share a variety of common biological, physical, social, and emotional characteristics with the rest of humanity, suggesting that there are certain attributes and characteristics that are universal. We also observed that certain kinds of behaviours and psychological characteristics are also found in other cultures, but are manifested differently – the expression of feelings and emotions being a prime example. Our concern for the moment is to consider briefly those behaviours that to a large measure are culture-specific. Once one is able to perceive the same event from within its unique cultural context, it soon begins to unfold and even explain itself in a rational and logical manner.

Each such event sheds its own light on the cultural-specificity of behaviours. Each event tells us about the nature and even the origin of that particular event. But it does not allow us to go beyond that event and draw any general conclusions. A collection of such events, though not without their intrinsic interest, does not serve a great purpose in our understanding cultural differences in an integrated holistic manner. Compiling a catalogue of events, however detailed and comprehensive, does not enable us to formulate a comprehensive theory. What one needs therefore is a conceptual framework, or a theoretical model, from which testable hypotheses can be deduced and tested. Such models are by no means easy to construct. They cannot, as it were, be snapped out of thin air. One might even start with a hunch, a guess, an observation, or a hypothesis. How one arrives at a hypotheses or a theory is immaterial. The history of science is replete with several fascinating and even bizarre examples of how scientists have arrived at theoretical formulations from which they have been able deduce hypotheses, which they have then subjected to rigorous critical tests.

Theoretical model of cross-cultural differences

Over the years I have been involved in constructing and validating a conceptual model which attempts to explain similarities and differences between Eastern cultures and Western cultures in terms of their major values systems, which guide and influence their behaviours. Values are the currently held normative expectations that underlie individual and social conduct (Laungani, 1995b). They form the bases of familial, social, religious, legal, and political order. This is not to suggest that values do not change. The process of change varies from culture to culture. Some cultures are slow to change and others, like the European cultures, have demonstrated rapid changes, which are associated with the vast social, economic, technological, and scientific developments that have taken place in the last 100 years or so.

As was stated at the end of the previous chapter, the reasons for electing to examine cross-cultural differences from an Indian and from an English perspective is due mainly to the fact that India is the largest elected democratic country in the world, with its current population at around 1.1 billion – and increasing. It is united by its secular politico-legal system and its written Constitution. It is also a country of refreshing diversity, which is manifest in its ecology, climate, language, religious beliefs and practices, diet, dress, patterns of worship, levels of affluence, education, lifestyles, and a variety of other cultural differences. It is, in a sense, a country that contains within it multiple cultures, the parallels of which are to be found in other Eastern countries, ranging from the Middle Eastern Arab States to countries in South East Asia and beyond. Similar observations can also be made about Britain. Although in size a relatively small country, Britain too contains within it multiple cultures and multiple religious groups, including the Irish, the Scots, the Welsh, Europeans, Australians, Asians, Afro-Caribbean, South Africans, East Africans, people from the Middle East, Nigerians, Ethiopians, Sudanese, and more recently the political refugees and asylum seekers from the Eastern European countries, including Russia.

The proposed model offers four interrelated *core values* or *factors*, which distinguish Western cultures from Eastern cultures, or more specifically, *British* approaches from *Indian* approaches to the understanding of cultural differences.

The four core values or factors are:

- Individualism — Communalism (Collectivism)
- Cognitivism — Emotionalism
- Free will — Determinism
- Materialism — Spiritualism

To avoid any misinterpretation of the above factors, the following ground rules need to be established:

1 The two concepts underlying each factor are *not* dichotomous. They are to be understood as extending along a *continuum*, starting at, say, Individualism at one end, and extending into Communalism at the other. A dichotomous approach tends to classify people in 'either/or' terms. Such an approach is limited in its usefulness. People seldom fit into neat theoretically formulated and/or empirically derived categories. The sheer complexity and variability of human behaviours and responses within and between groups, even within a single culture, precludes serious attempts at such categorical classifications.

2 Categorical taxonomies may offer neat quantifiable numerical values, but their usefulness in understanding and explaining differences and similarities in core beliefs, attitudes, and values between cultures remains problematic. Life does not fit in neatly in 'either/or' or 'yes/no' categories.

3 A dimensional approach, on the other hand, takes account of human variability. It has the advantage of allowing us to measure salient attitudes and behaviours at any given point in time and over time. It also enables us to hypothesize expected theoretical and empirical differences and changes in positions along the continuum both within and between cultural groups.

4 Each of the hypothesized dimensions subsumes within it a variety of attitudes and behaviours, which to a large extent are influenced by the norms and values operative within that culture.

5 It needs to be made clear that the four factors are by no means orthogonal. They are correlated.

The theoretical bases of these factors have been described at length elsewhere (see Laungani, 1990, 1992a, 1992b, 1993, 1995b, 1996b, 1997c, 1999b, 2000a, 2001a, 2001b). Sachdev (1992) has provided an empirical validation of the four factors. In her research study, by means of specifically designed questionnaires, Sachdev compared the beliefs and values of the British-born Indian school children with those of the Caucasian school children in West London. The two groups of children – although both born and socialized in a predominantly Western culture – showed marked preferences in terms of their favoured value systems. Her research also enabled her to predict the sets of conditions. Independent studies undertaken by Sookhoo (1995) and by Laungani and Sookhoo (1995) provide further empirical validity to the theoretical constructs.

Before discussing each factor it needs to be pointed out that the constructs to the left of each factor are applicable more to British culture (and to Western cultures in general) and those on the right to the Indian culture (and to Eastern cultures in general). Let us now discuss briefly each of the core constructs .

Individualism – communalism: individualism

The dominant distinguishing feature of contemporary Western society is its emphasis on individualism. From a theistic standpoint, the roots of individualistic philosophy can be traced in the writings of St Augustine in the fourth century, who asserted that one can and should be able to commune with God directly, without having to receive the sanctions of the clergy or the Church. Over the centuries theistic notions of individualism gave way to secular and humanistic notions of individualism as a result of a viable social and political philosophy, which came into being during the sixteenth century. This feature of Western society sets it apart from non-Western societies, which are characterized by their emphasis on *collectivism*.

In recent years, much has been written on the concept of individualism and collectivism (Hofstede, 1980, 1991; Hui & Triandis, 1986; Kagitcibasi, 1997;

Kim, Triandis, & Yoon, 1992; Kim, Triandis, Kagitcibasi, Choi & Yoon, 1994; Laungani, 1998b, 1999b; Matsumoto, 1996b; Schwartz, 1990; Triandis, 1994). The concept has come to acquire different meanings.

Main features of individualism

Individualism is seen as an ability to exercise a degree of control over one's life, to cope with one's problems, have reliance upon oneself, being independent, autonomous, responsible for one's actions, self-fulfilment and self-realization of one's internal resources. As Triandis (1994) points out, individualism is concerned with giving priority to one's personal goals over the goals of one's in-group, or of one's family members.

The notion has also aroused debate among Western thinkers (Bellah, 1985; Kagitcibasi, 1997; Lukes, 1973; Matsumoto, 1996b; Riesman, 1954; Schwartz, 1990; Spence, 1985; Triandis, 1994; Waterman, 1981). Some writers, however, have been wary and have argued that the ideas underlying individualism are incompatible with communal and collective interests. The 'dog-eat-dog' philosophy is seen as being divisive, inimical in terms of the promotion of communal goals. It alienates fellow-beings from one another. However, there are others who extol its virtues (Sampson, 1977). It is seen as being in keeping with the philosophy of humanism and secularism, which emphasizes, among other things, the notion of 'dignity of man/woman', its disentanglement from theology and religion, and its espousal of scientific enterprise as the fundamental bases for understanding the Universe (Cooper, 1996). Its increasing popularity has also been attributed to the Weberian spirit of capitalism and free enterprise. Sampson (1977) sees no reason why the philosophy of individualism should not also nurture a spirit of co-operation and coexistence.

Development of identity

The major role of genetics and biological factors in the acquisition of identity is beyond dispute. In Western societies, identity is construed largely in developmental terms. The process of identity formation starts in infancy and according to received wisdom passes through several *critical* (and potentially traumatic) stages, from childhood, to adolescence, and into adulthood. One can construe the development of identity in Eriksonian terms, in Freudian terms, and also in cognitive-behavioural terms. To acquire a stable, rational, and appropriate identity, which asserts one's strengths, which is located in reality, which separates the individual from others, and which reflects one's true inner being is by no means easy. In Freudian terms, there is a constant struggle (often unconscious) between the demands of the id and the ego and the pressures of the super-ego, which if left unresolved can lead to severe neurosis in the individual. Erikson too in his own theory of identity development refers to a breakdown in identity, which may be due to a hasty acquisition of an identity – 'identity closure' – or of a diffusion of identities.

The pressure to acquire a stable identity often results in conflict, which if unresolved leads to severe stress, and in extreme cases to an identity crisis (Camilleri, 1990; Erikson, 1963; Maslow, 1970, 1971; Rogers, 1961, 1980).

Existential dread and loneliness

By its very nature, the philosophy of individualism makes it difficult for persons to share their problems, fears, anxieties, and dread with others. As several existential philosophers, from Kierkegaard and Nietzsche to Husserl and Heidegger pointed out several years ago, individualism creates in people an existential loneliness, which as Albert Camus pointed out in his famous book, *The Myth of Sisyphus* (1955), is an integral part of the human condition. The emphasis upon self-reliance – the expectation of being responsible for one's success or failure – imposes severe stress upon the individual and can lead to severe psychiatric disorders. A similar theme of individualism runs through the writings of Jean Paul Sartre. Sartre too believed that as human beings we are free, not only free but *condemned* to being free in a world which is without meaning, other than what we as free individuals might bring to it by our actions. But to exist as a human being is inexplicable and wholly absurd.

Individualism and the freedom it entails come with a price. The absurdity of the human condition creates a sense of dread, anxiety, and *anguish,* and an acute fear of what Sartre refers to as 'nothingness', which becomes more acute when we contemplate the final nothingness: *death.*

Maintenance of 'boundaries' – physical and psychological space

One of the dominant features of individualism is its recognition of and respect for an individual's physical and psychological space. People do not normally touch one another, for that is seen as an encroachment of one's physically defined boundaries. Second, physical contact, particularly between two males – an innocent holding of hands in public – may also be misconstrued, if not in the present liberal political climate it certainly was in past. The taboos related to physical touch are so strong that even in times of grief they are not easily violated. Even eye-to-eye contacts between two people are normally avoided. Several studies have shown that the effects of violating another person's physical space lead to severe stress and, in extreme cases, to neurosis (Greenberg & Firestone, 1977; Rohner, 1974).

Closely related to the concept of physical space is that of 'psychological space'. This is concerned with defining boundaries that separate the psychological self from others, or as Martin Buber refers to it, a separation between I–Thou. It implies a recognition of and respect for another person's individuality. It is an idea of immense value in the West, respected in all social situations. It comes into play in virtually all social encounters, from the most casual to the most intimate. One hears of people feeling 'threatened', 'upset', 'angry', 'awkward', 'confused', and so on when they feel that their subjectively defined space is invaded. Even in the case of anxiety, grief, mourning, and depression, people tend not to intrude. They are reluctant to volunteer support for fear of invading the other person's 'psychological' space. Vine (1982) reviewed the major studies in the area related to crowding – the invasion of psychological space – and found that violating another person's psychological space gives rise to stress and other forms of mental disorders.

Changing family structures

In the past, a family unit normally consisted of the father, the mother, their two to three children, and even the grandparents. The father was seen as the patriarch, the proverbial 'bread-winner'. He had no major role to play in the day-to-day bringing up of children. But in the last three to four decades the situation has changed dramatically. Formalized marriage has lost its status in Western society (Dumon, 1992). Cohabitation without marriage has increased. The rate of divorces has risen. At least one-third of all families in England are single-parent families, headed by a female, and over 25 per cent of the population lives alone. Further changes have occurred in demographic trends, economic recessions, wars, famines, migrations, and technological innovations. The widening opportunities for women may also account for the changes that have taken place in families.

These factors may have 'destabilized' society, creating a sense of loss of community life, particularly in the urban metropolitan cities. From a psychological point of view, major changes have occurred in collective values, particularly those which support individualism where, as we have seen, the needs of an individual take priority over the needs of the family and the group. Although the family is recognized as the basic unit, the microcosm of society, the changes in society have altered the roles and functions of both men and women in families. It is clear that the 'traditional' role of the family as a self-sustaining, self-contained unified unit has changed almost beyond recognition. Given the fact that the number of one-parent families in Britain is on the increase, and given the steady rise in teenage pregnancies, one cannot predict the impact that these factors will have on the growth and development of children (Laungani, 2005b).

Individualism – communalism: collectivism

Although American psychologists prefer to use the word 'collectivism' because of its neutrality, I prefer the word 'communalism' instead. A culture is not just a motley crowd or a collection of people; it is much more than that. In selecting a word which is seemingly neutral in its social and political connotations, there is the implicit danger of reintroducing the old notions of 'group mind' which were abandoned several decades ago.

Main features of communalism

Family and community-centred society

Indian (Hindu and Islamic) society, not unlike other Eastern societies, is a family-based and community-centred society (Abd al Ali, 1977; Basham, 1966; Farah, 1994; Flood, 1996; Kakar, 1981; Klostermaier, 1998; Koller, 1982; Lannoy, 1975; Laungani, 1997c, 1998d; Lipner, 1994; Mandelbaum, 1972; Sharma, 2000; Zaehner, 1966b).

Most Indians grow up and live in *extended family* networks. As Farah (1994) points out, 'The family to Islam is the cornerstone and the mainstay of the community, as it has been to the Arabs before Islam' (p. 161). A typical extended family usually consists of the mother and the father. The father, in most parts of India and Pakistan and other Eastern countries, is seen as head of family. The extended family would normally include all their children: their married sons and their wives, and their children (if any), their unmarried sons, their unmarried daughters, and other relatives such as the father's younger brothers, their wives and children, the father's widowed sister, all of whom would live under the same roof. In such a family structure incomes are pooled and are redistributed according to the needs of the respective members within the family.

In a family-oriented society any problem that affects an individual – financial, medical, psychiatric, or whatever – affects the entire family. One's individuality is subordinated to collective solidarity, and one's ego is submerged into the collective ego of the family and one's community. A community in India has several common features. People within a group are united by a common caste and sub-caste rank *(jati)*. The members within a community generally operate on a ranking or a hierarchical system. Elders are accorded special status within the community and their important role is very clearly recognized. Elders, whether they come from rural areas or from large metropolitan cities, are generally deferred to. On important issues the members of a community may meet and confer with one another, and any decisions taken are often binding on the rest of the members within the community. In the event of a person being perceived as being mentally ill, it initially falls upon the individual's family to look after and support the individual concerned. Should that become difficult for financial or other reasons, it then becomes the responsibility of the community members, the family's sub-caste, or *jati*, to offer support.

However, it should be emphasized that for an individual to stay as an integral part of the family and of the community, it is expected that the individual will submit to familial and communal norms, and will not deviate to an extent where it becomes necessary for severe sanctions to be imposed upon the deviant or, as an extreme measure, for the deviant to be ostracized. The pressure to conform to family norms and expectations can and does cause acute stress in individual members in the family, leading, in some instances, to psychotic disorders and hysteria (Channabasavanna & Bhatti, 1982; Sethi & Manchanda, 1978).

The caste system

Although in many respects Indian society is similar to most other Eastern societies, its unique distinguishing feature lies in its *caste system*. Its origin dates back to over 3500 years. The four castes in their hierarchical order are:

- Brahmins: the learned, educated elite; guardians of the Vedas, the priests.
- Kshatriyas: the noble warriors; defenders of the realm.
- Vaishyas: the traders, businessmen, farmers, money-lenders.
- Sudras: their main function is to serve the needs of the upper three.

Members of the upper three castes are known as 'twice born' because their male members have undergone an initiation, a rite of passage. It is after the sacred thread ceremony that marks their 'second birth' – the rites of passage – that they are allowed to read and learn from the Vedas and participate in all religious ceremonies. This rite separates the three highest castes from the Sudras, who are not permitted such an initiation.

The Sudras are further sub-divided into touchables and untouchables. The touchable Sudras engage in occupations which are considered by the upper three castes to be demeaning and polluting: barber, hairdresser, masseur, cleaner, water carrier, and so on. (I can still recall my own astonishment at learning, when I first came to England, the 'celebrity status' enjoyed by a few hairdressers.) The untouchable Sudras (now known as *Dalits*) engage in activities which are considered to be spiritually polluting: garbage collectors, those working in abattoirs, in crematoriums, and so on.

Major features of the caste system

There are at least five important features of the caste system:

1 Hierarchy
2 Pollution and Purification
3 Performance of Rituals
4 Notions of auspiciousness and purity
5 Development of identity

Hierarchy: Since one is born into a given caste it is virtually impossible to move from one caste into another, particularly from the lower into the higher. It is possible to move downwards, from the higher to the lower caste, through actions which are caste polluting. The sub-castes, within a given caste, also operate on a hierarchical model. Hierarchy consists of gradations; each sub-caste is graded, ranging from the lowest to the highest. Gradations of castes, to a large extent, are organized around degrees of purity and pollution, which include endogamy, commensality, and vocational specialization. Brahmins, who are at the top of the caste hierarchy, wield spiritual and 'divine' power. The Kshatriyas come from the warrior caste. Most of the kings and noblemen of the past era came from the Kshatriya caste; despite their temporal power, they deferred to the spiritual and divine power of the Brahmins. The Vaishyas, who constitute the bulk of Hindu society, belong to the trading caste and are normally in business, farming, and a variety of other commercial activities.

Pollution and purification: The day-to-day religious and secular behaviours of Hindus make sense when seen within the context of purity and pollution. Hindus view purity and pollution largely in spiritual terms and not in terms of hygiene (Filippi, 1996; Fuller, 1992; Lannoy, 1975). The status of a person in India is determined by his or her position in the caste hierarchy and by the degree of contact with the polluting agent. Proximity to a polluting agent may constitute a permanent pollution. This would mean that certain occupations are permanently polluting. Such a form of pollution is *collective* – the entire family remains polluted. It is also *hereditary*.

Pollution may be temporary but mild, severe, and permanent. One is in a state of mild impurity upon waking up in the morning, prior to performing one's morning ablutions, when one has eaten food, when one has not prayed. Mild states of pollution are easily overcome by appropriate actions, such as baths, prayers, wearing clean, washed clothes, and engaging in appropriate cleansing and purification rituals. Severe pollution occurs when high-caste Hindus come into physical and/or social contact with persons of the lowest caste. Permanent pollution occurs when a Hindu belonging to the highest caste (Brahmin) marries a person from the lowest caste, thereby breaking the principle of endogamy that has always been regarded as one of the cementing factors that has held the caste system together. It is notable that over the centuries, the principle of endogamy has not been swept aside; it has continued to retain its stronghold over the Hindus all over

India, particularly in the rural areas of the country, and to a large extent even in Britain. Marriages are still arranged and organized by the parents of prospective spouses. Although the style of arranged marriages has undergone a modest change within Indian society, particularly among the affluent members of society in the urban sectors of the country, arranged marriages are still the norm.

Performance of rituals: In Western countries there is a clear distinction between the sacred and the secular. In Hinduism there are no sharp distinctions between the sacred and the secular. The lines are blurred. This can be observed even in the most mundane day-to-day activities, such as washing one's hands, having a bath, carrying out one's morning ablutions, accepting drinking water or food from others, or offering it to others, and so on. Although seemingly trivial, they have deep-rooted religious connotations. To a Westerner unversed in the day-to-day ritualistic practices of Hindus, such behaviours would seem strange and even irrational. To a Hindu, however, they fall within the orbit of necessary religious ablutions, which he or she has internalized from childhood and performs automatically. So much of day-to-day Hindu behaviour is influenced by religious beliefs that it is virtually impossible to identify behaviours which might be seen as secular (Pandey, 1948/1969).

The ritual activity is addressed to sacred beings, such as gods or ancestors. Ninian Smart (1996) refers to such rituals as 'focused rituals', where the focus is on worship. Rituals therefore are forms of personal communication with gods. Communication itself may serve different purposes: worship, giving thanks, asking for favours, expiation and atonement. Smart adds that a variant of the religious ritual is the yogic ritual where the performance of yogic exercises is seen as a means by which a person seeks to attain a higher state of consciousness. Failure to perform the rituals leads to a form of spiritual pollution (Sharma, 2000). Flood (1996) points out that it is ritual action which anchors people in a sense of deeper identity and belonging. The most important rituals are those related to birth, the initiation ceremony, marriage, which signals the beginning of the householder's life, and the final funeral rites and *after-death* rites.

The daily life of an orthodox Hindu is beset with all kinds of polluting agents, as though they lie in wait and are ready to 'pounce' upon the person should his or her vigilance drop even for a moment. But what protects a devout Hindu from pollution is the detailed attention paid to performing the required rituals during the course of the day. As was stated earlier, the performance of all the daily rituals are internalized at an early age and become functionally autonomous.

Notions of auspiciousness and purity: In Western thinking, the notion of auspiciousness does not hold the same meaning as it does for Hindus, Muslims, and Jews all over the world. In the West there are a few events (such as Easter, Christmas) which might be construed as being auspicious: baptisms, christenings, church weddings, sacramental rites, funerals, and so on.

In Indian philosophy, the two words 'auspiciousness' and 'purity' are inter-related. In Sanskrit, auspiciousness is referred to as *shub* and purity as *shudh*. In ordinary, every-day language auspiciousness also refers to time and temporal events (Madan, 1987). To Hindus there is an auspicious time for most activities: starting a journey, travelling, undertaking a pilgrimage, starting a new business, buying a new house, moving into the house, time of birth, marriage, burial, cremation, and other activities. Apart from time, auspiciousness is also associated with places, objects, or persons. Varanasi (or Benaras) is regarded as a holy city, and a pilgrimage to Varanasi is seen as being auspicious. Similarly, some metals – silver, gold, copper, brass – are also considered to be auspicious.

In contrast to auspiciousness, the term 'purity' *(shudh)* is not used in everyday speech (Madan, 1987). Purity and its opposite, impurity *(ashudh)*, are seen as attributes of persons, objects, foods, and places. For instance, ghee (clarified butter), a temple, a consecrated area of land, are all seen as being pure. On the other hand, contact with certain kinds of human beings (low-caste Hindus or non-Hindus) is seen as being impure. So are certain places, such as abattoirs, cremation grounds and brothels. Contact leads to pollution. It is therefore in the interest of a Hindu to avoid such impurities and pursue those actions and eat those foods that ensure purity.

The meticulous and precise performance of rites and rituals to avoid pollution and spiritual contamination is seen as being desirable for Hindus. It binds and preserves the caste system, which in turn provides a sense of continuity and belonging. Rites and rituals legitimize social order and uphold social institutions.

It is worth pointing out here that the majority of the Hindus living in Britain tend to abide by those caste-related norms on matters which are of importance to them, for example, in births, betrothals, marriages, funerals, visits to temples, pilgrimages, and so on.

To convey the powerful impact that the notions of purity and impurity have on the behaviours of Hindus, let me to recount, much to my mortification, an experience that I had when I first came to England.

Box 3.1

A few of my colleagues and I were sitting in the college refectory having lunch. One of my colleagues, who adores his food and is a 'big' eater, guzzled through his lunch and kept eyeing my plate, which was more than half-full. I played around with the food for a while and left the plate half eaten. He turned to me and asked me if I had finished eating. I nodded. He stretched out his hand and dragged my plate towards him. As he was about to start eating I screamed at him:

(Continued)

'Andrew! What do you think you are doing?'

'Finishing off your chips,' he replied, unperturbed.

'But you can't! They are impure. They are contaminated. I've touched them. Why don't I get you another plate?' I pleaded.

'How can they be impure, you fool! You've just eaten some of them.'

'That's precisely why they are impure! Because I've touched them.'

It was impossible to bridge the cultural gulf that separated us. I sat in mortified silence while Andrew ate the chips and discussed with glee what he thought was the funny side of this brief episode. What impressions my colleagues formed of me, what kind of an idiot my colleagues thought I was, I did not care to inquire. I had been acting in accordance with ancient Hindu custom: one does not eat food that has been touched and eaten by another person. To do so is to eat food which is impure, or *ashud.*

Development of identity: Identity in Indians, to a large extent, is *ascribed* and, to a lesser extent, *achieved.* By virtue of being born into one of the four hereditary castes (this applies mainly to the Hindus who comprise over 82 per cent of the total population of India), one's identity is *ascribed* at birth. An identity that is ascribed or 'given' to a growing child has the advantage of 'security', in the sense that the persons concerned 'knows' what is expected of them. But it also severely restricts the choices open to the individual. While personal choice is central to an individualistic society, it is seen as an exception in a communalistic society.

One's identity, to a large extent, tends to be a reflection of familial and social norms and caste expectations. Females are socialized into developing 'floating identities', for when she is born she is seen as a daughter; after marriage she is seen as someone's wife; then as a mother, and when her children get married, as a mother-in-law; finally, as a grandmother; and should her husband predecease her, as a widow. She appears to have no individual identity other than the changing identities she acquires through reflected role relationships. Her private persona remains submerged within these changing and conflicting identities.

With the exception of the caste system, which is a unique feature of Indian society, other collectivist cultures including China, Taiwan, Korea, Hong Kong, Philippines, Thailand, Nepal, Pakistan, Iran, Turkey, Portugal, Mexico, Peru, Venezuela, and Colombia also share most of the features described above (Hofstede, 1980; Matsumoto, 1996b; Ward & Kennedy, 1996b; Yang, 1997). For instance, Kuo-Shu Yang (1997) in his excellent analyses of the traditional

Chinese personality refers to the tight, close-knit bond between the individual and his or her family. He points out that:

> Chinese familism disposes the Chinese to subordinate their personal interests, goals, glory, and welfare to their family's interests, goals, glory, and welfare to the extent that the family is primary and its members secondary. (p. 245)

Again, Kuo-Shu Yang points out that in order to attain harmony within the family it is essential for the individual to 'surrender or merge into his or her family, and as a result, lose his or her individuality and idiosyncrasies as an independent actor' (p. 245).

The ubiquitous power of the caste system

One needs to emphasize here that one's caste origins are so strongly ingrained in the Hindu psyche that it is difficult for a large number of people to renounce it; one might attempt to do so as a cosmetic exercise, and for a variety of other social and financial reasons, for wanting to seem modern, educated, rational, and Westernised; but more often than not, it tends to remain intact.

Hinduism, unlike Islam and Christianity, is not a proselytising religion. But such is the awesome power of the caste system that variants of the caste system have spread over to other religious groups, including Muslims, Catholics, and Sikhs, in certain parts of India. Although, in theory, these religious groups would consider the very idea of caste as anathema to their own religious beliefs, caste and caste relations creep into social practices and relationships in extremely subtle ways. In India, it is not uncommon to notice that many Catholics, in addition to their own Christian names, also have Hindu names, and operate on a de facto caste system. Many Muslims too operate on a similar basis; their names are often indistinguishable from Hindu names. A person unacquainted with Indian names would find it difficult to tell from surnames such as Bahadur, Bhat, Bhatti, Bhimji, Chamar, Choudhary, Darzi, Ghani, Kamal, Mistry, Nawab, Raja, Ramji, Sutaria, Shah – to name but a few – whether the persons concerned are Hindus or Muslims, Parsees or Catholics! Even within Sikhism, which is a caste-free religion, many Sikhs operate on a de facto caste system in certain parts of India and Britain.

Despite the inequities of the caste system, the heavy burden it imposes on people, and the appalling prejudices in terms of occupations, areas of residence, social and marital relationships, which it unleashes on people of the lower castes, why has the caste system continued to survive? To examine this problem is beyond the scope of this chapter. It would need a separate book.

Table 3.1 Major features of individualism and communalism

Individualism	Communalism
Emphasis on personal responsibility and self-achievement	Emphasis on collective responsibility and collective achievement
Identity achieved	Identity ascribed
Anxiety is related to the *acquisition* of identity	Anxiety may be related to the 'imposition' of a familial and caste-related identity
Family life operates on a *horizontal* model	Family life runs on a *hierarchical* model
Emphasis on nuclear (and one-parent) families	Emphasis on extended families
Social behaviours 'class-related'	Social behaviours caste and religion-related
Pollution and purification seen in terms of hygiene	Pollution and purification seen in spiritual and caste-related terms
Religion tends to be less important; secularism important	Religion plays a dominant role in everyday life
Rituals, if any, tend to be secular	Religious rituals play a dominant role in day-to-day behaviours

The major features of individualism and communalism are shown in Table 3.1. Let us now turn to the second set of factors.

Cognitivism – emotionalism: cognitivism

Cognitivism is concerned with the way in which the British (the English in particular) construe their private and social worlds and the ways in which they form and sustain social relationships. In broad terms it has been suggested by Pande (1968) that Western society is a *work-and-activity-centred* society and in contradistinction, Eastern societies in general and Indian society in particular are *relationship-centred*. Our constructions of our social worlds are not accidental developments. They stem from our inheritance of our different philosophical legacies (Laungani, 2000d; Zimmer, 1951/1989).

Rationality and logic

In a *work-and-activity-centred* society, people are more likely to operate on a cognitive mode, where the emphasis is on rationality, logic and control, which extends to the display of emotions and feelings. Public expression of feelings and emotions – particularly among the middle classes in England – is often frowned upon. It is not as though negative feelings and emotions are never expressed, rather they are done so in a subtle way. Even in situations where it would seem legitimate to express feelings openly, without inhibition – at funerals, for instance – the English are guided by control, which suggests that one must not cry in public, one must at all times put on a 'brave' face, one must, above all, never lose one's dignity. Dignity lies in restraint. The unwillingness or the inability to express emotions openly is a theme that has caused some worry to many other writers in the field (Gorer, 1965; Hockey, 1993; Sarbin, 1986).

Relationships

In a work-and-activity-centred society, relationships outside the family are formed through shared commonalities. One does not take a relationship 'for granted'; one is expected to 'work at a relationship', in a marriage, in a family situation, with friends, with colleagues at work, and even with one's children. In such society, one's identity, one's self-image, and one's self-esteem grow out of one's work and one's attitude to work. Work defines one's sense of worth. Work promotes, fosters, and sustains relationships. Given the over-arching ideology of individualism, one's work and one's attitudes to work have a far greater impact on one's life than do relationships.

Conception of time

Our conception of time is both objective and subjective. At an objective level, time is seen in terms of an Einsteinium dimension, where each hour is divided into its fixed moments of minutes, seconds, and milliseconds. Each moment (at least on Earth) expires at the same speed – an hour passes not a moment sooner, not a moment later. At a subjective level, however, there are variations in our perceptions of time. In a work-and-activity-centred society, one's working life, including one's private life, is organized around time. To ensure the judicious use of time, one resorts to keeping appointments' books, computer-assisted diaries; one works to fixed time-schedules, one sets deadlines; one tries to keep within one's time-limits. One is constantly aware of the swift passage of time, and to fritter it away is often construed as an act of criminality.

Time therefore comes to acquire a significant meaning in a work-and-activity-centred society (McClelland, 1961). The fear of running out of time, the fear of not being able to accomplish one's short-term and long-term goals on time, is seen as one of the greatest stressors in Western society. Even casual encounters between friends, between colleagues at work, operate on covert agendas. Meeting people is seldom construed as an end in itself; it is a means to an end, with time playing a significant role.

Cognitivism – emotionalism: emotionalism

The close physical proximity in which people continuously live and share their lives with one another forces a *relationship-centred society* to operate on an *emotional* dimension, where feelings and emotions are not easily repressed, and their expression in general is not frowned upon. However, it should be stressed that relationships are also organized along hierarchical lines, and tend to be 'tight', 'closed', and rigid.

Relationships

In such a society crying, dependence on others, excessive emotionality, volatility, even verbal hostility, both in males and females, are not in any way considered as signs of weakness or ill-breeding. Since feelings and emotions – both positive and negative – are expressed easily, there is little danger of treading incautiously on others' sensibilities and vulnerabilities, such as might be the case in work-and-activity-centred societies. Given the extended-family structure of relationships, emotional outbursts are, as it were, 'taken on board' by the family members. Quite often the emotional outbursts are of a symbolic nature, even highly stylised and ritualistic. Given the extreme closeness of life, the paucity of amenities, the absence of privacy, the inertia evoked by the overpowering heat and dust, the awesome feeling of claustrophobia, it is not at all surprising that families do often quarrel, fight, and swear at one another and from time to time assault one another too. But their quarrels and outbursts are often of a symbolic nature, for otherwise such quarrels would lead to a permanent rift, the consequences of which would be far more traumatic than those of living together. There is in such outbursts a surrealistic quality: for at one level they are alarmingly real – the words and abuses hurled at one another, vicious and hurtful – yet at another, bewilderingly unreal. They serve no function other than the cathartic relief, which such outbursts bring.

But here a word of caution needs to be exercised. In a hierarchical family structure, feelings and emotions are not expressed indiscriminately. Each member within the family soon becomes aware of his or her own position within the hierarchy, and in the process of familial adjustment learns the normative expressions of feelings and emotions permissible to the person concerned. Even in such emotionally charged situations, the internalized familial norms often prevent the younger members of the family from openly expressing negative emotions towards their elders. In other words, 'who can say what to whom, how, and with what effect' is guided by a familial 'pecking order', which the members of the family learn to internalize quite early on in their lives.

However, in a relationship-centred society, one is forced into relationships from which one cannot or is unable to opt out of without severe sanctions being

Table 3.2   Major features of cognitivism and emotionalism

Cognitivism	Emotionalism
Emphasis on rationality and logic	Emphasis on feelings and intuition
Feelings and emotions tend to be kept in check	Feelings and emotions tend to be expressed freely
Emphasis on work and activity	Emphasis on relationships
Relationships are often a by-product of work	Work is often a by-product of relationships
Relations based on shared interests	Relations based on caste and family
'Rigid' attitude to time	'Flexible' attitude to time

imposed upon the individual. Several studies have shown that one's inability to break away, or even sever enforced relationships based on birth and caste, often leads to severe stress and neurosis (Channabasavanna & Bhatti, 1982).

Concept of time

Although at an objective level, time is construed in virtually the same way as it is in the West, at a subjective level, time in India is seen in *more flexible and even relaxed terms*. Time, in Indian metaphysics, is not conceptualized in linear terms. A linear model of time signifies a beginning, a middle, and an end, or, in other words, a past, a present, and a future. Time, in Indian philosophy, is conceptualized in circular terms, which means that time has no beginning (or its beginning remains unknown, or is unknowable), no middle, and no end. These differential conceptualizations have serious implications for our understanding of the nature of private and social behaviours.

Time in India is often viewed as 'a quiet, motionless ocean', 'a vast expanse of sky'. The only exceptions to this flexible construction of time are to be found in those situations which are considered auspicious: undertaking an important journey, fixing the time of christening, betrothals, weddings, funerals, and so on. Such events, because of their religious significance, are seldom left to chance; one seeks divine guidance in their planning and execution.

The major features of cognitivism and emotionalism are shown in Table 3.2.

Free will – determinism

All cultures, the world over, subscribe to ideas underlying free will and determinism. Logically the two sets of beliefs – free will and determinism – are incompatible. But it has never prevented people from subscribing to both sets of beliefs in varying degrees – and even the same behaviour being determined on one occasion and voluntary on another. From time to time the emphasis shifts, and a given culture may move from one set of beliefs to another. This would suggest that certain beliefs and behaviours, which in the past may have been seen as being voluntary and freely executed, may subsequently be construed as being determined by other 'forces', ranging from the divine, the theological, the religious, and the malevolent to the genetic, the biological, and the environmental.

Free will and determinism in the West

Free will and determinism are complex philosophical issues, which incorporate within them a variety of other constructs (Dilman, 1999; Russell, 1946/1961). Notions of free will and determinism until about the sixteenth century were entangled largely in their religious connotations. God was the creator of the Universe and was seen as being omnipotent and omniscient. God had knowledge of the past, the present, and of course our future. And the fact that the knowledge of our future was known to God – ahead of time – indicated that our future was fixed, much in the same way our past is 'fixed' in our memories. Thus, the idea of free will, namely that we determine our own future, by making choices, became an illusion. And the idea that God had created us free became a contradiction in Christian theology. Needless to say that philosophers through the ages, from St Augustine and St Aquinas, to Descartes, Spinoza, Hume, and Kant, have worried over this problem and each in his own way has endeavoured to find an acceptable solution.

However, it was not until after the publication of Newton's *Principia* in 1687 that the concept of determinism was partially freed from its theistic connotations and a non-theistic and mechanistic view of determinism in science, and indeed in the Universe, gained prominence. A scientific notion of determinism, with its emphasis on causality, or conversely, its denial of non-causal events, found favour among the rationalist philosophers who embraced it with great fervour (Popper, 1972). And with the emergence of quantum mechanics in the early twentieth century, determinism in science, if not in human affairs, once again came to be seriously questioned.

Despite the advances in science and quantum mechanics, the arguments related to free will and determinism have not been resolved; they keep re-emerging in different forms and guises even among eighteenth-, nineteenth-, and twentieth-century philosophers such as Schopenhauer, Nietzsche, Heidegger, Sartre and Camus, among others (Dilman, 1999; Honderich, 1999).

Notwithstanding the unresolved debates in philosophy on the subject, there is a strange form of dualism in Western thinking on this subject. Scientific research in medicine, psychiatry, biology, and other related disciplines, including psychology, is based on the acceptance of a deterministic framework – hence the concern with seeking causal explanations. On the other hand, the notion of free will becomes evident at a social, psychological, and common-sense level. This manifests itself in the constant use of proverbs, homilies, poems, and popular advice offered freely to children and adults – '*Where there's will, there's a way*', '*Pull your socks up*', '*It's all in your hands*', '*You can do it!*' and so on – occasionally, by the very people who adopt a deterministic model in the course of their professional and scientific work (Laungani, 1993).

The question is, what do we mean by free will? Free will might be defined as a *non-causal, voluntary action*. However, at a common-sense level it is defined as exercising voluntary control over one's actions. Thus free will allows an individual to do what he or she wills, and in so doing take 'credit' for his or her successes, and accept blame for his or her failures and mishaps.

The notion of determinism plays a major role within the Freudian framework. Every event, Freud argued, had a cause. There were no chance events. Freud was at pains to point out that even 'free associations', reaction formations, 'slips of the tongue', temporary amnesia, and all other 'defence mechanisms' are not really free. They arise out of past connections, which are located in the unconscious. One might in this context recall Freud's notion of *psychic determinism* (or psychological determinism), which suggested that chance factors could not explain these patterns of behaviours. They were a result of, or determined by, unconscious psychological processes. Although he posited very serious limitations on the notion of free will, he managed to escape from a tyrannical deterministic model by arguing that these issues have little bearing on the question of free will. It was within our 'character' to initiate desirable changes within our psyche, and acquire a strong, rational ego which was firmly located in reality.

Free will and determinism in Eastern cultures

Similar contradictions with regard to notions of free will and determinism are also to be found in Eastern cultures. Hindu and Buddhist thinking, for instance, are dominated by the belief in the law of karma. The role of determinism is also integral to Islamic thinking; everything that happens is due to the will of Allah. This idea is enshrined in the classic poem of the Persian poet Omar Khayyam (translated by Edward Fitzgerald, 1856/1972):

> The Moving Finger writes; and having writ,
> Moves on: nor all thy Piety nor Wit,
> Shall lure it back to cancel half a Line
> Nor all thy Tears wash out a Word of it.

The law of karma

The law of karma, in its simplest form, states that all human actions lead to consequences. Right actions produce good consequences and wrong actions produce bad consequences. At first sight, the law of karma seems to be identical with the law of universal causation, which asserts that every event has a cause, or that nothing is uncaused. Though seemingly identical, there are significant differences between the two laws. Unlike the law of universal causation, the law of karma is not concerned with consequences in general, but with consequences which affect the individual – the doer of the action. Second, the law of karma applies specifically to the *moral* sphere. It is therefore not concerned with the general relation between actions and their consequences but 'rather with the moral quality of the actions and their consequences' (Reichenbach, 1990: 1). Third, what gives the law of karma its supreme moral quality is the assertion that the doer not only deserves the consequences of his or her actions, but is also unable to avoid experiencing them (Prasad, 1989). It should be made clear that the actions of the doer may have occurred in his or her present life, or past life. Similarly, the consequences of the doer's actions may occur during the person's present life or future life. The main point is that it is impossible to avoid the consequences of one's actions. In his analysis of the law of karma, Hiriyanna (1949) explains that the events of our lives are determined by their antecedent causes. Since all actions lead to consequences, which are related to the nature and the type of actions, there is absolute *justice* that falls to our lot, in the sense that good actions lead to happiness and bad actions to unhappiness.

The doctrine of karma is extremely significant because it offers explanations not only for pain, suffering, and misfortune, but also for pleasure, happiness, and good fortune. Each of us receives the results of our own actions and not another's. Thus, the sins of our fathers are not visited upon us. The deterministic belief that one's present life is shaped by one's actions in one's past life (or lives) allows them to explain and accept a variety of misfortunes (and good fortunes) which befall them through the course of their journey through life. It engenders within their psyche a spirit of passive, if not resigned acceptance of misfortunes, ranging from glaring inequalities of caste and status, disease and illness, poverty and destitution, to exploitation and prejudice and sudden deaths within the family.

Interestingly, the law of karma does not negate the notion of free will. As Christoph von Furer-Haimendorf (1974) has pointed out, in an important sense karma is based on the assumption of free will. The theory of *karma* rests on the idea that an individual has the final moral responsibility for each of his or her actions, hence the freedom of moral choice.

The law of karma stands out as the most significant feature of Hinduism. Although there is no basis for establishing its empirical validity, Hindus in general have an unswerving faith in the workings of the law of karma. It has shaped the Indian view of life over centuries. One might even go to the extent of saying that the Hindu psyche is built around the notion of karma (O'Flaherty, 1976, 1980; Reichenbach, 1990; Sharma, 2000; Sinari, 1984; Zaehner, 1962). The influence of the law of karma manifests itself at every stage in a Hindu's life: at birth, in childhood, during adolescence and adulthood, in marriage, in illness and health, in good fortune and misfortune, in death, and bereavement, and *after death*.

Box 3.2

Knowledge of the law of karma, even in its most rudimentary form, is known all over India. Several years ago, when I visited India, I used to notice a group of street urchins who, along with their parents, had taken shelter a few doors away from a large palatial mansion with electronic iron gates that swung open when the owner drove past in his chauffeur-driven Mercedes. On seeing the gates swinging open, the urchins would run to the gate, and as the car drove past them, would salute the owner, who from time to time threw a few coins from the open car window. In my misplaced reformative and revolutionary zeal, I felt a sense of outrage at the condescending and patronising manner of the owner. One day, on an impulse, I rounded up the urchins, about a dozen of them – they were hungry little creatures, illiterate, emaciated, unkempt, dirty, between the ages of 5 and 13. When questioned why they bowed down to the owner of the mansion, they explained in their own limited way that they felt no rancour, no anger, no animosity towards the owner when the coins came flying through the car window. In fact, they were proud to be associated with such a great man, the *Burra Sahib*. He must have performed deeds of great virtue in his past birth to achieve such an eminent position in his present life! It turned out that he had become their role model. They were convinced that if they too engaged in righteous and virtuous actions in their present life, they would reap the fruits of their endeavours in their future lives. So convinced were the children in their beliefs that one of them, using an old Indian proverb, boasted that when God decided to give him wealth, it would come crashing through the roof. Such a view allowed them to accept their own destitution, if not with equanimity, certainly without rancour. It also allowed them to sustain the hope of a better life in their next life. The belief in the munificence of God cuts across all castes and classes in India.

Humbled by their beliefs, I realized that to try to change centuries of encrusted religious and spiritual beliefs of devout Hindus by a sermon was as futile as attempting to change the beliefs of devout Muslims and devout Catholics concerning the day of judgment.

There are disadvantages too in subscribing to a deterministic philosophy. Let us now summarize the main advantages and disadvantages in subscribing to the law of karma:

Table 3.3   Major features of free will and determinism

Free will	Determinism
Emphasis on freedom of choice	Freedom of choice limited
Proactive	Reactive
Success or failure due largely to effort	Although effort is important, success or failure is related to one's *karma*
Self-blame or guilt is a residual consequence of failure	No guilt is attached to failure
Failure may lead to victim-blaming	No blame is attached to victim
Luke-warm beliefs in birth, rebirth and after-life	Very strong beliefs in the cycle of birth, rebirth and after-life

1   A belief in determinism is likely to engender in the Indian psyche a spirit of passive, if not resigned acceptance of the vicissitudes of life. This prevents a person from experiencing feelings of guilt – a state from which Westerners, because of their fundamental belief in the doctrine of free will, cannot be protected.

2   It often leads to a state of existential, and in certain instances, moral resignation, compounded by a profound sense of *inertia*. One does not take immediate *proactive* measures; one merely accepts the vicissitudes of life without qualm. While this may prevent a person from experiencing stress, it does not allow the same person to make individual attempts to alleviate his unbearable condition.

3   A belief in the unending cycle of birth and rebirth, a belief that one's life does not end at death but leads to a new beginning, and that one's moral actions in one's present life or past lives will lead to consequences in one's future life, may create in the Hindu psyche a set of psychologically protective mechanisms in the face of death. A belief in an after-life helps to reduce the terror of death and the fear of extinction.

4   The acceptance of the doctrine of *karma* instils in one the idea that in the final analysis, no one but we ourselves are ultimately responsible for the consequences of our actions. *This brings the notion of individualism to its highest level.*

5   The unshakable belief that upon one's death one's indestructible spirit (*atman*) will survive the body and at some point during the individual's *karmic* cycle of birth and rebirth find abode in another body (hopefully a more pious and august one) makes the acceptance of death less painful.

6   The belief in the cycle of birth and rebirth creates an aspiration of hope. They 'know' that they need to engage in meritorious acts of piety and in so doing they would reap the rewards of their actions in their present life or in

their future life by being born into a 'better' family and into a higher caste in their next birth.

The major features of free will and determinism are shown in Table 3.3

Materialism – spiritualism: materialism

Materialism refers to a belief in the existence of a material world, or a world composed of matter. The idea that there is an external reality, an external world, which is 'out there' and that human beings by the exercise of their intellect and reason can attempt to unravel its mysteries, runs through the entire history of Western philosophy. This theme, in its many variants, reached its apogee during the spectacular rise of the Renaissance and post-Renaissance period which, given its adherence to the philosophy of humanism, also managed, to a certain extent, to disentangle Western philosophy from its religious dogmas (Cooper, 1996; Pater, 1986). But such debates have, in the main, been confined to journals of philosophy and science. Nonetheless, these philosophies have had a profound influence on the shaping of the Western mind and of course the dominant Western values, which, to a large extent, guide, sustain, and regulate private and public behaviour.

At a practical, day-to-day level, however, one accepts the assumed solidity of the world which one inhabits. But one pays a heavy price for such acceptance. For such an acceptance gives rise to the popular myth that all explanations of phenomena, ranging from lunar cycles to lunacy, need to be sought within the (assumed) materialist framework. This is evidenced by the profound reluctance among psychiatrists, medical practitioners and psychologists in general to entertain any explanations which are of a non-material or supernatural nature. Non-material explanations are treated at best with scepticism, and at worst with scorn.

A materialist philosophy also tends to engender in its subscribers the belief that our knowledge of the world is external to ourselves; reality is, as it were, 'out there', and it is only through objective scientific enterprise that one will acquire an understanding of the external world and, with it, an understanding of 'reality'. The few psychiatrists and psychologists who have steered away from materialistic explanations, or have shown the willingness to consider alternative non-material explanations, comprise a very small minority. Most of them are painfully aware that anyone offering non-material explanations of phenomena is in danger of incurring the wrath of the scientific community. Non-material explanations fall within the purview of the pre-scientific communities, or in other words, superstitious and backward societies, to be found mainly in underdeveloped countries and, by implication, in collectivist societies.

For over 2000 years *yogis* in India have made claims about their abilities to alter their states of consciousness at will, thereby bringing their autonomic nervous system under voluntary control. Western scientists dismissed these claims as unsubstantiated exaggerations. It was not until 1969 that Neal Miller successfully trained his laboratory rats to lower and raise their blood-pressure levels by selective reinforcement (Miller, 1969). Miller found that he could train his students to exercise voluntary control over their autonomic responses. Miller's findings opened the doors to yoga in American universities, and research into altered states of consciousness, followed by its applications into techniques of biofeedback, became respectable. But the philosophical and spiritual underpinnings of yoga, the variations within different forms of yoga, the teleological purposes in yoga, have to a large extent been ignored. Yoga has been put on a business footing. Commercialism has replaced spiritualism.

Materialism – spiritualism: spiritualism

In striking contrast to the philosophies in the West, Indian philosophy has been concerned not with information but with *transformation* (de Riencourt, 1980; Embree, 1988; Radhakrishnan, 1939; Zimmer, 1951/1989). It is not concerned with exploring, describing, and understanding the visible world, as is evident with Western philosophy. The reason for this neglect is due to the strong Hindu belief that the world is illusory, and although bound by time and space, it is subject to change and decay. Therefore nothing is to be gained by studying and exploring this changing, transient, illusory world. Thus, the notion of materialism is a relatively unimportant concept in Indian thinking. The external world to Indians is *not* composed of matter. It is *maya* (Zimmer, 1951/1989). The concept of *maya*, as Zimmer points out, 'holds a key position in Vedantic thought and teaching' (p. 19). Since the external world is illusory, reality, or its perception, lies *within* the individual and not, as Westerners believe, *outside* the individual.

The supreme concern of the Indian mind therefore is on the discovery of the self, wherein lies 'ultimate reality' or *ultimate truth* (de Riencourt, 1980; Radhakrishnan, 1939; Sinari, 1984; Zaehner, 1984). The ultimate purpose of human existence is to transcend one's illusory physical existence, renounce the world of material aspirations, attain a heightened state of spiritual awareness, and finally liberate oneself from the bondage of the cycle of birth and rebirth, thereby attaining *moksha*. It is then that one's soul *(atman)* merges with the ultimate *brahman*. Any activity that is likely to promote such a state is to be encouraged. But how is such transcendence – inward-seeking spiritual consciousness – to be achieved, which will lead to *moksha*? *Moksha* (or *nirvana*, according to Buddhist philosophy) cannot be achieved overnight. It can only be

Table 3.4   Major features of materialism and spiritualism

Materialism	Spiritualism
The world is 'real', physical	The world is illusory
Rejection of contradictory explanations of phenomena	Co-existence of contradictory explanations of phenomena
Reality is external to the individual	Reality is internal to the individual
Reality perceived through scientific enterprise	Reality perceived through contemplation and inner reflection
Emphasis on seeking information about the Universe	Emphasis on spiritual transformation: on becoming a better being

achieved through continuous effort and adopting a meditative perspective. The search for *moksha* is long and arduous. It may involve a series of lives and deaths in the process.

It is only through the discovery of the self that transformation becomes possible. Everything that we normally know and express about ourselves is subject to change and decay. But the discovered *self (atman)*, as Zimmer points out, is forever changeless, beyond time and space, beyond the normal (scientific) methods of human understanding. It transcends intellectual and rational understanding. Thus the main goal of Indian philosophy – epitomized in the Upanishads, formulated in the post-Vedic period – has been to know and understand this self, which leads to a *total transformation* of the individual or, as Zimmer calls it, a 'transmutation of the soul'. The main object of Indian philosophy is to bring about a radical change in human nature, a change that eventually leads to human perfection, a divine God-like state. This, according to Zimmer (1951/1989), tends to make Indians more *inward looking* and Westerners more *outward looking*.

Also, given the illusory nature of the external world, the Indian mind remains unfettered by materialistic boundaries. It resorts to explanations where material and spiritual, physical and metaphysical, natural and supernatural explanations of phenomena coexist with one another. What to a Western mind, weaned on Aristotelian logic, nourished on a scientific diet, socialized on materialism, empiricism, and positivism, might seem an irreconcilable contradiction, leaves an Indian mind relatively unperturbed.

The major features of materialism and spiritualism are shown in Table 3.4.

Conclusion

We have come a long way. It was necessary to undertake such a long journey because of the complexities involved in the correct understanding of differences and similarities between Eastern and Western cultures. As has already been mentioned in the first chapter, one needs to avoid trading in stereotypes and/or offering simplistic and ill-founded explanations of different cultures. Such explanations are ill-conceived and potentially dangerous. Instead of ushering in an era of genuine multicultural understanding and co-existence, they may act as divisive forces among cultures.

Cultures exercise a powerful influence on the development of one's identities, one's worldview. The normative prescriptions of a culture help in initiating, sustaining, and controlling private, familial, and social behaviours. Behaviours which fall outside the established conventional norms may be seen as deviations, and depending on the importance and the functional value of the behaviour concerned, pressures – from mild to severe – may be brought to bear upon the individual to conform to the norms. And when that fails, sanctions may be imposed upon the deviant individual, ranging from confinement, incarceration, to ostracism, and so on. Certain forms of deviations in certain instances may be construed as forms of mental aberrations, and once identified are dealt with in culturally appropriate ways, for example, confinement, medication, exorcism, yogic exercises, and so forth, by a culturally accepted 'expert' who is trained in such practices.

Thus each culture devises its own internally consistent set of rules. To understand a given pattern of behaviour in another culture, it is necessary to understand the system of rules and the assumptions that guide the private and social behaviours of people in that culture.

Thus there would be no need to 'order' cultures on a measurable scale of superiority or inferiority, civilized or primitive, advanced or backward, religious or secular, superstitious or scientific, and so on. Such an approach would also help to dilute, if not dissolve altogether, the oft-voiced accusations of scientific, educational, and economic imperialism which have been levelled against Western countries by the developing countries.

4

Research in Cross-Cultural Settings: Ethical Considerations

E thics is an integral part of philosophy. It is concerned with human conduct in terms of deciding how we shall live our lives. How shall we decide what constitutes a good life was the question Socrates raised in the fourth century BC. How shall we distinguish between good and bad, between right and wrong, between just and unjust, between fair and unfair, and between kindness and cruelty? This fundamental question was also raised by the philosophers in India, thus pointing to a historical parallelism in philosophical thought between two ancient civilizations (Radhakrishnan, 1923/1989, 1927/1948).

Ethics, as we know, is concerned with questions of what *ought* to be the case rather than what *is* the case. *How ought we to behave not only towards ourselves but also towards our fellow human beings?* Even a cursory examination of the above statement poses a formidable problem: how does one move from what 'is' to what 'ought?' It is a feat which has defeated many a moral philosopher (Frankfurt, 1988; Williams, 1985).

Although ethics is an integral part of philosophy, the study of ethical behaviour has been of considerable interest to psychologists. Their investigations, however, have been of a *descriptive and explanatory nature* (Eysenck, 1964; Kohlberg, 1984; Naito & Gielen, 1992; Piaget, 1948). They have each attempted to understand the development of moral behaviour and have offered a variety of theoretical perspectives, ranging from cultural relativism, socialization processes, to conditioning and personality characteristics in explaining the acquisition of moral behaviour. Psychologists have been concerned mainly with *descriptive ethics*, and have stayed clear of moral prescriptions, which they believe lie outside the field of psychology and fall within the domain of moral philosophy and religion. But large cracks have begun to appear in their scientific stance, and ethics rather belatedly has caught up with psychology. Psychologists including all other social, biological, medical, and natural scientists have become acutely involved in ethics.

In the natural and the physical sciences, research does not always depend upon the co-operation and the willingness of human subjects. And therefore the question of causing distress to human subjects or exploiting them in any way does not arise. One could hardly accuse a physical scientist of showing cruelty to sub-atomic particles! But it is the applications (or misapplications) to which the scientific findings may be put that cause very serious concerns (Beauchamp & Childress, 1994). They assert that ethics is a generic term for 'various ways of understanding and examining the moral life' (p. 4).

In the biological and medical sciences, there is a danger from two fronts: in the witting and unwitting exploitation of human beings, and the benevolent or malevolent applications of the findings (Beauchamp & Childress, 1994; Lifton, 1986; McCormick & Ramsay, 1978). But in the social sciences ethical concerns take on even greater significance. They arise from three sources: (a) due to the process of scientific inquiry itself, (b) glaring misdemeanours, ranging from thoughtlessness and bullying, hurt, trauma, and pain, which the subject might be exposed to (Milgram, 1974) during the investigation, and (c) as a result of the application and misapplication of the research findings (Berreman, 1972). Since social science research depends entirely on the willing co-operation of the people who assist us in the gathering of our data and the testing of our hypotheses, scientists need to be aware of the actual and/or the potential harm they can cause the very people without whose help social science research would, in all likelihood, come to a stand still.

Concern with the ethics of social science research is a fairly recent phenomenon. In the past, little attention was paid to ethical questions by social scientists because first, there was an unquestioning acceptance of *the natural science paradigm* within the social sciences, and therefore the subjects could be treated as objects who had no rights and towards whom the scientist had no obligations. Second, as Barnes (1979) points out, the acceptance of the natural science paradigm was complemented by the political context in which the paradigm was applied in practice. Both in anthropology and sociology, scientific attention was focused on the study of the powerless rather than the powerful, on the poor working classes at home rather than on the aristocracy, and on the *conquered* tribal peoples and the 'natives' in the colonies.

It was not until the late 1940s and early 1950s that social scientists, particularly anthropologists, began to express some concern over the ethical issues involved in social science research in general and in anthropological research in particular. The earliest glimmerings of concern with ethics were to be found in the use of pseudonyms, which protected the identities of the subjects studied. There was a recognition that the citizens who had been the objects of scientific enquiry might perhaps suffer if the findings of the study were published in their undisguised form.

Four major factors contributed to an increase in concern with ethical issues:

1 There was a growing disenchantment with the natural science paradigm as the ruling paradigm in the social sciences. It had serious limitations. One could not, on the one hand, treat the participants in the research as self-determining individuals upon whose willing co-operation depended the outcome of the research enterprise, and on the other, treat them as mere objects of research, who had no rights whatever and who could be manipulated at will by the investigators. The history of research within the social sciences is replete with sad examples of glaring misdemeanours, ranging from thoughtlessness and bullying, to hurt, pain, and suffering which researchers have wittingly or unwittingly inflicted upon the fellow human beings who have participated (Laungani, 1996c). This brought into question the entire business of treating subjects as objects of research and also the nature of the relationship between the researcher and the researched (Barnes, 1979; Berreman, 1969, 1972, 1973; Judd, Smith, & Kidder, 1991; McNamara & Woods, 1977; Silverman, 1977; Zimbardo, Haney & Banks, 1973).

2 As far as anthropology was concerned, there was a changing perspective in the role of anthropologists in the colonies, particularly in those British territories that were committed to a policy of indirect rule. In those colonial settings, anthropologists often found themselves in an uncomfortable position. The colonial administrators, who saw them as experts, had a vested interest in furthering the work of anthropologists. However, the quality of their work depended on the type and nature of relationships they were able to establish and sustain with the citizens of the colonies they had come to study. Thus, on the one hand, the anthropologists were dependent on the assistance offered by the colonial administrator, and on the other, they were dependent on the trust and goodwill of the citizens they had come to study.

The two interests, the anthropologists found, were mutually incompatible. The reactions of the anthropologists to these issues were mixed. Some anthropologists advocated that the tribal peoples should be left alone to continue living undisturbed and were prepared to opt out (Barnes, 1979). A few of them slipped into the role, which the colonial administrators had partly designed for them, a role with which they also felt inherently comfortable. Their formulations, based on the then popular theory of social Darwinism, were essentially Eurocentric. Implicit in their formulations was the underlying belief in the innate inferiority of the non-European races (Klineberg, 1980). However, most of the anthropologists steered clear of the two extremes.

They ignored the problems of imperialism (and with it, their own unwitting role in its perpetuation) and chose to see themselves as the paternalistic protectors of the indigenous social institutions of the people they had come to study (Barnes, 1979). But the paternalistic posturing fooled no one, least of all the 'natives'; real power, as everyone knew, lay in the hands of the colonial administrators.

3 The third factor, which led to a serious concern with ethics, was the direct result of the findings of the Nuremberg trials of ex-Nazi war criminals, among whom were several medical practitioners convicted of conducting inhuman medical experiments on innocent victims in German concentration camps. The world awoke to the horrors, the cruelties, and the brutalities of medical research, and the Nuremberg Code of medical ethics for human experimentation was set up in 1948. The Code stated clearly the responsibilities and the duties of the scientists towards their fellow human beings. The Code stated that all experiments must serve a humanitarian purpose, that the participation in an experiment or a research study should be voluntary; under no circumstances should the participants be subjected to any psychological and/or physical harm; the participants must be given the option to withdraw from the study if they so wished.

The Nuremberg Code set into motion the creation of several codes of ethical practices, including The World Medical Association's Declaration of Helsinki, 1964 and 1975; AAA, 1973; APA, 1973, 1992; APSA, 1968; ASA, 1971; BPS, 1993; and so on. The White House, through its Office of Science and Technology, issued a set of ethical guidelines entitled *Privacy and Behavioral Research* (1967) and in 1974, the US Congress established a National Commission for Protection of Human Subjects of Biomedical and Behavioural Research. Over the years, ethics committees and sub-committees have been set up in universities, hospitals, educational establishments and those governmental organizations sponsoring and promoting research activities. Ethics committees are expected to vet research proposals, and in so doing they serve an important function.

4   The fourth factor, which led to a concern with ethics, was the arrival of cross-cultural psychology on the international scene (Jahoda, 1970). It was, as Jahoda argued in the same paper, a belated arrival, but its emergence brought with it a serious concern for the ethical issues involved in research in developing countries.

Has the situation changed since? Has it become easier (or more difficult) for cross-cultural psychologists to visit the Eastern cultures and undertake uninterrupted research, unhampered by bureaucratic interference? Since the problem is entwined with politics, bureaucracy, government policy, there are no straightforward answers to this question.

The problems of cross-cultural psychologists start even before they leave their own country. If the research was to get off the ground, it was necessary for us to deal with the following problems.

Negotiations with governmental agencies and/or academic institutions

It is incumbent upon the scientist to explain the nature of the entire research project including the sets of hypotheses and the methodology to be used to test them. Any area that might be considered to be sensitive or might be perceived by the government as delicate or embarrassing or as evidence of Western opportunism or academic colonialism should be ironed out well before the scientist leaves his or her own country. It is necessary to win the goodwill and the approval for the project in advance. Failure to do so can lead to needless bureaucratic delays, and in some cases may even jeopardise the project permanently. Some have argued that the governmental agencies in developing countries tend to be needlessly touchy, if not paranoid in their structures.

But this is an unfair argument, for one has only to examine the consequences of some of the disastrous research projects of the past to appreciate their need for caution. The most iniquitous example of such a research project was the infamous *Project Camelot,* which was sponsored by the United States Department of the Army (Deitchman, 1976; Horowitz, 1973; Sjoberg, 1967). The project employed sociologists, psychologists, anthropologists and political scientists from Chile, Columbia, and from other countries, including Sweden. The fundamental aim of the project was to *help the United States government* to understand the nature of insurrection and internal revolutions in Chile and other Latin American countries – knowledge that would then enable them to cope with and manipulate such internal revolutions to their own political advantage. The project was designed with great care and from a methodological point of view it was impeccable; but the aims of the project, from an ethical point of view, were indefensible. Some of the

Chilean academics commissioned to work on the project had serious misgivings; they were aware too that they were working in a ruthless and totalitarian political climate, which could put their work and, in some instances, even their lives in extreme danger were they to express their misgivings in public. Yet a few did. News spread. Questions were raised. Inquiries were made. Documents were rifled. Whistles were blown. The world suddenly became aware of *Project Camelot*. The international outcry that *Project Camelot* raised brought about its premature abandonment. The Americans withdrew, their image tarnished, their morality beyond redemption.

One can therefore understand and even sympathize with the concern, bordering on paranoia, of developing countries when vetting and considering the viability of research projects submitted to them from Western countries.

Under certain conditions, the relevant governmental agencies and/or academic institutions may object to parts of the research programme. Upon closer examination, it may transpire that the objection is not so much to the project but to the political affiliations and views concerning the country in which the principal investigator(s) have chosen to undertake their research. Sometimes a question might be raised. Who is best qualified to see and interpret social reality? Do outsiders, coming as they do from the affluent West, possess the necessary insight, empathy, and sensitivity in understanding the problems of peoples of developing countries? Would they be the right persons to investigate them objectively?

Some psychologists, like Lewis (1973), take the view that non-members, *even though from the same country*, lack the personal experience or commitment necessary to understand the group culture. This argument is based on a position of *cultural relativism*. Such an approach, as I have argued elsewhere, 'although fashionable within certain areas of trans-cultural psychiatry, is misguided' (Laungani, 1996d: 31). Such a position is not only untenable but it is also potentially dangerous because its adoption would put an end to all socio-cultural research by persons *not* identified as 'in-group' members. But nonetheless, unsatisfactory answers to questions concerning the bona fides of the principal investigator(s) could cause serious delays in the commencement of the project, or, in exceptional circumstances, could even jeopardise the entire project.

Bona fides of the principal investigator(s)

Occasionally, academics and governmental agencies in the developing countries insist on vetting research proposals, including the potential investigators in terms of their political and social affiliations. Such an insistence, apart from a 'flexing of muscles', does not serve any significant purpose. The idea that by probing into the political and social affiliations of the principal investigators one will weed out a potentially dangerous research worker and potentially dangerous research projects, lacks substance. It assumes that the value systems of scientists influence the outcome of their research findings. Admittedly no scientist works in a social and moral vacuum. The very desire of a scientist to undertake this study and not that, to pursue this discipline and not that, is a reflection of the deep-rooted values of the scientist. In that sense, no research is value-free. It is clear therefore that our values often, though not always, dictate the choice of our research projects. But it does not follow that our values also influence the outcomes of our research projects. Such a conclusion is false, for it rests on the acceptance of a mistaken subjectivist epistemology (Lakatos, 1978; Lakatos & Musgrave, 1970; Popper, 1972). If research outcomes were directly influenced by one's values, there would be little point in undertaking research in the first place. All one would need to do would be to spell out one's conclusions based on one's cherished values!

Finding collaborator(s)

According to Warwick (1980), this is an extremely delicate problem where failure to exercise care and diplomacy can seriously jeopardize the entire research project. How does one choose a collaborator? Should one select one who is 'politically safe', is 'acceptable' to the academic establishments of his country, has impeccable credentials and sound research publications, and is not likely to arouse the jealousies and rivalries of other academic staff within his or her department as a result of the prestige value attached to Western-funded research projects? If so, how does one find such a collaborator? The problem arises because in most developing countries, including India, the number of researchers in a given field is quite small. In some countries there are no more than five or six psychologists who 'count' as scholars in their field. Warwick (1980) suggests that the factors which explain this situation include limited professional training, heavy teaching loads, low pay, lack of research facilities, *lack of a tradition of research,* the paucity of publication outlets, severe academic infighting, and often a high level of political turmoil in the universities and, at a larger level, in the countries. Thus it is the few who are well known that will attract the attention of the directors of a cross-cultural or cross-national research projects. It is possible therefore that seeking the help of a local collaborator into research projects formulated outside the country *might* distort local research priorities.

Notwithstanding the practical difficulties in finding local collaborators, it is absolutely essential that cross-cultural research projects are *planned, designed and executed together.* It would be presumptuous, to say the very least, on the part of foreign investigators to believe that they have a clear understanding of the *emic formulations* of the concepts and hypotheses which they are planning to investigate. If meaningful research is to be done and complex hypotheses are to be meaningfully tested across cultures, it is necessary that the concepts are conceptually equivalent and serve a similar function in the other culture, and that they are capable of being measured meaningfully, and that reliable and valid cross-cultural comparisons can be made, and so on. It is through the local collaborator's first-hand knowledge of the cultural nuances, the subtle use of language, an awareness of the local customs, rites, and rituals, networks of social and familial relations, patterns of beliefs, values and social behaviours, and so forth that a foreign investigator can hope to study the problem meaningfully and intelligently. For a foreign investigator to decide to 'go it alone' (as some have chosen to do) would seem unwise. Or else the findings from such isolated research endeavours are likely to be so trivial as to be socially or psychologically insignificant, such as some of the early cross-cultural studies on intelligence, visual perception, and visual illusions (Rivers, 1901, 1905).

Let us put the same argument in reverse. Let us assume that a research investigator from (say) Pakistan, who has never been abroad, who has lived all his life in Lahore, comes to England and undertakes *all by himself* a study on social class differences among the English in terms of their attitudes to work, marriage, and leisure pursuits. One wonders how the English psychologists would view such a research enterprise!

Research sponsorship

Most cross-cultural studies require some type of financial support from a research sponsor. It need hardly be stressed that funding agencies exert a crucial influence over what is done in cross-cultural research, who does it, how and where the studies are conducted, and the channels through which the findings will eventually be disseminated. This 'pressure' by the sponsoring agency increases significantly if the sponsoring agency has a particular interest in the outcome of the research project. What could delay the commencement of the research project is when the sponsoring agency itself comes under the scrutiny by the academic and/or governmental agencies of the country where the study is to be undertaken. The sponsor's name and image are crucial to the reception accorded to a study in the field. In addition to the outcry, which followed *Project Camelot*, a similar problem arose over Berremen's (1972) research project in India. The Himalayan border countries' project of the University of California was initially financed from private American sources. In 1968 a member of the Indian Parliament disclosed that the project was now to be partially financed by the United States Department of Defence (DOD) for a period of three years. The project was abandoned because of the Indian government's opposition to the project.

It is only after the preliminary negotiations for the study and the problems of sponsorship, the visas required to enter and live in the country, the accommodation and the duration of stay, and so on have been satisfactorily concluded that the cross-cultural research project is ready to move to the field.

The ethical problems confronting the investigator do not end there. New ones occur as soon as the researchers arrive in the country. The researchers now find that they are confronted with three types of ethical issues:

- The personal values of the investigator(s).
- The process of enquiry.
- Applications of research findings.

Personal values of the investigator(s)

Unless they have totally inured themselves from a series of culture shocks, foreign investigators coming from the affluent West are more than likely to be affected by the conditions of life around them. It will not be long before they experience a serious clash of values and may find it increasingly difficult to maintain a stance of 'scientific neutrality' (in keeping with the natural science paradigm) and pursue a supposedly value-free investigation. In human terms, they might decide that sitting on the fence, so to speak, is not the best policy and might consequently wish to get 'involved'. This could happen in several ways; the increasing difficulty of maintaining power relationship between researcher and researched, the inability to adhere to a natural science paradigm, the desire to get involved in the community or village by contributing to the welfare of the villagers, the need to change the structure of the society that they have come to study, and so forth. On the debit side they might find that they are not made to feel welcome, they may be accused of promoting academic imperialism or colonialism, they may be criticized for not consulting enough with the local experts and granting them equal status in the research design, they may inadvertently get drawn into departmental jealousies and rivalries, they may be exploited by their collaborators either in terms of additional monetary 'expenses' or in terms of joint publications for which the local collaborators may not have undertaken their required share of work. In extreme cases, they might be accused of being foreign agents and might, in fact, be declared *persona non-grata* and be asked to leave the country (Berreman, 1972).

In addition to the ethical problems within the social, economic, and political context, which all research workers would need to find satisfactory solutions to, they may also experience a variety of personal ethical problems, which might best be described as 'sins of omission and commission'. This refers to the problems of understanding, acceptance, and, to a certain extent, internalization of the cultural norms and mores operative in that particular culture. Mistakes which might seem trivial to the researcher may, in fact, have extremely serious repercussions on the maintenance of cordial relationships and the eventual pursuance of the research project. It is important that one learns to perform culturally relevant courtesies in the manner in which they are traditionally performed within that culture.

A few examples from Indian society will help to clarify the problem. For instance, one would need to observe appropriate codes of dress: to enter an orthodox Indian home wearing shorts would be considered inappropriate. One would need to be aware of and respect their dietary practices, forms of greeting, the taboos related to any form of physical contact between unrelated males and females. One also needs to be particularly sensitive and attentive to the traditional forms of greeting, but more importantly, who may address whom, how, under what conditions, and with what levels of deference, formality, informality, intimacy, and so on.

Each culture has its own norms, values, and mores which have a significant bearing on the religious beliefs, kinship patterns, and social arrangements of the people of a particular culture (Laungani, 2004c, 2004b). Unless researchers are familiar with such norms, their communications with members of the host culture are likely to be restricted and superficial. Cultural misunderstandings can so easily lead to people taking offence and/or causing offence when none was intended.

The process of enquiry

Cross-cultural research is a form of social intervention which alters the characteristics or relationships of individuals or groups. The main problems that arise from such an intervention are the duties and obligations of the researchers to the people they have chosen to study. The extent to which the researchers impinge upon the people that they study would naturally vary according to the nature of the study, the duration of stay, and the implemented research design. On the one hand, the impingement may be minimal as when the subjects are asked to fill in a one-item questionnaire (see Hofstede, 1976, 1980), and on the other, they may be deceived into believing that they are going to be harmed or are likely to cause harm to others (Milgram, 1974), made to feel extremely anxious, guilty, and experience stress (Schachter, 1959), or when they are asked the most personal, intimate and embarrassing questions, or made to reveal information about themselves which they would rather withhold, and so on. This, as Baumrind (1964) points out, is a grave and serious problem not just in psychological research but also in psychiatry where it is incumbent upon the psychiatrist to explain the nature of the investigation and seek informed consent. Concerned researchers object to these forms of research.

What are the duties and obligations of the researchers to their citizens? There are at least three conflicting arguments that have been suggested in response to the above question:

1   Some scientists have argued that the 'subjects' may legitimately be made to suffer for the benefit of mankind. This ancient 'means-and-ends' argument follows from the premise that was stated earlier, namely that knowledge is preferable to

ignorance, and therefore if in the process of acquiring knowledge which, it is assumed, is going to be beneficial to mankind in the long run a few people are caused unavoidable distress, it does not become an argument for the abandonment of the pursuit of such knowledge. Support for this argument can be found in the field of bio-medical research. For instance, McCormick (1976) strongly supports this argument on the basic principle of justice. He believes that we all ought to bear minimal or negligible burdens for the common good. Such burdens are not just charitable acts; they are demanded by the principle of justice. Thus we ought to consent to participation in certain forms of research under appropriate conditions. He defends his position by arguing that we would need to carefully weigh the benefits and the risks before consenting to participate in a research study. Such an argument is not easy to settle. Whether the principle of natural justice should override considerations of personal risks would depend upon whether this commonly accepted moral principle should or ought to be replaced by another (Beauchamp & Childress, 1989). There does not appear to be a legitimate way by which one might settle this argument.

2   The second argument proposes that the participants in any research enterprise *must* be given the option to refuse to participate in the research study. At first glance, the argument has much to commend it. It is in keeping with the Nuremberg Code. It is an argument that recognizes and respects the rights of individuals to make up their own minds concerning their involvement in a research undertaking. But when seen from a cross-cultural perspective, the argument seems flawed because it exempts the scientist from his or her personal obligations and duties towards the participants and places the responsibilities for participating or refusing to participate on the research subjects. Since research subjects are seldom given complete information concerning the nature, the rationale, the methodology, and the testable hypotheses of the research project in which their co-operation is being sought, they are hardly in a position to make a rational choice related to acceptance or refusal to participate in the project. Moreover, a large number of social psychology experiments, field studies, and so forth rely on deception because to reveal the true purpose of the study in advance would invalidate the study. Though the investigators might in principle be willing to 'come clean' with their subjects, in practice they would abstain from doing so. Thus, in a large number of cases the subjects are not given a true option other than one of blanket acceptance or refusal to take part in the study.

Notwithstanding the arguments against the use of deception (see Baumrind, 1964; Bok, 1978; Kelman, 1967; Mixon, 1977), deception in psychological research is seen as a powerful methodological and manipulative variable which can be used effectively in research design. As Adair, Dushenko, & Lindsay (1985) point out, the use of deception allows complex and sensitive studies of social behaviours to be undertaken which otherwise would not be possible.

Notwithstanding the protestations against deception, Adair et al. (1985) argue that 'the use [of deception] has not only increased in frequency and intensity – it has become the accepted model for social psychological research' (p. 70). From a cross-cultural point of view, it becomes even more difficult for subjects to refuse to participate in a study. This is true of Indian subjects as well. First of all, Indian children are socialized into obedience of the authority of their elders and their teachers, therefore refusal to participate in a research study does not come easily to them. Refusal is likely to be construed as a form of defiance, a show of which may incur negative sanctions being imposed on the person concerned. Second, being requested by a *foreign investigator* to particpate in a research study might be seen as acquiring added status in relation to those who have not been so approached. Third, the lure of receiving monetary payment, which relative to Western standards might not be insubstantial, for assisting with the research may make refusal impossible. Finally, the insistence that subjects be given the right to refuse to participate in a research project might be in keeping with the required standards of ethical behaviour accepted in Western countries, but such a caveat may be of little relevance in other cultures. Thus the argument that the subjects must be given the option to accept or refuse to participate in a research study does not have much to commend it in practice. It just doesn't work.

3   The argument that the social scientists do not seriously interfere with the well-being of the subjects is an empirical one. There is some research evidence available that shows that the participants in research which involves deception and the use of stressors *do not* experience the negative effects which one might be led to expect (Sullivan & Deiker, 1973). This finding is further supported by a survey conducted by Gray, Cooke, and Tannenbaum (1978). Ring, Wallston, and Corey (1970), who replicated Milgram's original experiment, found that only 4 per cent of the subjects who had been debriefed regretted participating in the experiment and indicated that the experiment should not have been allowed to continue.

It is possible that in so far as psychological research which involves the use *of college* students as subjects is concerned, the above argument is valid because (a) the college students in Western countries have become increasingly aware of their rights; (b) psychological experiments among the student fraternity have lost their aura and have even to a certain extent become tarnished (Barnes, 1979; Kelman, 1972); and (c) students tend to look upon psychological experiments as little more than necessary course requirements.

But again, in cross-cultural settings, the situation might well be different (Pryzwansky & Wendt, 1999). The cross-cultural psychologist may be ignorant of the unique features of each cultural setting, including its political context, and this may lead him or her into unwittingly causing distress, anxiety, or offence to the subjects of the research. Let us take an example: to ask unmarried women in Britain about their sexual behaviour may result in mixed responses ranging from amusement, impertinence, to offence. But the same questions put to unmarried women in India would be regarded as extremely insulting and immoral. There are strong taboos against pre-marital sex in India.

There is no denying that the investigator has certain duties and obligations towards the subjects of his study. The investigator simply cannot afford *not* to discharge them because failure to do so would, in the long run, become counter-productive. Warwick (1980) has suggested a series of ethical guidelines for cross-cultural psychologists. As a first step, he believes that research projects should involve equal-status collaboration right from the planning stage to its execution and eventual publication. Warwick also believes that all collaborators should be fully informed of the sponsorship, funding sources, purposes of research, as well as the intended uses of the data. It should be pointed out that the idea of equal collaboration, although desirable, is not always possible to implement because, to a large extent, 'he who pays the piper calls the tune'. It is the foreign investigators who arrive with funds at their disposal. This cold fact alters the basis of relationships between the foreign investigators and the local collaborators. Under these conditions, equal-status collaboration may easily turn into an asymmetrical relationship, where power implicitly passes into the hands of the foreign investigators, leaving the local collaborators dependent upon the foreign investigator in terms of the progress of research, the collection and analyses of data, and the eventual publication of the research findings.

However, given the practical difficulties of collaborative research, it raises an important question: is there any particular virtue in equal-status collaboration other than its political one? Academically, it might not be defensible. Equal-status collaboration may then turn out to be a myth.

The responsibilities of investigators to their research participants is a subject that has been of serious concern among psychologists; several thought-provoking guidelines, in keeping with the spirit of the APA *Ethics Code* (1993), have been offered. With regard to the responsibilities of the investigator to the populations studied, Tapp, Kelman, Triandis, Wrightsman & Coelho (1974) list six broad areas of ethical concern:

1   The research activity undertaken should be ethically acceptable.
2   The rights of subjects must be respected.
3   There should be open communications.
4   The researcher should respect the host culture.
5   Care should be taken to protect the subjects' welfare and dignity.
6   The research must be of benefit to the participants.

Once again it should be pointed out that these are *ideal conditions*. In practice, they may not be implemented in the spirit in which they are formulated.

Applications of research findings

Turning now to the ethical issues related to the uses, actual and potential, to which the research findings are to be put, one finds that the investigator is in a dilemma. On the one hand, the scientist has an interest in the pursuit of knowledge and its dissemination, which can be most readily achieved by publication. The scientist is also interested in furthering his or her own career, which is also facilitated by publication. On the other hand, the scientist may realize the potential dangers of publication, particularly if the research happens to be in a socially and/or politically sensitive area. One might recall the controversies surrounding the issues related to the inheritance of intelligence and the racial and ethnic differences in intelligence, which were fiercely debated in the 1970s. Though the dilemma has been posed in its ideal context, in reality, however, the situation is quite different. A large proportion of social scientists, it might be argued, *do not* spend a great deal of time deliberating over the ethical issues related to publication. They get on with their work and after its completion they attempt to get it published. Also, a large proportion of the published work of the social scientists (luckily) passes unnoticed. The outcry which follows some published work covers at least three salient areas of criticism:

- those concerning the process of research, for example, the problems of deception encountered in Asch's and Milgram's work;
- those concerning the findings of the research, for example, racial differences in IQ (Jensen, 1969); and
- those related to the potential or actual deleterious applications of the research findings, for example, the putative applications of the sensory deprivation research on suspected IRA members in Northern Ireland (cf. Shallice, 1972).

The first of these three criticisms has already been dealt with. The public outcry that followed the publication of Jensen's (1969) well-known paper was directed not so much at the process of inquiry but at the findings of the paper. The findings were questioned, denied, ridiculed, attacked, rejected; Jensen himself was accused of promoting racism by his 'pseudo-scientific' demonstrations of the innate inferiority of the American blacks on measured IQ in relation to the Caucasian whites in America.

Upon sifting through the barrage of criticisms related to Jensen's work and other research of a similar nature, one finds that the negative criticisms themselves fall into two categories. One set of criticisms was levelled at the process of research and the research findings. The critics pointed out that there was a variety of flaws, fallacious assumptions, discrepancies, and shortcomings in the research designs of those psychologists who claimed to have discovered genetic differences in measured IQs. Thus their conclusions were totally unwarranted. The second set of criticisms were ideological in nature. The critics subscribed to a form of liberal ideology that is antithetical to considerations of genetic differences in races and ethnic groups and which tends to explain any observed behavioural differences within and between groups of people in environmental terms. The important question is not whether the findings were spurious or genuine, but whether such findings ought to have been published in view of the potential misuse to which such findings could be subjected – such as when the National Front party in Britain quoted, or rather misquoted, the findings to justify their policy of white supremacy.

It is no doubt true, as Barnes (1979) argues, that even in cross-cultural research, publication may cause considerable harm to the subjects in several ways: it might reinforce existing negative stereotypes; it might also become a regular 'hunting ground' for future investigators. It is possible too that the subjects portrayed in the study might be easily identified, notwithstanding all precautions at preserving their anonymity undertaken by the investigator (cf. Berreman, 1973), thus violating their rights to privacy. In some instances the subjects studied might become potentially exploitable by different governmental agencies, and also by foreign governments. This was true of the anthropological study undertaken by Condominas (1973). He published an account of Sur Lak, a Montagnard village in South Vietnam. Five years later the US government sent a troop of Green Berets to Sur Lak, and the village was destroyed.

To publish or not to publish is the question. It is obvious from this that there is a conflict of interests; those of the scientist who understandably is keen to publish, and those of the subjects whose rights need to be respected and protected. The social scientists need to consider this issue with great care. They should be able to foresee the adverse consequences which might befall the participants, who themselves may be unaware of such hazards when offering their willing help to the research scientists. Knowledge is a public commodity, which can be used for good or ill (Barnes, 1979). The scientists simply cannot shrug off their moral responsibilities towards their subjects once the data have been collected and they are ready to return home.

Is there anything that can be done? Some social scientists, in view of the conflict of interests, have advocated a policy of refraining from social research completely. Others have argued that rather than study the social inequalities that abound in the world, the scientist should show a greater degree of political commitment, and should take constructive action to end them. They maintain that a scientist cannot now afford to adopt a value-free stance of scientific neutrality. According to Kelman (1968), scientists should take an active role in humanizing society. But as was pointed out earlier, the scientist is a guest in the country and is hardly in a position to advocate and/or initiate social changes which would help ameliorate the social and political evils within that society.

What compounds the problem further is the fact that a greater proportion of social science research is carried out by commercial organizations, with their team of entrepreneurial business consultants. Their primary concerns are pecuniary; ethical consideration, *if* they enter into their research framework, are of minor importance. Other than governmental legislation, there appears to be no easy solution to this serious problem.

It should be made clear, though, that not all publication is potentially harmful. On the credit side, publication might bring about the desired positive changes in social policy; it might bring a particular problem to public attention, thus generating private and public conscience; and it might lead to the ultimate welfare of the subjects studied.

Conclusion

There does not appear to be a readily acceptable solution to all the ethical issues surrounding research in the social sciences – particularly in the field of cross-cultural psychology. There is an obvious need to set up ethical committees (such as the ones formed by the American Psychological Association, the British Psychological Society, and so on) where the needs and interest of the cross-cultural psychologist, the rights of the subjects, and the obligations and interests of the sponsors can be discussed and negotiated to the mutual satisfaction of all the parties involved in the transaction.

Methodological Issues in Cross-Cultural Psychology

Methodology, in its simplest form, is concerned with the questions: How shall we study a given problem? What techniques should we employ which would get us near the truth? Can we arrive at an objective and valid understanding of a problem through rational reflection alone – without having to bother about methodology? The rationalist philosophers of the seventeenth century – Descartes, Spinoza and Leibniz – believed that one could, through the exercise of reason alone, arrive at truth. Their faith, however, was misplaced and the truth of their assertion turned out to be untrue. Reason alone does not allow us to arrive at truth. Combined with reason, one needs to, as the saying goes, 'dirty one's hands' and use empirical methods to try to ascertain truth, or at least an approximation of truth (Popper, 1963). To a large extent even the choice of the research methodology is influenced by the social, political, technological conditions *and particularly by the existing states of knowledge within the culture at a given period of time.* All the above factors influence us in our construction of a research problem, and in finding viable ways of solving the problem. Good research is not done in a social vacuum.

Chapters on methodology can often seem notoriously dry, drab, and dull. Despite their importance, several readers often tend to skim through or even skip over such chapters and focus on those that deal with specific problem areas, as we shall no doubt do in the subsequent chapters. But to skim through chapters on methodology is a dangerous practice, for without a proper understanding of how a particular study was conceived, what assumptions were made, how they were investigated and tested, how the data were analysed and interpreted, and so on, one can never be certain of the findings, namely their validity. It is therefore important that a chapter on methodology be written in a manner that holds the reader's attention and interest and allows the reader to look upon it as an integral part of any research undertaking, rather than as an appendage, 'tacked on' because it is the expected thing to do. It also ought to convince the reader that his or her knowledge of the subject under study, without a proper understanding of the methodology, would have been superficial, not to say unreliable, at the very least.

Let me therefore start this chapter with a scenario with which most Western readers are unlikely to be familiar. Let us go through the scenario and see what we make of it.

Box 5.1

Imagine you have been transported to Bihar in India, where you have come to visit the ancient University of Nalanda and the famous Buddhist and Hindu temples of India. Bihar, a large populous state, is situated to the north-east of India. During your trip through the famous temples in Gaya, you find yourself wandering through a small village. Although you have some knowledge of village life in India, you welcome the new experiences in store. As you wander through the fields, you see a man, unkempt and unwashed, sitting at some distance away from a well, with a couple of brass pots by his side. On seeing a young woman approaching the well, he joins his hands in supplication, and bowing down to her, points to the empty pots lying besides him. He looks at her pleadingly. She ignores him completely, fills her two brass pots from the well and, balancing them on her head, walks away. The man looks heavenwards in despair. Eventually he gets up, collects the two empty pots and shuffles away.

Some preliminary questions

Let us ask a few questions. How would you interpret this scene? Who is the man sitting by the side of the well? Why does he bow to the woman? Why does he not draw water from the well himself instead of asking her to fill them for him? Why does she ignore him?

To an outsider, unacquainted with the cultural drama being played out, this must seem a strange experience. You might be tempted to assume that the man asking the woman to fill up his pots might have been physically handicapped and consequently lacked the strength to draw water from the well. But seeing him heave his empty pots on his shoulders and walk away disconfirms the 'physical handicap' hypothesis. You might then assume that the woman may have had a difficult encounter with the person in the past and may have decided not to enter into any contact with him. You might also wish to believe the woman was in a rush and therefore couldn't be bothered, or that she was frightened of him, and so on. You might also wonder that being seen talking to a stranger might lead to village gossip. There are several other explanations that spring easily to mind. Which of the above explanations would you bet on? I'm afraid you'd lose on all counts.

Interpretation of Box 5.1

The fact of the matter is that the man asking the woman to draw water for him is a Sudra – a person who belongs to the lowest caste within the Hindu hierarchical caste system. Sudras (now known as *dalits,* the oppressed ones) were considered – and in some parts of India still are considered – to be untouchable (Laungani, 2002a). To come in any form of physical contact with a Sudra is to become spiritually polluted. Persons belonging to the higher caste take special care to avoid physical contact with an untouchable. The woman obviously belongs to higher caste and is unwilling to come into any contact with the Sudra. In many remote villages in India, an untouchable is even prohibited from drawing water from the village well. The prohibition is not a legal sanction; it carries the oppressive weight of tradition. For the untouchable to immerse his pot into the well would 'contaminate' the well, making it impossible for the high caste Hindus to use it without engaging in elaborate purification rites. Such an act of defiance would unleash the wrath of the high caste Hindus upon the helpless untouchable. Centuries of such appalling inequities have socialized them into mute submission. Had she taken pity on the untouchable and consented to draw water for him, she would then have used her own pot and then poured the contents into his pot, ensuring that her pot did not touch his pot. To immerse the untouchable's pot into the well would also have resulted in the spiritual contamination of the well (Laungani, 2002b).

It is clear from the foregoing incident that hypothese formulated to explain behaviours cannot be pulled out of thin air. They form part of one's cultural milieu. Unless one had prior knowledge of the history and the workings of the Hindu caste system, the workings of the law of karma, and of village life in India, one would not be able to make sense of the incident. One needs to place the incident within its cultural context. It is only then that the pattern of behaviour of the woman, and of the man, fall into place. This incident described is unique to an Indian setting. It has no parallels in any part of the world or in any other culture. One might point out the seeming similarities or approximations of such behaviours that were observable in South Africa and in the United States, where the black Africans and black American were segregated from the whites. But such a comparison is without meaning, for it ignores the historical context and the powerful influence of ancient traditions on people's behaviours.

One of the major tasks of cross-cultural psychology, as was pointed out in the previous chapters, is to locate those behaviours which are universal, those that are exclusively culture-specific, and those which transcend a few clearly defined cultural boundaries and share commonalities with other cultures and are thus partly universal and partly culture-specific. According to Triandis (1972), cross-cultural psychology is concerned with the systematic study of behaviour and experience as it occurs in different cultures, is influenced by culture, or results in changes in existing cultures (p. 1). The above definition is neat and precise. It encapsulates quite succinctly the nature and scope of cross-cultural psychology. The emphasis is primarily on studying *psychological phenomena*. Cross-cultural psychologists tend to treat cultures as independent variables and examine the effect of those variables on relevant psychological phenomena.

This distinguishes cross-cultural psychology from anthropology, where the main concern – at least in the past – was to *describe cultures in their totality* and compare them in terms of theoretically and empirically derived parameters. However, with increasing collaboration, the sharp dividing lines separating the disciplines have blurred (Bochner, 1986; Jahoda, 1982, 1992; Munroe & Munroe, 1997).

But before we examine the major research strategies used in cross-cultural studies, a few points need to be made concerning what constitutes *genuine* cross-cultural research. A few examples might help clarify the problem. Which of the following studies would constitute a genuine cross-cultural study?

- Comparative studies of American whites and American blacks in the United States.
- Comparative studies of Bangladeshis and Caucasians in England.
- Comparative studies of Bangladeshis and Indians, both living in England.
- Comparative studies of Pakistanis in Pakistan and Caucasians in England.
- Large-scale studies comparing Americans with the Japanese.
- Comparative studies of Britain and Denmark.

To put cross-cultural research on a more rational and logical footing, psychologists in the 1960s and early 1970s expended great effort to compile systematic information of more than a hundred societies dotted round the world, in terms of their specific cultural attributes (Murdock, 1967). The *Ethnographic Atlas* contains lists of societies that are carefully coded on a variety of cultural attributes, which allow the researcher to select societies and compare them on those attributes. Despite the availability of this valuable information, the decision to regard one form of research as cross-cultural and another as cross-national is often arbitrary. Quite often what might seem a specific cultural unit might, on subsequent analysis, turn out to be a biological factor. And if so, is one them genuinely involved in understanding culture-specific differences? These are powerful influences, which come in the way of undertaking 'pure' uncontaminated studies.

This point has been discussed by Whiting (1968), who suggests that there isn't any one 'ideal' type of unit for cross-cultural comparisons. The unit of analysis is often determined by the problem that is to be investigated. For instance, comparative studies between Britain and Denmark would be referred to as cross-national, and those between Pakistan and Britain would be seen as cross-cultural.

General methodological approaches to cross-cultural psychology

Experimental methods in cross-cultural research

Cross-cultural psychologists, as we noted in the last chapter, are concerned with testing hypotheses. The hypotheses may be specific and relatively easily testable, or they may be complex, involving a series of interrelated sub-hypotheses which may call for a great deal of ingenuity for testing them. Their approach in many ways is molecular rather than molar. They specify and isolate variables of theoretical significance and design appropriate ways of testing them. Experimentation is seen as the ideal research method because of its putative advantages over other methods of investigation: it allows the experimenter to exercise control over his or her observations, manipulate variables of interest, eliminate extraneous or irrelevant factors, and, above all, tease out causal relations (Christensen, 1980). Cross-cultural psychologists avoid the grand sweep of the anthropologists, who to a large extent are concerned about describing a system.

However, it needs to be pointed out that the advantages of the experimental method as a source of obtaining valid knowledge have been a subject of serious controversy. Its efficacy even within a single culture has been questioned. It has been argued that because of its enforced artificiality it is sterile; it does not reflect real-life situations, lacks ecological validity, and its findings may be confounded by 'experimenter effects' (Bannister, 1966; Barber, 1976; Brunswick, 1956; Rosenthal & Rosnow, 1974). There are a number of anomalies in experimental research. It is also seen as being unethical because it involves the manipulation of human subjects. The experimental method is also seen as a 'left over' of the antiquated model of nineteenth-century physics.

All the above criticisms apply to experimental studies undertaken in a *single* culture. But when the experimental method is used in cross-cultural research, it tends to be compounded by a host of other problems. Cross-cultural studies, if they are to be meaningful, need to contend not only with the above criticisms but also cope with the additional problems which are characteristic of cross-cultural research.

Non-experimental methods in cross-cultural research

Though the experimental method is seen as being ideally suited for testing functional relationships, in practice it is *infrequently* encountered in cross-cultural studies. It appears to have gone out of fashion. To start with, a large number of cross-cultural studies have been the result of opportunism and expediency. Sechrest (1977) points out that investigators appear to pursue their own idiosyncratic directions in their research and that 'too much cross-cultural research is done by, more or less, blind uninformed comparison of members of two or more cultures on some variable of interest, with very little thought given to the way in which culture might be linked to that variable' (p. 117). It would seem that there has been very little attempt at co-ordinated research efforts and the net result has been that 'little reliable systematic knowledge has been gathered' (Finifter, 1977: 151).

What has added to the confusion is the fact that research in cross-cultural psychology is undertaken by psychologists of all kinds of persuasions, with diverse theoretical leanings. In the past, the field was dominated by researchers with psychoanalytical orientations and in their studies they focused largely on problems related to the influence of culture on personality. Now the situation has changed. It attracts clinical psychologists, psychoanalysts, psychiatrists, developmental, social, experimental and cognitive, psychologists, psycholinguists, psychometricians, and so on. They all study different problems, espouse different theories, and employ different research strategies in their investigations. Questionnaires, observational techniques, psychometric instruments, psychological tests, field studies are the popular techniques used in cross-cultural research.

Theoretical approaches to cross-cultural psychology

Cross-cultural research is certainly not devoid of theories. In fact there is a proliferation of theories. But they are best seen as approaches than theories in the strict sense of their meaning. Miller (1997) lists a variety of such theoretical approaches, which serve as markers for contemporary research: culturally diverse approaches to self, psychological functioning, emotion, personality, motivation, development of identity, morality, mental health, social appraisal, processes of socialization, self-management, and so forth. Several other theoretical approaches, including the investigation of mental illness, anxiety and healing strategies, have also been suggested, which would allow researchers to investigate similarities and differences in behaviours across cultures. *But what appears to be lacking in cross-cultural research is a good and robust guiding theory – a unifying paradigm.* Whether such a unifying theory will emerge and how such a theory will be tested are questions to which no clear answers are available.

One might be tempted to argue that given the vast variations within and between cultures, in terms of their ecology, resources, social, political, biological, and other cultural factors which impinge upon the individual, it makes little sense to talk about one major unifying theory. But several valiant attempts have been made by many research workers to encapsulate research within a theoretical context. For instance, Sechrest (1977) in the late seventies classified cross-cultural research into three types (he referred to them as Type I, Type II, and Type III). Each type of research was concerned with different sets of issues, asked different sets of questions, and used different techniques for answering those questions.

Type I research according to Sechrest is concerned with *global cultural effect*. Here one is concerned with phenomena of general interest. The aim is to determine whether the phenomenon, for example, mental illness, is in any way influenced by cultural factors. Such a finding, Sechrest states, 'would affect our understanding and the interpretation of the phenomenon' (1977: 105). On the other hand, a demonstration of a *lack* of cultural influences would suggest a biological explanation of the phenomenon. In Type II studies the cultural origins of the phenomenon remain unquestioned. Here the aim is to demonstrate the importance of specific cultural variables. For instance, the study of the specific variables that influence the development of personality in a culture would constitute Type II research.

In Type III research the investigator is more interested in the culture itself than in any dependent variable being studied. Vassiliou and Vassiliou (1973) studied the meaning assigned to the Greek word *philotimo* (the nearest English translation of the word is 'code of honour') by Greek subjects. They found that the concept, though it had different shades of meaning within the Greek sample, could nonetheless be understood only with reference to Greek culture; it had no equivalent meaning outside Greek culture. Similarly, the word 'untouchable', which we referred to at the start of the chapter, has no meaning whatsover outside Indian culture. Such a finding would suggest that there are certain concepts, attributes, behavioural patterns, which are unique to a particular culture and acquire meaning only within the context of that culture.

Let us take another example, which is concerned with hospitality. In India there is an unwritten custom that a guest invited to dinner will leave a spoonful of food on the plate uneaten, whereas in Western countries the situation is reversed. There the guest is expected to make every attempt *not* to leave any food on the dinner plate. In an Indian context, the guest, by leaving a spoonful of food on the dinner plate, conveys to the host that he or she is neither greedy nor starving. Within a Western context, the guest displays appreciation of the hospitality by not leaving bits of food on the plate.

Segall et al. (1999) have provided an interesting conceptual framework that serves as a good guide to cross-cultural research. They argue that the framework needs to be understood in terms of two major factors – background variables and process variables – which influence psychological outcomes. The background variables are referred to as ecological and socio-political, and the process variables refer to cultural adaptation and biological adaptation. The two sets of variables have an impact on behaviour. Behavioural changes can occur as a result of changes in background and/or process variables. This is facilitated by a feedback loop: changes in one area – such as changes in ecology, sharp climatic changes, depletion on mineral resources, oil reserve, political instability – bring about changes in the other areas within the culture, and these in turn influence changes not only at a group level but also at an individual psychological level. Thus, according to Segall et al. (1999), cross-cultural psychology operates both at population and individual levels. And given the complex multi-disciplinary nature of inputs and their various influences, other disciplines, including anthropology, linguistics, biology, sociology, also have a major input in the study of human behaviour. The study of human behaviour across cultures is thus not the sole preserve of psychologists.

Process of research in cross-cultural psychology

After the thinking and the planning stages have been sorted out, one is involved with the actual business of undertaking research. And this in itself poses serious methodological problems. Let us deal with them by planning a hypothetical study, which you and I shall undertake in India, a country of which I have some knowledge.

In our study we shall attempt to examine the relationship between culture and personality. The study of culture and personality is a well-ploughed field. Therefore it might be prudent to stay with it. Our goal is to undertake a comparative study in personality between English subjects in England and Indian subjects in India. You would be right in arguing that this research could have been undertaken in any part of the world, or even in England, using a group of Indian subjects and comparing them with English subjects. Such a study would, of course, have been cheaper and speedier. These are valid objections. But whether such a study would classify as a genuine cross-cultural study is a debatable point – hence the trip to India.

From the scores of personality theories, which have been formulated by Western psychologists over the last hundred years, *which* theory of personality shall we opt for? Personality theories range from the Freudian, the neo-Freudian, the developmental, the biological, the existential, the motivational and the cognitive, behaviourist, to several others. Each theory makes its own assumptions, adopts its own methods of investigation, explanation, and interpretation. Obviously we have our own personal preferences. But regardless of which theory we select, we need to bear in mind that *all theories of personality that we have knowledge of are Western constructions. They have been formulated, designed, and tested by Western psychologists, largely on Western subjects.* How can we be sure that a particular theory – or any of the theories we opt for – will 'transcend' cultural boundaries and will be found to be relevant for subjects from Eastern cultures as well? How can we be sure that the notions of personality in non-Western cultures do not vary from those in Western cultures – particularly when one remembers that there are wide conceptual, theoretical, and methodological gulfs in personality theories in Western cultures? It is possible that their notions of personality may vary from those accepted in the West. It is also possible that Western approaches, tried and tested techniques, may be of little use when used in other cultures. This is a serious methodological problem. It is referred to as the 'emic–etic dilemma'.

The emic–etic dilemma

It was Pike (1966) who first suggested that the linguistic distinction between phonemics and phonetics served as a useful analogy for distinguishing between two significantly different approaches to the study of cross-cultural phenomena. Phonemics is concerned with the study of sounds used in one particular language and phonetics is concerned with generalizing from phonemic studies in separate languages to a universal science relevant to all languages. This analogy may be extended to cross-cultural research. Triandis (1972) suggests that the emic approach best describes items of behaviour occurring in a particular culture. It utilizes concepts drawn only from that culture. However, the emic approach has one serious limitation. By its very nature it does not allow us to compare cultures because the concepts developed in a single culture may be relevant *only to that*

Table 5.1   Emic vs. etic approaches

Emic approach	Etic approach
Studies behavior from within the system	Studies behavior from a position outside the system
Examines only one culture	Examines many cultures, comparing them
Structure discovered by the analyst	Structure created by the analyst
Criteria are relative to internal factors	Critirea are considered absolute or universal

Source: Berry (1969).

culture. This lack of universality of concepts prevents any meaningful cross-cultural comparisons.

The etic approach, on the other hand, investigates a phenomenon by utilizing universal concepts. The selection of universal categories facilitates cross-cultural comparisons. The etic approach, therefore, is particularly useful for testing the generality of psychological theories across cultures.

The emic–etic distinction has been further enunciated by Berry in Table 5.1.

All is not well with the classification systems in Table 5.1. The terms 'studies behaviour from within the system' and 'from … outside the system' seem to be arbitrary. All cultures consist of several interlocking systems, which may be examined at several levels: kinship, caste, linguistic, political, and so on. They need to be seen as systems rather than a system. Furthermore, as Jahoda (1983) points out, the words *discovery* and *creation* are not opposites, as Berry assumes them to be. Attempts to find acceptable solutions to the emic–etic dilemma, sadly, have not been very successful (Davidson, Jaccard, Triandis, Morales, & Diaz-Guerrero, 1976).

From an epistemological point of view, Berry's formulation is mistaken. It implies that structure (namely, truth) is 'out there' and will sooner or later *reveal itself* if one's observations are uncontaminated by various biases and artefacts. The factor that Berry misses is that all our observations, as Popper (1963, 1972) points out, are theory-laden. To adopt a position of pure, uncontaminated observation as a source of valid objective knowledge is a return to a form of naïve empiricism of the kind which David Hume had proposed in the seventeenth century. Structures are not self-evident. They are not discovered. They are created or invented constructs.

Despite the ambiguities underlying emic–etic classifications, the importance of testing the generality of psychological theories cannot be overstated. Unless psychological theories are tested cross-culturally, the findings of the Western theories will always remain culture-bound. Let us therefore stay with the emic–etic distinction and return to our research proposal.

We explore the range of personality theories and eventually decide to work with Eysenck's theory of personality (Eysenck, 1952, 1960, 1963, 1967; Eysenck & Eysenck, 1969). Without going into the details, suffice it to say that Eysenck proposes a bio-social theory of personality, which encompasses three independent, uncorrelated dimensions of personality: introversion–extraversion, neuroticism–stability, and psychoticism. Over the years, Eysenck and his associates have designed and refined several psychometric tests including the Eysenck Personality Questionnaire (EPQ). The EPQ consists of simple, easy-to-administer, easy-to-understand, and easy-to-answer questions. The pattern of scores on the tests reflects the nature of the personality characteristics of the subject being tested. Eysenck argues that his theory of personality, despite certain limitations, succeeds in measuring personality cross-culturally. In fairness to Eysenck, it needs to be pointed out that *several hundreds* of carefully designed cross-cultural studies based on his theory have been undertaken. Although the findings from all the studies are by no means unequivocal, there is a significant degree of consensus in the findings. A limited claim to universality suggests that although the test was designed in the West, and therefore needs to be seen as an emic test, there is partial applicability of the test across cultures. The extent of its applicability is determined by factor loadings and other complex statistical analyses of the scores obtained on the tests. To use an analogy, a personality test is like any other scientific instrument, for example, the clinical thermometer. Regardless of who constructed the clinical thermometer, where, when, and how, it has universal applicability. Temperatures are invariant across cultures. But unlike scientific instruments, personality tests and other psychological instruments are extremely sensitive to cultural nuances. The question that is of concern to us is this: are there ways of resolving the emic–etic dilemma? Under what conditions can a test formulated in one culture be legitimately used in another culture? Cross-cultural psychologists have proposed two strategies to deal with the emic–etic dilemma: the pseudo-etic approach and the combined etic–emic approach.

Pseudo-etic approach

The researchers need to satisfy themselves on the following points.

Conceptual equivalence

It is important that the concepts underlying the test (or the instrument) have a similar shared meaning in another culture. In other words, one must ensure that 'like is being compared with like'. This is not always easy to establish, particularly when translated versions of the test are to be used. For instance, the concept 'pollution' has two meanings in Hindu culture. It refers to hygienic pollution, the meaning of which is shared by people in other cultures. But more importantly, the term 'pollution' is often referred to as spiritual and religious pollution. As an example, for a high caste Hindu to come into contact with the lowest caste Hindu (Sudra) is to become *spiritually* polluted. The concept of spiritual pollution does not exist in European culture; its nearest equivalent term would be 'desecration' – which of course does not have the same connotation. Again, words such as 'cheeky', 'scrumping', including a variety of metaphors commonly used in English (for example, *Draconian, Stoical endurance, Quixotic, Oedipal, Confucian, being in limbo, the patience of Job,* etc.) which are easily understood in England, have no meaning whatever within an Indian cultural context and therefore are difficult, if not impossible, to translate meaningfully. Failure to understand the implied meanings in the concepts may seriously compromise the validity of the test. Despite the care that has gone into translations of psychological instruments, many such translated tests tend to be flawed.

Metric equivalence

Once again it is necessary to ensure that the subjects to be tested in both cultures clearly understand the nature of the measuring scale and what it purports to measure. While Western subjects are used to understanding the workings of a 5-point Likert-type scale, or a Thurstone scale, or other types of variations of the scales on questionnaires, subjects from non-Western cultures are unused to being tested and may fail to understand what is required of them.

Ethical equivalence

A questionnaire designed to measure (say) attitudes to pre-marital sex, or gay marriages, or the use of contraceptives, may be found to be unacceptable by both men and women in non-Western cultures, and consequently may engender serious ethical conflicts in the subjects being tested. One must not assume that patterns of behaviours considered to be ethical (or unethical) in Western cultures will be perceived similarly by people in other cultures. The ethical problems underlying cross-cultural research have already been examined in the previous chapter. But suffice it to say for the present that the issue of ethics needs to be taken into very careful consideration when planning and designing cross-cultural studies.

Combined emic–etic approach

Here the first step is to identify an etic construct that is assumed to have universal status. The next step involves developing emic ways of measuring the concept in the culture. This approach, although it sounds reasonable, creates further problems. As was stated earlier, if the research involves the use of linguistic material it is difficult to be certain if the translated material has linguistic equivalence. Words, when translated into another language, may lose their connotative meanings (Brislin, 1981). Even if one were to abandon linguistic equivalence and opt for conceptual (or psychological) equivalence, one could run into similar difficulties. A search for conceptual equivalence presupposes a very intimate knowledge of the cultures concerned. This is not always possible. Comparability of cultures then becomes a matter of intuitive judgment instead of objective standardization. Under these conditions there is the uncertainty of whether the concepts are in fact psychologically equivalent.

It would therefore appear that the innumerable problems related to the emic–etic distinction are not particularly easy to overcome, and in most cases psychologists arrive at a reasonable compromise. Jahoda (1977) wonders whether there might not be something wrong with the concept. He believes that the combined etic–emic approach with its postulated sequence of moving from etic to emic to derived, etic is 'little more than a pipe dream' (p. 61).

Let us summarize the main points related to undertaking cross-cultural research. It is clear that any research strategy used to investigate a cross-cultural problem is seldom a matter of arbitrary choice. It needs to be carefully planned before it can be executed. The planning should include most, if not all, the following factors:

1   The nature and type of problem being investigated:
   - Is it an exploratory, descriptive study ?
   - Does it involve hypothesis testing?
   - Is it a replicative study?

2   The nature and type of culture being investigated:
   - Complex versus simple
   - Developed, developing, or underdeveloped
   - Large or small
   - Unilingual or multilingual
   - Secular or non-secular
   - Mono-religious or multi-religious.

3   The theoretical underpinnings of the problem:
   - The theoretical orientation of the investigator.

4   Practical considerations:
   - The feasibility of using electronic devices; experimentation.
   - Time and duration of stay of the investigator in the culture.
   - Funding and other resources.
   - The availability of local resources: access to 'subject pools'.
   - The availability of translators, local informants, interpreters, other experts.

5   The prevalent zeitgeist to which the investigator implicitly subscribes.
6   Facilities for collaboration with indigenous academics.

Conclusion

We seem to be reasonably prepared for our cross-cultural trip. Are there any other factors that we would need to take into consideration to ensure that the study is meaningful, viable, and is likely to yield results in which one might place a fair degree of confidence?

We shall assume that the study will be undertaken in Bombay (now known as Mumbai). It will be done on a large sample of English-speaking university student population (males and females) randomly selected from a variety of local colleges affiliated to the University of Mumbai. Using English-speaking students will enable us to use the English version of the personality test, instead of using a standardized, translated version of the EPQ. We shall further assume that the negotiations for collaborating with Indian academics, permissions to undertake the study, problems concerning accommodation and living arrangements have all been dealt with successfully. We shall also assume that no objections will be forthcoming from any governmental agencies concerning our bona fides as research psychologists attached to a recognized British university, and will be given the necessary visas for the duration of our stay in India. We shall also ensure that the test material to be used has already been despatched in advance, awaiting us at one of the colleges that has agreed to host our work. We have also taken all the required health-related precautions.

It has taken us six months to sort out these problems. We are now ready to set off for a two-month stay in India. Can anything go wrong?

Lots!

There are a variety of problems – social, political, personal, and ethical – that we shall encounter during the course of our stay in India. To come from an advanced, liberal democratic country to an overpopulated, multi-religious, multi-cultural, multi-lingual, developing country is to expose oneself to a variety of experiences which, despite prior preparation, may lead to social, moral and ethical 'culture-shocks'. These are some of the personal issues that one would need to contend with during the entire period of one's stay. It is inevitable that we shall experience bewildering sets of problems, which may affect us personally at a deeper emotional, social, and ethical level. However hard one tries, it is not be always easy to separate one's own personal values from professional ethics involved in research.

Part II

Applied
Perspectives

Doing Research in India: Cultural and Ethical Considerations

Since this is a fantasy trip to India, it seemed perverse not to travel First Class. During the flight, my associate – Stuart Dent, abbreviated to Student – and I enjoyed the opulent hospitality in the form of champagne, caviar, smoked salmon, *paté de foie gras*, mountains of cheesecake, dark chocolate, and other delicacies which I knew would be hard to come by in India, not without paying a king's ransom. I feared for my young research colleague. Would he, I kept asking myself, be able to make the required culinary adjustments during his stay in India? However, I was reassured by the fact that Indian cuisine, in the last two decades, has had a powerful impact on the hitherto bland English palate, and felt he would cope. But those would only be the first of many adjustments that would be required of him during our proposed three-month stay in India. I was more concerned about the social, climatic, practical, moral, and ethical adjustments that would be required of him. I felt he would need to acquire the sensitivity to do a 'gestalt switch' and learn to see the world from what to him would be a strange, if not alien perspective. During the flight I asked him if he had read some of the books that I had recommended him as background reading on India, Indian culture, and Indian religions. He had done his homework well. He rattled off the titles of quite a few books he had devoured, and those that he hadn't he had packed in his suitcase.

I then expressed my own views on some of the ethical and moral dilemmas that both of us would in all probability encounter in India, not only at a deeply personal and experiential level but at a research level as well. I knew from past experience that at times it would become impossible to separate one set of ethical problems from the other.

Our research project had been honed to perfection. The major aim of our study was to examine the relationship between personality, conformity, and obedience to authority. It was to be a comparative study, which involved testing students from England and India. The 'English' part of the study had already been completed. Our trip to India would help us to complete the remainder of the study.

Prior to our leaving England I had entered into elaborate negotiations with Professor Pandit, who was Head of Department at the University of Bombay. All the test papers, the documents, and other required paraphernalia, including our requests for suitable accommodation during our proposed three-month stay in Bombay, had been sent out in advance to Professor Pandit. He had expressed his willingness to help us with our research project. Since our study was to be done in several different colleges affiliated to the University of Bombay, all the documents had been sent in advance. From the correspondence that I had had exchanged with Professor Pandit, everything was in order. All possible arrangements had been made.

Professor Pandit, despite the late-night arrival of the plane, had taken the trouble to meet us at the airport in Bombay. I was touched by his kindness and concern. Being the Head of the Psychology Department, he could easily have requested one of his junior colleagues to receive us at the airport. He smiled, shook our hands and instructed his chauffeur to deal with our luggage. The change in the weather upon leaving the air-conditioned airport was dramatic! The icy blasts of London winter suddenly gave way to a damp, perspiring, heat. Our overcoats seemed like millstones round our neck. Student looked miserable.

Professor Pandit had arranged two rooms for us in the university campus, which was about a 20-minute drive from the airport. He instructed his chauffeur accordingly. I had first met Professor Pandit a couple of years before, during my last visit to Bombay. And a year later he had come to England on a brief lecture tour, where I had had the privilege of having him as my guest at home. We had got on extremely well together and he had more than volunteered – insisted – that he would make all the arrangements for our stay in India and would also ensure that a couple of his junior staff members would be available to assist us in our research.

His main area of research is in cultural psychology, or what has come to be seen as 'indigenous psychology'.

Without the slightest awareness, Professor Pandit and I slipped into talking in what is referred to as 'Hinglish' (Das, 2002), a combination of Hindi and English. In 'Hinglish', the two languages merge in a unique idiosyncratic way: one starts a sentence in Hindi (or in English) and halfway through slips into English (or into Hindi), ending the sentence once again in the other language. In some instances, one speaks a mixture of three languages – I call it Tringlish – all in one sentence. English, in a sense, has been Indianized. A foreigner unacquainted with this type of speech is quite often mystified by it and is seldom able to decipher the correct meaning of a sentence. The point to bear in mind is that India is a multi-lingual country. There are over 30 officially recognized Indian languages and over 1000 dialects spoken in India (Manorama, 2003). Communication between different linguistic groups would become quite difficult, if not impossible, were each group to retain its linguistic purity.

The hall of residence, we noticed, had only been very recently constructed. It was a four-storey building with a wide, well-lit, well-furnished entrance hall. The night-duty porter, with a couple of telephones on his desk – there were no television monitors that we could detect – rose as soon as we entered. We were each allocated a room with an en-suite bathroom, a small desk, and the other usual comforts which, in the West, one would take for granted. The rooms seemed reasonably clean and well furnished. This was to be our home for the next three months.

Professor Pandit explained that the hall of residence had been built very recently. There were two such halls. This one was for male post-graduate students and foreign scholars. The other, a couple of miles away, was meant for female postgraduate and post-doctoral students. This was done in accordance with the wishes of the donors, who were unwilling to countenance mixed halls of residence. He hoped that our stay there would be would be comfortable. There was a refectory in the basement where we could have our meals. He warned us that the food served in the refectory was strictly vegetarian – not even eggs were permitted into the building. Also no alcohol was served on the premises, nor was one permitted to smuggle any into the rooms. The funds for the construction of the hall of residence had come from a charitable institution, which had made this caveat conditional. However, he assured us that there were several restaurants and bars within walking distance, which would cater to our carnivorous culinary comforts and inventive inebriating indulgences. He had informed Mr Desai, the warden of the hall of residence, of our arrival. Dr Pandit, lifting an old-fashioned phrase straight out of the P. G. Wodehouse era, said that Mr Desai was a good bloke – a 'damn nice chap'. He assured us that Mr Desai would be of great assistance to us during the course of our stay in Bombay. He promised to meet us within the next couple of days after we had settled in and had overcome the travails of jetlag. So saying he took his leave. We both thanked him profusely and withdrew to our respective rooms.

The following day, after Student had had his first taste of a hot, spicy, and pungent South Indian breakfast, which brought an unusual glow to his face and beads of sweat to his brow, I suggested that he should explore the city by himself. It would be a good experience: he'd make mistakes, he'd lose his way, he'd commit social blunders, but he would start to learn at least at a day-to-day level the ways of the people in developing countries. Initially he seemed nervous about setting out on his own and disappointed at my reluctance to accompany him, but with gentle persuasion he fell in with my suggestion and left.

The following morning Student narrated a few of his experiences over breakfast. (I noticed that he assiduously avoided the Indian dosas and the *idlies,* which the waiter placed before him, and asked for a couple of slices of toast and coffee.) The poor fellow had had a torrid time. Without actually putting his fears into words, it was clear that Student was intimidated by the crowds, the noise, the roar of traffic, the bustle, the chaos, and the confusion all round him, which he found difficult to escape from or comprehend. He persevered. He rode on the local railway, terrified at seeing the passengers hanging on for dear life on the footboards of the overcrowded trains. He travelled on buses, he took the dangerously rickety three-wheeler auto-rickshaws, on the backs of many of which was painted the sign *'Trust in God'* – one would need to, he said to himself, smiling wryly. He walked through crowded bazaars, saw the higgledy-piggledy collection of hawkers, street vendors, selling fresh vegetables, flowers, fruit, sweets, rusty tools, household wares, electric goods, and a mixture other domestic appliances. Beggars swarmed around him. Hawkers beckoned him. Pimps solicited him. Moneychangers sidled up to him. His white skin was the magnet that attracted others to him. He ignored them all, and walked by. Little street urchins played around in the gutters and the puddles by the roadside, heedless of the traffic thundering past as they darted across the road. Although their mothers kept a vigilant eye over their antics, they were busy sniffing and rummaging through huge piles of smelly rubbish, in search of any food or any discarded item of clothing that could be salvaged. Further down the road, he saw in the distance magnificent high-rise skyscrapers looming over the slums and the shantytowns all around them. He spent a few hours wandering through the slums, ignoring the overtures of several people who sidled up to him.

Like the proverbial Siamese twins, poverty and affluence seemed inseparable. At the corner of every third or fourth street, he noticed a Hindu temple, each of which varied in size and construction. Worshippers went in, rang bells, prostrated themselves before the gods, recited hurried prayers, and dropping a nickel or two into the plate placed next to the deities, left. He recalled the famous phrase attributed to Karl Marx: religion being the opium of the masses. Tiredness sapped his energy and enthusiasm; he returned to the hall of residence.

Professor Pandit had sent his car to collect us for our appointment at the University. Student seemed listless, even unwilling to talk. I wondered if the spicy food had upset him. When I questioned him on his trip to the city, he answered my question in a desultory, roundabout way. Suddenly, he turned on me and asked, rather angrily, if there was any point in studying personality characteristics of university students in Bombay and then doing a comparative analysis with a similar sample of English students. I knew it was not a rhetorical question. He was very disturbed. There were problems of far greater importance to be investigated, he added, his voice cracking. One could tell that something was bothering him deeply. I was sure that his day's trip into the city had something to do with his sudden change in attitude. He seemed very distressed. Being the kind person that Student was, carrying his liberal, humanitarian values on his 'sleeve', it did not to surprise me to see him in such a state of distress. If half a day's trip into Bombay had affected him so deeply, I wondered at the variety of shocks he would have experienced had the study been based in one of the poorer, deprived villages around Bombay, or elsewhere. I kept my counsel to myself and decided not to enter into a discussion at this stage, perhaps later.

Our meeting with Professor Pandit the following day was cordial and extremely fruitful. Presently, the peon entered the room, bearing a tray with a teapot, five cups and saucers, and a large dish brimming with a variety of sweet and savoury Indian snacks, which he placed at a nearby table. He looked at the Professor, who shook his head. The peon withdrew silently.

'I'm waiting for two of my colleagues to join us', he explained. Just then, there was a knock on the door, and we were introduced to two men who entered the room. They were Professor Pandit's junior colleagues: Dr Joshi and Dr Khan. The peon re-entered the room. Tea was served. Snacks were passed round. Student was about to decline when he caught my disapproving eye. He accepted the fried Indian snacks that the peon placed on his plate.

Presently, Professor Pandit turned to Student and asked him jovially, 'Tell me, have you had any exciting adventures in Bombay?'

Taking his words literally he replied, 'I'd hardly call them exciting. Not after my visit to Dharavi.'

'Ah, a man of great courage,' replied Professor Pandit approvingly.

'Not many people venture out into Dharavi,' said Dr Khan.

Box 6.1

Dharavi, for the uninitiated, is the largest, the dirtiest, and perhaps the most overcrowded slum in Asia. Within an area of about 7.5 square kilometres, it holds a population of over 1.2 million souls. Malaria, dysentery, tuberculosis, and a hundred other infectious diseases conspire with malnutrition, poverty, and destitution to make life a living nightmare for the slum dwellers. Basic amenities such as safe water, toilets, fresh food, milk, electricity supply, which the people of the developed countries take for granted, are often seen as luxuries. People live in small hovels, made of – rather assembled together – corrugated metal, old moth-eaten blankets, sacking, cardboard, bits and pieces of wood, steel pipes, and whatever other material that the slum dwellers can get hold of, which will keep the pollution, the noise, the insects, the heat, and the monsoons away and give them some peace and a semblance of privacy. But these measures do not work. During the monsoons the rains lash through the slum dwellings, bringing down many such hutments. The grounds turn into slushy, muddy settlements – breeding grounds for infectious diseases which bring death and devastation to children and adults alike. Mosquitoes invade their dingy, poky little rooms, feeding on children and adults alike with indiscriminate abandon. Cockroaches come out of their hiding in droves, and large scavenging rats dart about from one sewer to another, from one hovel to another, in search of food. Living in these mean and wretched slums, as they do, from birth to death, one cannot but wonder how the people who are born and brought up there survive. It is impossible *not* to feel numbed by what one sees, impossible to blot the bleak landscape and the human misery out of one's consciousness.

Author's note: The reader needs to be informed that the conditions described above existed several years ago. During my last visit to Dharavi, in 2002, the slums had been modernized; the conditions of living have undergone a change for the better and several cottage industries have been established.

'Even horses in stables in England lead a more comfortable life!' said Student with intense sorrow and anger in his voice.

'You might be interested to know that in the last 18 years since I have been Professor and Head of Department, I have met scores of Western psychologists from America, Canada, England, Germany, Australia, New Zealand and elsewhere.' Barring one or two exceptions, he explained, not one of them had shown the slightest interest to visit Dharavi, let alone undertake any research there. It was not as though they were not aware of Dharavi. How could one not be? And yet when one considered Dharavi, despite its moral and humanitarian problems, including those of death and destitution, it was the most fertile ground for valuable research – both of a theoretical and applied nature. There was not a psychological problem in the world that could not be investigated in Dharavi. Hindus and Muslims, Sikhs and Christians; high castes and low castes, educated and uneducated, beggars and bandits, social workers and health workers, barbers and tailors, tanners and weavers, potters and furniture makers, drug dealers and junkies, priests and sinners, pimps and prostitutes, exploiters and the exploited, they all, *all* lived together, all sharing, so to speak, the same fate. Dharavi was more than a slum; it was India, on a reduced scale. A thousand research workers could be kept gainfully employed in Dharavi for decades.

'How do they do it? How do they survive? Why don't they resist, rebel?'

'There are no easy answers to these questions. That's for you to find out,' answered the Professor.

'I don't know.'

'There is within the Indian psyche an ingrained characteristic of acceptance – a form of resigned acceptance.'

'Of what?'

'You would call it fate. In Hindu philosophy we call it karma. It is bolstered by our unswerving belief in the law of karma. It is this belief that gives us the strength to accept and survive against all odds. Muslims call it *naseeb* or *kismet*, or the will of Allah. And we call it karma. Our society would disintegrate if we did not possess this safety valve. It is our sanctuary, our refuge.'

He then tuned to his two colleagues, Dr Joshi and Dr Khan, and said, 'These two gentlemen have worked in Dharavi for over a year and could tell you stories which would freeze your bone-marrow.'

Dr Joshi had a flowing beard and was dressed in a knee-length saffron robe; a beaded garland hung over his neck; it was clear that he was a Hindu swami. It turned out that he had been a Sanskrit scholar and had graduated in Sanskrit from the Banaras Hindu University. Later on he had moved into the field of psychology. Dr Khan, on the other hand, who as I learnt subsequently was a devout and deeply religious Sunni Muslim, was dressed in a white safari suit. They were both in their early thirties and had been attached to the Department of Psychology for about a decade each, first as students and then as members of the faculty. After their year's assignment in Dharavi, they got deeply involved in the experimental study of yoga and meditation, particularly in its therapeutic effects, assisting Professor Pandit who was the Director of the research project. Cross-cultural psychology per se was not their area of specialization, but indigenous psychology was. Through an extremely generous grant they had acquired a modern, well-equipped experimental laboratory where they could undertake the sophisticated studies, which involved the use of EEGS, ECG, and other measurement devices. Their laboratory was part of a yoga Institute, which was at a hill station about 100 miles to the south of Bombay. They normally spent their weekends in the experimental laboratory.

Professor Pandit pointed out that they were more than willing to help us with our research project. He explained that he had just finished writing a book entitled *Yoga and Indigenous Psychology*, and he would be happy for us to read the manuscript if we so desired. There was a chapter or two, he felt, that would be particularly pertinent to our own research project, particularly the ones related to the social, cultural, and ethical problems of undertaking cross-cultural research. We jumped at his offer with alacrity.

What follows now is a summarized account from Professor Pandit's chapter entitled 'Doing Research in India'.

Each culture, each nation presents its own sets of problems. Unless the researcher is fairly conversant with the problems of the culture that he has chosen to investigate and knows how to cope with them, it is doubtful that the research will be of any great value both in its theoretical and applied sense. Paradoxically, many Western researchers never visit the country of their chosen study. In such cases, the study is often undertaken by local indigenous collaborators. The advantages of such an approach are easily visible, but they tend to be outweighed by the disadvantages. The principal investigator based abroad has no control over the study, is often ignorant of how the data were gathered, and is entirely dependent on the collaborator for this information. The value of this form of collaborative research often tends to remain questionable.

It needs to be emphasized that it is not the aim of this chapter to provide a comprehensive account of the physical and commercial geography of India, nor is it concerned with the economy, its industrial and technological development, its social and political history, demographical and epidemiological indices, and current political affairs. The chapter concentrates on the practical, social, academic, and ethical problems which a research psychologist is likely to encounter during the course of research.

Fundamentally, an investigator has two main choices open: he or she could either choose to work in cities or in villages – although the two need not be seen as mutually exclusive. Let us discus the kinds of problems that an investigator is likely to face on his or her arrival in Bombay.

Understanding day-to-day social behaviours of Indians

Here there are a few ground rules which facilitate social interaction that need to be learnt. They are not cast in stone. But nonetheless the interested foreigner will find that they come in handy in social situations. They are summarized below:

1   Indians tend to strike up social conversations with total strangers quite easily. In their social interactions, Indians, unlike Westerners, tend in general to be a 'touching' people. The also stand quite close to one another, and do not keep the kind of distance which Westerners tend to maintain in social situations. However, there are taboos concerning males touching females and vice-versa.
2   indians can often ask – and do – without any embarrassment, very personal and delicate questions concerning one's age, marital status, the number of children one has, their age and sex, one's occupation, income, religious beliefs, and so on. One needs to learn to fend these questions without seeming to cause offence.
3   One learns that to meet people it is not always necessary to make a prior appointment. One calls on them and waits if the person one has come to meet is busy or not available. Not being put out if one is kept waiting far beyond one's appointed time is a necessary social skill, which needs to be acquired.
4   Indians often tend to display a seeming unconcern for privacy. Indian society is a family-oriented society and since individuals live in extended family networks, where life is shared, the need for privacy is not felt with the same level of intensity as it is in

the West. A Westerner unused to this feature of Indian family life may see lack of privacy as a painful intrusion. The relative unconcern with privacy is a specific cultural phenomenon.

5   Extending hospitality is an integral part of Indian culture. However, the issue is more complicated. Who extends hospitality to whom, with what frequency, is often determined by factors related to caste, creed, family connections, and so on [issues which are discussed in depth in the following chapter].

6   The notion of time among Indians differs sharply from Western notions. Time is seen in flexible, even relaxed terms. There isn't thus the frenetic rush that is noticeable in the West. One needs to learn not to be put out by their differential conceptions of time.

7   Indians, in general, do not shy away from expressing feelings, displaying emotions among friends, within the family, and even in public. It arouses no inhibitions, nor is it seen (within certain limits, of course) as a sign of ill breeding.

8   The daily life of Indians (Hindus, Muslims, and Sikhs) is organized around their religious beliefs, prayers, and worship. This includes participating in all the varied religious festivals, performing all the required prayers, and thereby seeking the blessings of all the gods and deities.

9   Religious practices often tend to be reduced to ritualistic behaviours. The performance of rituals plays an important part in the daily life of Indians, Hindus, Muslims, and Buddhists. Rituals need to be seen as a form of personalized communication with cosmic deities. Not to perform the required rituals can lead to spiritual contamination. Elaborate purification rituals need to be performed to regain a state of purity.

10 Indians, particularly orthodox Hindus, operate on a fairly rigid caste system. Inter-caste interactions serve a functional value, but intra-caste interactions are more intimate and are of greater importance, in terms of meetings, invitations, marriage, illness, death and bereavement, and several other social and familial activities.

Conflicting social and ethical problems

There are a variety of other serious social and ethical problems which investigators, unless they are totally insensitive, would find impossible to ignore during the course of their stay in India. In the West, to a large extent one is 'sheltered' (or one can insulate oneself) from witnessing problems of such severity. But to come face to face with unimaginable poverty, destitution, malnourishment, exploitation of children, dirt, pollution, noise, overcrowding, illness, disease, and several other social ills such as corruption, child labour, child prostitution, exploitation of labour, religious bigotry, caste and communal prejudice, one is as though etherized by what the eye sees, the mind registers, the heart feels, and the soul sinks into despair. It comes as a shock to learn that over 40 per cent of Indians living in large metropolitan cities are homeless; like foetid flotsam, they spill on to the streets and makeshift slums, heirs to all the ills mentioned above. It is impossible to offer any guidelines on these issues. How a Western research worker would react or ought to react to such ills and iniquities is best left to individual consciences and coping strategies.

Doing research in cities

The ideal time to come to India as far as the weather is concerned is in winter, when in most parts of India it is cool and pleasant and there is neither the heat nor the monsoons to contend with. But academic institutions in India start their academic terms in June–July, just when the academic year in Britain and America is coming to a close. This of course assumes that the research will be based in an academic institution.

The colleges in and around Bombay are affiliated to the University of Bombay, and a few to the SNDT University, a women's university. The affiliated colleges do not normally offer postgraduate courses; there are exceptions, though. Every member of the staff, from a humble laboratory technician to the head of department is normally called Professor; acquisition of a PhD changes one's status and one is thenceforth addressed as Doctor. Research degrees and postgraduate degrees are normally offered by the University departments, each of which is headed by a bona fide Professor.

A normal sized classroom in an affiliated college may consist of over 130 students, making it easy for researchers to find and work with large samples. Recruiting students for one's research project hardly ever poses a problem. After they have overcome their initial shyness, the students are quite keen to volunteer as subjects. Unlike students in Western countries, who often have to be cajoled into volunteering as research subjects (or in some instance are paid to participate), the students here are eager to co-operate with the research.

Since most of the teaching at the Universities in Bombay is done in English, it overcomes to a certain extent the problems of translations of test materials. In that sense, undertaking research in large metropolitan cities in India poses a slightly lesser problem than undertaking research in the rural areas, particularly in villages, where language is one of the biggest barriers to this form of paper-and-pencil research. But this is not to say that the tests constructed in Western countries can be used at will in other cultures. All psychological tests even within a single culture are beset with innumerable problems, which of course become more pronounced when used in other countries. One would need to ensure, therefore, that sound and suitable strategies have been designed to determine their usefulness across cultures.

Doing research in an Indian village

General issues

It is not often recognized by Westerners that over 72 per cent of the Indian population lives in villages wherein as Gandhi was known to have remarked '... lives the soul of India'. Given the present Indian population at about 1.1 billion, it is clear that over 720 million people live in villages in India, which is 12 times the population of Britain and about three times the population of the United States. Villages in India vary in size, population, economy, levels of education and literacy, soil, geography, climate, farming and other agricultural produce, religion, language, dialects, social customs, dietary practices, health, illness, under-nourishment, and last, but no means the least, levels of poverty.

The decision to select a particular village is often influenced by two major factors: academic and practical. At an academic level, the choice of a particular village may be left to the local collaborator. It is possible too that the village may have been the subject of an earlier study. Practical considerations would include factors such as living accommodation, supply of electricity, availability of safe water, food, transport, communication facilities, access to medical care centres and the distance from its nearest township or city. Needless to say, it would be prudent to take these known problems into serious consideration. But unknown problems cannot be accounted for in advance. The village chosen for the study could be stricken by drought, plagued by an epidemic, devastated by floods and other natural disasters.

Often, because of these insurmountable problems, cross-cultural psychologists tend to restrict their stay to the barest minimum period. They also choose to investigate those problems that are methodologically simple, require little or no instrumentation, and can be completed speedily. It is hardly surprising that cross-cultural psychologists from Western countries have often concentrated, more so in the past than at present, on what might be termed 'sterile' problems, such as the differences in perception of shapes, sizes, depth, figures, visual illusions, between two neighbouring villages and/or tribes in India, Africa, and elsewhere. Several critics of cross-cultural research (Bock, 1980; Segall, 1979) have expressed the opinion that cross-cultural research projects have often been designed *not* because of their theoretical relevance or useful practical applications but because they have been methodologically simple and easy to investigate.

Psychologists from the developing countries have construed this type of research as a disguised form of racism. In fairness to Western psychologists, it must be acknowledged that the indigenous psychologists have often aided and abetted this form of research because, as Durganand Sinha (1993) points out, there was until recently among many Indian psychologists, an inability to dislodge the yoke of their colonial past. Happily, the situation has changed and Indian psychologists have started to investigate those psychological problems which are (a) unique to an Indian setting, and (b) have a positive applied end in view, which would lead to positive socio-economic changes and development in the country. They also began to question the usefulness of Western models within their own cultural context.

Problems of languages

The problems of language are far more important than is often assumed by Western cross-cultural psychologists. It needs to be realized that in order to understand an alien culture it is important to distinguish between its simple and superficial aspects and the deeper colloquial ones. The culture that one elects to study needs to be examined as a whole rather than picking up unconnected bits and pieces because of their methodological convenience. Western psychologists in general have ignored this advice and have sought to study cross-cultural problems from a Eurocentric perspective, rather than vice-versa (Halbfass, 1981/1988). Given the multiplicity of languages and dialects spoken and the varying levels of literacy in India, the use of written tests is unlikely to be of any significant advantage. And even if the tests were to be translated, the conceptual and empirical equivalence, including their relevance to an Indian setting, would be questionable. Under certain conditions it may be possible to use non-verbal tests, but they too can be problematic. Again, timed tests in any form do not have much relevance in Indian villages. As has already been mentioned, time in India does not have the same connotations as it does in the West. In a village one's life is confined for the most part to a clearly defined physical area, most of which lies within walking and cycling distance. One's vision of the world seldom extends beyond the boundaries of the village. One lives in the abode of one's ancestors; one's children and grandchildren will continue to live long after one has died. Indians tend to see time in cosmic dimensions; it has no beginning, no end. In keeping the philosophy of the law of karma, one's present life is seen as one of many lives that one has lived in the past, and the present life will be followed by further lives to come. The cycle of birth and rebirth is strongly ingrained in the Indian psyche.

Finding appropriate samples for research

There are several practical problems which research workers would need to contend with, such as:

1 The difficulties in getting subjects of different castes (and religious groups) to join in a combined research project. It would have to be an extremely liberal Brahmin who would consent to sit next to an untouchable to engage in, for instance, joint perceptual, cognitive tasks designed by the investigator.
2 Persuading female subjects to participate in the research study.
3 Never having participated in a research study before (in many cases, never having spoken to or even seen a Westerner), the villagers might feel intimidated, harbour unvoiced resentments, demand payments for their participation in the research, and so on.

Ethical issues

A Western investigator working in an Indian village is in a very powerful position vis-à-vis the research sample. To a peasant, a tenanted farmer, the researchers represent power, authority, and affluence. It is in this area that they would need to exercise the highest degree of rectitude, lest they misuse their power for their own ends. A question that is obviously difficult to answer but should remain at the forefront of the investigator's mind is: whose interests are being served by the research? Is there any likelihood of any short-term or long-term benefits for the people of the village? The investigator would also need to ensure that under no circumstances the findings of the study are likely to have any deleterious effects on the villagers.

Professor Pandit's engrossing chapter did not end there. He had gone on to discuss a variety of other issues, including the nature and the iniquities of the caste system, inter-caste relations, government-aided schemes set up in several villages related to the promotion of social and economic welfare, the eradication of untouchability, contraception and population control, social welfare, and so on. He did, however, open our eyes to a variety of human and fascinating problems that were as though waiting to be investigated. But since those problems do not have a direct bearing on the problem of methodology, there is little point in dipping further into the Professor's chapter.

Our own research project went according to plan. The Principals of those colleges where our research project was to be undertaken were co-operative; rooms had been allocated, the volunteers had been lined up, and barring several unavoidable delays, Student and I were able to collect a vast amount of data during the three months of our stay in Bombay.

Prior to returning to London we spent a day with Drs Joshi and Khan at their Yoga Institute at the hill station to the South of Bombay and were deeply impressed by the experimental work that was in progress. It was refreshing to see indigenous problems, such as meditation techniques, levels of concentration, *samadhi,* and a variety of yogic exercises, being investigated with the use of Western scientific instruments and the data accumulated analysed by sophisticated statistical packages.

The East and the West appeared to have inched closer to one another.

Author's note

The curious reader might wonder why I chose to write this particular chapter a) in the first person singular and b) as a fantasy chapter. However, writing academic books in the first person singular is not entirely strange or unusual. Bertrand Russell's *History of Western Philosophy* (1946/1961), among several other great and profound works in philosophy, psychology, and psychoanalysis, has been written in the first person singular. There is no enshrined rule that an academic book *has* to be written in the third person singular. To write in the first person singular is just a break from a well-established convention. Thus, the first point related to writing in the first person singular does not require any justification.

But more to the point, it is important to understand why I chose to write it as a fantasy chapter. I did this for a variety of reasons. A fantasy chapter has certain advantages: it removes the constraint of having to use carefully formulated words and sentences, which constantly need justifying and even cross-referencing. Released of such a constraint, one can take a few chances and write with the kind of verve and vigour which makes the reading of the text more interesting, even exciting. Second, in a fantasy chapter one can describe and discuss ideas and issues in a language that allows one to use dialogues, emotions, feelings, similes and metaphors. My idea was to bring to the reader's consciousness the flavour of what it is like to come a foreign country that one has never visited before: I wanted to convey the atmosphere of being in a developing country, which would allow the reader to identify with the 'characters' and see the world as they see it. I hope, in this respect, I have succeeded.

There is a third important reason too. Several Western (British, European, American, Canadian, Australian) cross-cultural psychologists who come to the developing countries in order to undertake cross-cultural research do not always expose themselves to the country in which they undertake their studies. Prior to taking the trip they enter into negotiations with local academics and it is through their expertise that the research is actually undertaken. Unlike the anthropologists, who regard it as their moral and professional duty to live in the country they visit, the cross-cultural psychologists do not feel obliged to stay in the country, learn the language and the customs and become participant observers.

As reiterated by Professor Pandit earlier, I too can quote several instances of Western psychologists who have come to India, have stayed there for a period ranging from a week to a month, completed their 'largely paper and pencil research' with the help of the local academics and returned to their own countries. Their interest, as one can see, is not in the country, hardly in the people they have come to study, but in testing their own, largely Western theoretical assumptions, and publishing their findings in their journals. The local collaborators with whom they work in tandem are quite pleased, even flattered, to be asked, for it then allows them to publish jointly with their foreign academics, and at some later stage enable them to obtain research and travel grants to undertake research in Western countries. Working with an academic from the West has distinct pecuniary and career advantages. Whether such an approach leads to a genuine understanding of cultures and promotes a feeling of universal brotherhood is a debatable point. My own feelings on this matter are those of intense pessimism.

However, it is my hope and unsung prayer that the Western cross-cultural psychologists reading this critique of Western approaches to research in Eastern cultures will, at some stage, reflect on this extremely important issue, examine their psyche, perhaps even look into the depths of their soul, and attempt to understand and learn to perceive cultures as they are perceived by the people living there.

7

Family Structures and Child-Rearing Practices

Children are children are children, the world over. They are all born helpless and defenceless. They all need care, comfort, food, and shelter for their biological survival. Their biological survival also runs parallel with their cognitive, linguistic and emotional development, which is indispensable in order for them to become part of the society and the culture into which they are born. Without human care and guidance, it would be impossible for children to acquire any human characteristics. Several remarkable opportunistic case studies have shown that in the case of abandoned infants who were brought up in the 'wild' by wolves, when brought back into human society, failed to acquire any of the positive human emotions such as smiling or laughing, and none of the physical attributes such as being able to walk on their feet, being able to use implements and tools with their hands, nor indeed the most rudimentary linguistic skills. Further studies, such as those of Bowlby, Wayne and Dennis, Ainsworth, Sluckin, and others, in keeping with an ethological perspective, have also demonstrated the deleterious effects of deprivation of children, brought up in orphanages and in homes where their care has been minimal or virtually non-existent. In recent years, similar findings have been reported on studies of refugee children from Romania, Bosnia, Serbia, and other eastern European countries (Young, 1999, personal communication).

It is obvious therefore that the biological, social, linguistic, emotional, and cultural development of children is totally dependent upon their being nurtured and cared for by humans in a human society. That is the only way by which one becomes 'humanized'. It is possible though, that in so far as the acquisition of language is concerned, as Chomsky's research has endeavoured to demonstrate, that it may be based on a 'universal' genetic programming code inherited by humans the world over. However, this does not explain the inability of the abandoned children mentioned above to acquire even the simplest of linguistic codes. In defence it has been argued that the abandoned children may have been very severely mentally retarded to start with, thus making it impossible for them to have acquired the most basic linguistic skills. It need hardly be emphasized that the most powerful influences on the growth and development of a child are those of the child's family members or, in their absence, the child's carers.

Defining a family

The very notion of what constitutes a family has become a subject of intense debate (Altman & Ginat, 1996; Bumpass, Raley, & Sweet, 1995; Low, 2005; Luker, 1996). In the not too distant past – just over half a century ago – a family unit in Western and in Eastern cultures consisted of the father, the mother, their two to three children, and even the grandparents. The father was generally seen as the patriarch and the proverbial 'bread-winner'. He had no major role to play in the day-to-day bringing up of children, which was left largely in the hands of the women at home. Day-to-day life revolved around the family and their community members and the Church. But in the last four to five decades the situation has changed, so much so that the concept of what constitutes a family in the West has become difficult to define with any degree of accuracy (Trost, 1996). Several factors have contributed to the confusion:

- in Western societies, formalized marriage appears to have lost its status (Dumon, 1992);
- cohabitation without marriage has increased;
- the rate of divorces has been rising in most European countries, including Britain (Edgar, 1992);

- it is estimated that in England at least one-third of all families are single-parent families, headed by a female;
- and over 25 per cent of the population lives alone;
- an increase in lesbian/gay, transsexual, and transgender relationships; and
- other extraneous factors such as changes in demographic trends, economic recessions, wars, famines, migrations, technological innovation, urbanization, and widening opportunities for women also account for the changes that have taken place.

An interesting contradiction presents itself when one considers the findings of the survey of different human societies undertaken by Murdock (1967, 1981). Murdock's research reveals a variety of family types. His *Ethnographic Atlas* (1967) and *Atlas of World Cultures* (1981) shows that more than 90 per cent of societies listed in the world are polygamous. In addition to these there are mother-and-child families; monogamous families that live with the husband's parents, with the wife's parents, with other relatives, or in a new location; polygamous families in which men marry sisters, marry non-sisters, capture women from other groups, in which co-wives live in the same household, or live apart; and polyandrous families in which brothers marry one woman. It needs to be stressed that human beings show the greatest degree of within-species diversity. Such diversity is unknown in any other species (Low, 2005: 16). Would any such arrangements constitute a family?

Sex, gender, and family

Right throughout the world and right throughout history, from ancient times to the present, people have been fascinated and even obsessed with human sexuality in its diverse manifestations. Sex changes, genital mutilations, castration, circumcision, cross-dressing, unconventional sexual preferences, sodomy, sex with animals, birds, children, and inanimate objects, multiple sexual acts, sado-masochistic sexual acts – there is hardly a form of sexual behaviour that has not been fantasized and enacted. Since our concern is with understanding the notion of family and not with sexuality and sexual preferences in general, let us tease out those areas that have a bearing on the notion of family.

Lesbian/gay, transsexual and transgender families

In addition to those who prefer to engage in lesbian and gay relationships, there are those who wish to be what they are not and attempt to change their sex. There are others who display unconventional sexual preferences and engage in cross-dressing. In many Eastern cultures there are groups of people who voluntarily or are coerced into getting castrated and live with groups of other castrated persons.

In recent years, the impact of the gay civil rights movement has brought about a proliferation of lesbian-gay families. Patterson and Freil (2000) estimate a range of between 800,000 and 7 million lesbian/gay parents bringing up between 1.6 and 14 million children in the United States. In France, for instance, 40 per cent of all first births in 1990 occurred outside of marriage (Leridon & Toulemon, 1995). Silverstein and Aurbach (2005) point out that in Scandinavia it is not uncommon to see wedding dresses made with bodies that allow a mother to breastfeed her infant during her wedding ceremony.

Scientific and technological advancements in the area of transgender and transsexual changes have also led to increasing demands; they have become quite popular in certain parts of America, particularly in California, where a variety of clinics specializing in this type of work have been set up. Several counselling and therapeutic services are also on offer to persons seeking guidance. Our concern, however, is not with the proliferation of such services, nor are we concerned with the moral, the familial, the legal, the social, and the hitherto unpredictable long-term social consequences which such changes are likely to bring about. Our main concern is to clarify how such changes affect our understanding of the notion of what constitutes a family. When one takes into account transsexual families, where fathers become male-to-female, and mothers become female-to-male, the problem of accurately defining a family becomes even more problematic.

Let us try to understand what it must feel like for a six-year-old child to live with his or her parents, both of whom have undergone transgender changes recently. What effect is such a dramatic change likely to have on the psyche and on the future development of the child?

Box 7.1

To understand the problem of transgender, I would like to engage you in a creative role-playing exercise. Imagine that you are the six-year-old child. You live with your mother and your father. In your own childish way you find that your parents blow 'hot and cold', which you cannot understand but find intensely distressing. Excessive care and love often give way to indifference, anger, and neglect. Although you love your parents deeply, you cannot figure out their changes in moods and behaviours.

To add to your distress you notice changes in your parents, which you are unable to understand and therefore unable to explain to yourself. Your mother, you notice, has had her hair cut short, and now combs it with a side parting. Gone is her make-up. Her dresses have given way to shirts and trousers. She has even taken to wearing men's suits. Her ample breasts have as though shrunk and have virtually disappeared. She has developed facial hair and has started to shave, like your father. Her voice too has become deeper and heavier.

(Continued)

And exactly the opposite changes have begun to appear in your father. His body, you notice, is getting rounder and softer, his hair has grown longer, his face is becoming smoother, he applyies facial creams and make-up, his voice softer, his shirts, trousers, and suits have been replaced by skirts and dresses. Unbeknown to you, both your parents have had a gender change: your mother is not your mother; she is now your father. And your father is not your father; he is now your mother. You have become one of the 'elite', children of a modern American transsexual family!

As a six-year-old child, how would you be expected to make sense of what has transpired and deal with these changes – at a personal and at a social level? How would you explain this rare and disturbing phenomenon to yourself, your classmates, the children next door, and the guests who occasionally drop in at home? You search in vain for satisfactory answers. You turn to your parents, but other than cuddling comforts and pretty presents, no explanations that would make sense to you are forthcoming. From time to time they take you to see and talk to a nice, friendly person. She sits with you for an hour or so, plays a few games with you with dolls and drawings, but you are still frightened, bewildered, and lost.

Try to visualize the kinds of problems you would encounter during the course of your own attempts at personal adjustment to the changes in the gender identities brought about by your parents.

Interpretation of Box 6.1

There are several issues of grave importance that need to be considered in this situation. For both the parents wishing to change their own gender identities is a classic affirmation of the philosophy of individualism at its highest peak where the interests of the individual (in this case, two individuals) override and take precedence over the needs and concerns of the child. Although the parents appear to have spared no effort in showering their child with love and affection and have even initiated counselling for their child, there remains a serious unanswered moral question. Are the parents ethically justified – *do they have the right* – to put the child through an experience which *may* turn out to be extremely traumatic, leading to extremely distressing short-term and long-term post-traumatic stress disorders? The fact that the child is taken to a counsellor or a therapist does not in itself guarantee successful 'treatment' – despite the syrupy claims of success that are made by several counsellors working in this field. It should be made clear that no attempt is being made to chastize the parents by wagging an accusing moral finger at them. What is being stressed is that the moral problems are serious; they ought not to be swept under a carpet of indifference.

I do not know what the right course of action would be in such a situation – if, there *is* a right course of action. Would one expect the parents to 'sacrifice' their own desires and private ambitions for the sake of their child? Would they consider having their child adopted? Would they live in the hope that their child over a period of time

(Continued)

would get over the problem and learn to see and accept them in their newly invented gender identities?

Before ending this vignette, let me turn the discussion on its head and engage you in a role-reversal. Instead of being the six-year-old child, imagine now you are one of the parents: what would you do in this situation? This form of inquiry is not meant to be a moral criticism. In defence of the parental decisions to undergo sex changes, one might contend that prior to the changes the family consisted of the father, the mother, and the child, and that after the changes the family still consists of the father, the mother, and the child. The fact that the father is now the mother and the mother is now the father should make no difference to one's conception of family; they still remain a family, albeit, a unique family. But it would be naïve to assume that no psychological changes are likely to occur as a result of such changes.

From a cross-cultural point of view an interesting question that comes to mind is this: are such transgender and transsexual families a unique phenomenon found only in modern Western societies? Or are similar families also to be found in Eastern cultures, such as India, Pakistan, Bangladesh, Malaysia, Thailand, Japan, and in the Middle East?

A close examination of the literature reveals that sex changes in Eastern cultures are equally, if not more popular than in Western countries. They have a long history, which dates back to the eighteenth century and even earlier. Let us discuss this briefly with reference to a specific group of people found in India, Pakistan, and Bangladesh, and several other Islamic countries in the Middle East. They are referred to as 'hijras'.

Hijras

The term 'hijra' is an interesting concept. It does not have an equivalent in Western lexicons. In Western countries, gender is generally defined in dichotomous terms: male or female, boy or girl. There is also a special term – hermaphrodite – which is used to explain an animal (or a person) displaying both male and female characteristics. But the term 'hermaphrodite' does not fully convey a similar meaning to the term 'hijra'.

Who is a hijra? A hijra is a person who belongs to a group that is often referred to as the 'third sex' or the third gender – a term with which Westerners are not particularly familiar. Hijras often describe themselves as neither men nor women. They are people born with a male body but with a non-male or female gender identity. Some undergo crude sex-change operations, including castrations (Jaffrey, 1996; Nanda, 1998). In India a sex-change operation is seen as a ritualistic ceremony because of its association with Hindu religion. In Pakistan there is a strong belief that hijras have the power to curse, referred to as 'bad-dua', and also to bless, referred to as 'dua'. Most hijras are homosexual transvestites. It is not just in India and Pakistan but in several other Eastern countries, including Bangladesh, Indonesia, and other Muslim states in the Middle East, that one finds large groups of *hijras*. The *hijras* of Pakistan look upon themselves with a sense of exclusivity; they tend to see themselves as the cultural descendents of the court eunuchs of the Mogul Empire.

Hijras in general do not lead a conventional family life. Most hijras leave home or are abandoned by their families and live in separate clans or communal households that are presided over by a leader or a guru (Freilich, Raybeek, & Suvishinsky, 1991). Hijras normally tend to dress in female clothes, acquire female names, and refer to themselves as females. Despite the lukewarm acceptance of hijras within society, they remain at the bottom of the social hierarchy. They are a marginalized group of wanderers, and from time to time they are subjected to harsh discriminatory attacks from others. They are also seen as objects of fun, ribaldry, and mockery. Most of them live in slums on the fringes of poverty and destitution, scraping a living by prostitution, begging, and by performing traditional ceremonies, which occur whenever a new baby is born in a community or when a marriage is about to take place.

I can recall very clearly a band of about 25 hijras, all dressed as females, wearing colourful saris, gold necklaces, bangles, and earrings who, having heard of my forthcoming marriage, forced their way into our family home in Bombay to dance with me and the other members of my family. Much to my embarrassment but to the intense glee and amusement of my friends and family members, the hijras, their bangles jingling, their eyes a-twinkle, their arms around me and those of the other male and female guests in the room, in songs, innuendoes, and gestures which were unmistakably lewd and erotic, wished me well and hoped that the marriage would lead to the creation of several children. It was only after I had paid them enough money for each to buy a sari with, that they hugged me, fondled me, and with gestures of undisguised obscenity, blessed me, offered their prayers, and left.

One might ask why I permitted the hijras to enter our house. To deny entry to a band of hijras into your home to celebrate an auspicious occasion is culturally unacceptable. One is expected to fall in with such historically established cultural practices. Besides, as stated above, there is a strong belief that hijras have malevolent and benevolent 'powers' to lay curses or shower blessings. Not to have yielded to their entrapment would also have deprived my family members and friends the expected conventional, ribald pleasures which they believed were their due when the hijras barged their way into the house.

It is only in recent years that hijras have begun to make demands for fair and just treatment. The recent election of a hijra as Mayor in Uttar Pradesh in India would seem that they are beginning to gain a collective political voice in the country. But it would be unwise to conclude that one political event, major though it may be, is likely to bring about a change of heart in the rest of the people in India. Prejudices clog intellectual 'arteries', and like clogged arteries are not easily dislodged – not without some form of drastic 'psychic-surgery'. The expected change in terms of tolerance and acceptance of hijras into the mainstream of society for the present, seems a utopian dream. Also, one would be stretching the point if one were to refer to the hijras as a family or a group of families.

It seems we are back to square one. We are still unable to offer a satisfactory definition of what constitutes a family. Given the variations in sexual preferences, sexual changes, gender redefinitions, lesbian and gay marriages, changing relationships, the concept of what constitutes a family becomes increasingly difficult to define with any degree of accuracy. Is there a way out?

Low (2005) suggests that two factors need to be taken into serious consideration in understanding the concept of family: *genetic relatedness and co-residence in a household*. Hamilton (1964) argues that from a biological and ecological point of view, relatedness is absolutely central for making and testing predictions about familial behaviour. In other words, what differentiates a family from other social groups, are the emotional, socio-cultural, and legal relationships between the various members: spouses, parents and children, siblings, and other relatives. Taking the above factors into consideration makes sense. Let us take the above two factors – *genetic relatedness and co-residence* – as our working definition of a family.

Variations in family structures

Experience tells us that families vary along several characteristics: size, affluence, levels of education, occupation, intelligence, attitudes, beliefs, values, and so on. Families undergo change, which is often brought about by ecological factors, industrialization, urbanization, economic depressions, war, famine, natural disasters, and so on (United Nations, 1996).

Each family is a microcosm of a wider section of our community, which in turn is a microcosm of the society within which each family lives. Society provides us with a structure which regulates our lives, our beliefs, and our practices, and as a result we are able to make sense of our own lives, of others, of our own culture, and of the world around us. We tend to see society in tangible terms because it consists of groups of people who also occupy a given territory and live together. Given the wide variations in families around the world, the question that arises is this. Even within a single culture people vary along a variety of characteristics – skin colour, language, dietary preferences, religious beliefs, attitudes, and practices, levels of education, affluence, and so on. The variation also extends into ecological, political, social, economic, physical, and other environmental domains. But despite the differences there is a sense of belongingness, a feeling of 'oneness' with people of one's own culture. This occurs when one understands that all the diverse groups in one's society, to a large extent, are united by past historical associations and by sets of core values. Value systems have a significant bearing on a variety of factors, including child-rearing techniques, patterns of socialization, development of identities, emotional development, cognitive development, kinship networks, work-habits, the social and familial arrangements, and the religious beliefs and practices of people of that society.

Contemporary family structure in Western cultures

The changes in the size and the structure of families, combined with high levels of social and occupational mobility, may have 'destabilized' society, creating a sense of loss of community life, particularly in the urban metropolitan cities (United Nations, 1996). From a psychological point of view major changes have occurred in collective values, particularly those that support individualism, where the needs of an individual take priority over the needs of the family and the group (Laungani, 2005a). Although the family is recognized as the basic unit – the microcosm of society – the changes in society have altered the roles and functions of both men and women in families. It is clear that the 'traditional' role of the family as a self-sustaining, self-contained unified unit has changed almost beyond recognition. What impact a nuclear or a one-parent family (or a family of 'changing' parents due to living with different partners or remarriage) combined with increasing occupational, physical, and social mobility has on the future growth and development of the child is an open question. In the absence of any clear, longitudinal evidence, it would be pointless to express a firm opinion on this issue. It needs to be said, however, that in such a changing family situation the child is more than likely to be denied a sense of continuity and familiarity, not just in terms of being brought up by the same parents, but also in terms of friends and acquaintances.

In addition to the above changes, significant changes have also occurred in the size and the type of families in Britain and other Western countries. For instance, there is a different picture of family structures in England and Wales. There are a rapidly growing number of people living alone or as lone parents; one-third of adults remain single, and one-person households now represent 30 per cent of all households. Lone parents account for about 12 per cent of all households, and nine out of ten parents are women. What impact a one-parent family (or a family of 'changing' parents due to living with different partners, or remarriage, or sex-changes) is likely to have on the health, education work, and the development of the children can be gleaned from several research reports (United Nations, 1992, 1996). It is estimated that of the children from single-parent families in America:

- 66 per cent will fall into poverty before they reach the age of 18, compared with 20 per cent of children from two-parent families;
- 50 per cent are more likely to have learning difficulties;
- 20 per cent are more likely than children from two-parent homes to suffer from emotional and behavioural problems;
- over 80 per cent of adolescents admitted to hospital for psychiatric reasons come from single-parent families;
- almost twice as many high achievers come from two-parent homes as from one-parent homes;
- the most reliable predictor of crime and teenage pregnancy is not income or race, but family structure; and
- 70 per cent of imprisoned United States minors have spent at least part of their life without fathers.

It has also been argued that families in Western countries, particularly in the United States, have been unable to develop positive ways of adjusting to these rapid changes, and 'the speed of change alone is a major factor of stress in families' (United Nations, 1996: 10).

Family structure in India and other developing countries

Indian (Hindu) society, not unlike other Eastern societies, is a family-based and community-centred society (Basham, 1966; Flood, 1996; Kakar, 1981, 1979/1992; Klostermaier, 1998; Koller, 1982; Lannoy, 1975; Laungani, 1997b, 1998; Lipner, 1994; Mandelbaum, 1972; Sharma, 2001; Zaehner, 1966a, 1966b). In non-Western cultures, particularly in India, Pakistan, Bangladesh, and several other countries in South East Asia, including Malaysia and Indonesia, the size of the average family tends to be much larger. In China, although the present population is in the region of 1.27 billion, concerted attempts are being made by the Government to restrict and control family size to one child per family. But whether such an embargo on family size will lead to the expected diminution in the size of families in China is a long-term policy issue. The projection figures tend to show that in 2010 the population will rise to 1.357 billion, and in 2020 it is expected to reach 1.433 billion (*Encyclopaedia Britannica*, 2003).

Non-Western cultures even today follow an extended family network, which often includes the child's parents, grandparents, uncles, aunts, sister-in-laws, nieces, nephews, and other siblings in the household. In many affluent Indian homes, there would also be a retinue of faithful and long-serving servants (or 'faithful retainers', to use a Victorian phrase) involved in the care and the upbringing of children (Laungani, 2001d; United Nations, 1996). Thus a child learns right from an early age to be tended to by a variety of persons of different ages in the household. The child learns too the nature of his or her individualized relationships with different members in the family.

From my personal experience, I may point out that even at a rough count there were over 20 members in our household, not counting the retinue of servants who, as far as I can remember, have always been around. And far from a decline in numbers, the number of members staying at home rises regularly as a result of more children being born into the family. One of the obvious consequences of such a cultural arrangement is that it creates a sense of continuity *and* permanence in the mind of the growing child. Even after 30 years of living in the West, a return to India to the decaying ancestral family home creates a sense of sameness, which I find far more reassuring than the changes wrought by time in the country. The same faces, many of them wizened, lined, bent, and even arthritic, create a sense of permanence, illusory and duplicitous though it might be. The past and the present – thesis and antithesis – merge together, creating an interesting synthesis. On each of my visits to India, the individualistic lines of 'I' and 'thou' which are kept separate in the West, get blurred and much to my surprise I find that the 'I' and 'thou' merge into a 'we-ness'.

Given the large number of members in the family, children of course become the beneficiaries of multiple caregivers. The child living in an Indian home is likely to be subjected to a variety of influences (both contradictory and complementary) in the process of socialization. In other words, a growing child is also likely to acquire a variety of role models in the course of socialization.

The sense of sameness and permanence is also perpetuated by the fact that divorces in India are rare. They are not unheard of, but the rates are extremely low, particularly among Hindus, who comprise 82 per cent to 84 per cent of the total Indian population. Nowhere, not even in large urbanized metropolitan cities, do they reach the kind of epidemic proportions which they do in the West.

Marriage in India (particularly among Hindus, Catholics, Sikhs, and Parsis) is seen as a sacred religious ceremony and the couple is expected to remain together till 'death do them part'. That is the socially accepted view. The 'sacredness' of a Hindu marriage is often seen as the standard against which marriages in Western countries are judged – *and are found wanting*. Reality, however, does not in many cases reflect such high-sounding moral claims. A strong and pernicious social stigma is associated with divorce – particularly for the female, who in most cases is economically and socially dependent upon the husband and his family members and their network of relations *(baradari)*. She is not even in a position to countenance the idea of a divorce, let alone take any steps towards achieving it. The serious consequences, for example, loss of status, the possible loss of custody of her children, homelessness, threat of poverty, the danger of being referred to as a 'loose' woman (and thus 'easy game'), conspire to exert the required pressures to keep the marriage institution intact. So strong and powerful are the social pressures that most women, even under the most appalling domestic conditions (maltreatment, violence, abuse, lack of independence, subjugation at home, overwork, lack of political and legal awareness and recognition of their 'rights', and so on) elect to stay within the confines of a tyrannous family as silent sufferers rather than break away.

Features of extended families in India

Westerners in general tend to construe extended families in India largely in 'structural' terms. It has been argued that the extended family network in India, particularly in the large metropolitan cities, is gradually breaking down and is beginning to undergo a change, even giving way to a Western-style nuclear family structure.

It is doubtless true that several families in the larger cities of India have adopted a nuclear family network; one can in many instances see a replica of the 2.4 family-member structure, to which we referred earlier. But these exceptions notwithstanding, it needs to be stressed that Indian family life operates predominantly on an extended family network.

The misconception is based on how the term 'extended' family is defined. In the West an extended family is generally understood in 'structural' terms, namely, all members of the family, living together, sharing jointly the kitchen, the income, and other resources. The patriarch in most instances is seen as the head of the family, and the other members within the family are expected to defer to the wishes, the authority, and even the dictates of the head of the family. In some instances, his authority remains absolute. This type of a family is best referred to as a *joint family*.

But an extended family, although sharing most of the above characteristics, may not always live under the same roof and share all the resources. Thus, not all extended families are joint families. While the system of joint families still prevails in many parts of India, particularly in the rural areas, monumental changes have taken place in large cities. A desperate attempt to escape from the evils of debt, poverty, starvation, disease, lack of medical care, caste-related exploitation, and so on, has led to massive migrations from the rural to urban sectors in India. This, of course, has resulted in large cities being choked for space, fresh air, and accommodation. Only a few of the migrant families manage to find a roof over their heads. And the slums in which they live are often so small and cramped as to make it impossible for the entire family (of, say, eight persons) to live in them. The rest of the migrants survive by the roadside, next to a bus stop, on the pavements, in the lee of a boundary wall of a building, under a tarpaulin sheet tied to overhanging branches of a tree, or in illegally constructed mean hovels, which are often razed to the ground by the police, the local municipal authorities, and by the lashing rains during the monsoons. What these families subsist on can only be left to conjecture. How they manage to survive under these indescribable conditions is in itself a miracle. It is estimated that over 40 per cent of the urban dwellers in large metropolitan cities live by the roadside. These factors have led to a physical separation of families. But such a state of affairs has by no means led to an erosion of the extended family system.

In addition to its 'structural' features, the extended family needs to be understood in its psychological and functional terms as well. For a start, the patterns of relationships tend largely to be intra-familial. Family life is organized along age-and-gender-related hierarchical lines, with male elders being accorded a privileged position and a position of power. Each member, right from childhood, learns to understand and accept his or her own position within the family hierarchy. Who can take 'liberties' with whom, who can shout at whom, who will defer to whom, who will seek comfort and solace from whom, who can 'confide' in whom, are subtle emotional patterns of expressions which one learns in an extended family network.

Since relationships play a central role in extended families, it is worth pointing out that in India, each relationship has a specific name attached to it. For instance, the word brother-in-law and sister-in-law can mean any one of three relationships in English. Without further information, the Westerner would not know which of the following three persons were being referred to as under:

English term	Indian (Hindi) term
My wife's brother	*Salaa*
My sister's husband	*Bhanoi*
My wife's sister's husband	*Saandu-bhai (or Jeejaji)*

Each of these relationships in most Indian languages is identified by a specific name. The above examples refer to fairly easy-to-understand relationships. Complex relationships, such as *my mother's brother's daughter-in-law's son* is easily identifiable because of a specific name attached to it. Such, as one can see, is not the case in the English language. It is clear from this that specific words have been invented because of their functional importance within the cultural system. It does not take long for children to learn not only the exact nature of such complex relationships, but also the range and types of feelings and emotions which they may or may not be allowed to express within their large extended family network. These are common lessons that children of both sexes learn at home.

Gender differences in socialization of children in India

There are significant differences in socialization processes between boys and girls. Male children enjoy a more privileged position than their female siblings. The elders in the family allow a male child to 'get away' with behaviours, which they would find hard to condone in a female child (Kakar, 1981). The privilege also extends to food, clothing, toys, and play. In an impoverished home or a home of less than adequate means, a larger share of food is given to the male children; they may also be fed first by the family members. The needs of the female child seldom or never take precedence.

In accordance with ancient Hindu scriptures, the birth of a male child in a family is considered to be a blessing, for a variety of reasons (Laungani, 1997b). First, it ensures the perpetuation of the family name. Second, the son is seen as an economic asset and upon marriage would 'bring in' a handsome dowry. Third, he would also be expected to support and look after his parents when they become old and frail. Fourth, it is the son who, on the death of his parents, is expected to perform all the funeral rites and also light the funeral pyre, to ensure the safe passage and the eventual repose of their soul.

The birth of a daughter, on the other hand, is treated with mixed feelings and even with some misgivings. As Kakar (1981) points out, the daughter in a Hindu family hardly ever develops an identity of her own. Upon birth, she is seen as a daughter; she is expected to remain chaste and pure; upon reaching marriageable age she may be seen as an economic liability because of the dowry she is expected to take with her to her husband's home. On entering her married home, her status changes. She is seen as a wife, as a daughter-in-law, as a sister-in-law in the new home, and then as a mother, a grandmother, and should her husband predecease her, as a widow. Like a snake casting off its skin, the daughter upon marriage is shorn of her own name. She acquires a new persona and is given a new name by which she is addressed in future. While the snake's discarding of its old skin and acquiring a new skin is a natural event, which has certain biological and evolutionary gains, the Hindu bride, upon entering her new home – her own feelings notwithstanding – is expected to bury her past, which includes her identity, and start her life with a new identity which is *ascribed* to her by her husband and her in-laws. Such a staggering metamorphosis serves no biological or evolutionary advantages. On the contrary, it reinforces the defenceless if not 'subjugated' role which she is expected to play after marriage. Thus, her maiden name Geeta may be turned to Seeta, and Mohini to Rohini, Rajini to Sajni, Reena to Beena, and so on. She appears to have no individual identity other than the changing identities she acquires through reflected role relationships. Her private persona remains submerged within these changing and conflicting identities. Right from birth to death she does not possess an identity of her own. However, it is important to stress that several enlightened parents look upon the birth of a girl as 'a gift of the gods' and see it as their sacred duty, which is part of Hindu *dharma,* to have their daughter(s) handsomely and 'happily' married.

Despite the seemingly pitiful nature of the daughter-in-law's position in her husband's family home, there are compensatory psychological and power-related dramas that are played out in extended families in India. Imagine a scenario: three brothers with their respective wives living in an extended and joint family network. The oldest daughter-in-law (the oldest daughter-in-law is referred to as *jethani),* by virtue of being married to the oldest son, is often in an extremely dominant position to exercise power – delegating cooking, cleaning, washing, and such other household tasks to the two younger sisters-in-laws (the younger sister-in-law is referred to as *derani)* – even the care of her own children may be relegated to her younger sisters-in-laws. The power exercised can in certain instance be extremely tyrannical. The second sister-in-law can exercise a certain amount of power over the youngest sister-in-law, and so on, moving down along age-related hierarchical lines. However, the power structure can change dramatically in a variety of subtle ways, which often remain unnoticed to an outsider. For instance, the eldest sister-in-law may be childless, or may not have produced a male child; the younger sisters-in-laws may have produced sons; they may also have come from affluent homes, and may also be highly educated, or their respective husbands may have a far superior earning capacity to their oldest brother, and so on and so forth. The balance of power is by no means fixed; it is flexible, subtle, and changes from time to time. However, all the three sisters-in-law are expected to defer to the unquestionable power of their mother-in-law, who often 'rules' the house.

Upon the death of the mother-in-law, the balance of power shifts quite dramatically. Covert (and sometimes not-so-covert) battles may be fought by the three daughters-in-laws, with each jockeying for a position at the top. At times, the husbands too may be brought into the 'fray', leading to severe turmoil within the family, until the dust settles and the family situation reaches a new equilibrium.

Such subtle psychological dynamics are difficult, if not impossible, to investigate objectively; even the idea of using any of the qualitative methods of social research – handing out a questionnaire, for instance – is too ludicrous to demand serious consideration. One would need to be part of the ongoing family drama to arrive at some understanding of the problems and the intrigues involved and the manner in which they are handled.

Several writers (Flood, 1996; Kakar, 1981; Klostermaier, 1998; Koller, 1982; Lannoy, 1975; Laungani, 1997a, 1998; Mandelbaum, 1972; Roland, 1988) on this subject have pointed out that despite a large number of persons involved in the socialization of children, the part played by the mother in the bringing up of children is of paramount importance, particularly in her relationship with her son; a special relationship develops between the two. Whether this relationship can be construed in Oedipal terms is arguable, although several writers, including Kakar, Lannoy, and Roland, and others operating from within a Freudian framework, have asserted that that is often the case. The male child is indulged, pampered, protected, and as far as possible is denied very little. While the mother may attempt to strike a balance between the male and female child's demands, it often transpires that the male child's impulsive wishes, wants, and desires often take precedence over the needs of the female child. The father, on the other hand, remains detached from the day-to-day cares related to the upbringing of the child, male or female. His role, at least during the first few years, tends to be minimal.

It is generally after the 'sacred thread' ceremony of the male child that the father may start to take a keen interest in the son's education, socialization, and the acquisition of those qualities and behaviour patterns which will turn him into a model Hindu as prescribed in the ancient Vedic scriptures.

While boys are pampered and accorded privileges, girls are often brought up on a relatively strict regime. A girl is made aware of the role she is expected to play both at home, during adolescence, and more importantly after her marriage. Verily is virtue and virginity venerated. To convey the concept of virtue the children are taught lessons from ancient Hindu texts, including the two Indian epics, *The Ramayana and The Mahabharata*, and *The Upanishads*. Glorious stories of the virtuous and religious acts performed by Hindu women are held up as the ideal to which the female child is expected to aspire. Virtue consists of obedience (initially to parents and then to the husband and to the husband's family), doing one's duty, truthfulness, prayer, and ensuring the health and security of the husband and family. She is also trained in the necessary culinary and other domestic skills so that when she is married no criticisms befall her and she is looked upon as an ideal wife, a dutiful daughter-in-law, a compliant sister-in-law, and when she has children of her own, a loving and caring mother and indulgent grandmother.

In an extended family network, there are no clear demarcating boundaries between 'I and thou'. Boundaries merge. Thus, living together in a confined physical area, combined with the fact that most of the day-to-day activities are done jointly and are shared, the need for psychological and physical space and privacy, which is of such paramount importance to Westerners, does not have the same value among Indians. It might be true to say that people walk in and out of each other's rooms – even lives – without qualm, without any fears or intrusion. One might even go to the extent of arguing that one acquires a *collective* identity, which reflects all the norms and values shared by the family, their caste and sub-caste members.

Let me illustrate this with a personal example. On each of my trips to India, one of the things I found annoying and even quite irritating was the fact the people walked into my room, without knocking. There was little I could do to change ancient family customs; I accepted them as a long-suffering martyr.

However, I thought I might have some success with our servants, particularly our cook who has been with us for over 40 years. One morning, as he barged into my room with a cup of tea, I suggested to him as gently as I could that he should knock, wait for my response, before entering my room. He seemed genuinely bewildered by my request. He scratched his head, thought for a minute or two and replied, 'But, Sahib, I *know* you are in your room. What is the purpose of knocking?' I was chastened by his innocent good humour and never repeated my request for privacy – an idea that made no sense to him whatsoever. The notion of privacy, the desire to seek it, the fear of intruding on another person's privacy, does not in general have the same functional value as it does with people in most Western countries (Laungani, 1999b, 2000b).

The sacred and the secular

In Western countries there is a clear distinction between the sacred and the secular, but in Hinduism there are no sharp distinctions between them. The lines are blurred. This can be observed even in the most mundane day-to-day activities, such as washing one's hands, having a bath, carrying out one's morning ablutions, accepting drinking water or food from others, or offering it to others, and so on. Although seemingly trivial, they have deep-rooted religious connotations. To a Westerner unversed in the day-to-day ritualistic practices of Hindus, such behaviours would seem strange and even quite bizarre. To a Hindu, however, they fall within the orbit of necessary religious ablutions, which he or she has internalized from childhood and performs automatically. So much of day-to-day Hindu behaviour is influenced by religious beliefs that it is virtually impossible to identify behaviours which might be seen as secular (Pandey, 1948/1969).

Rituals therefore are forms of personal communication with gods. Communication itself may serve different purposes: worship, giving thanks, asking for favours, expiation and atonement. Smart (1996) adds that a variant of the religious ritual is the yogic ritual, where the performance of yogic exercises is seen as a means by which a person seeks to attain a higher state of consciousness.

The efficacy of rituals is believed to rest on their repetition; their meticulous performance provides a source of comfort to those practising them. Failure to perform the rituals leads to a form of spiritual pollution. Flood (1996) points out that it is ritual action which anchors people in a sense of deeper identity and belonging. Although there are varying numbers of rituals recorded in different texts, the rituals appear to be organized in a sequence which expresses the Hindu social order, or *dharma*. The most important rituals are those related to birth, the initiation ceremony, marriage, which signals the beginning of the householder's life, and the final funeral rites and *after-death* rites.

Furthermore, what binds families in India is the fact that virtually all the major social and religious festivals and activities, such as christenings, betrothals, marriages, pilgrimages, are performed together. Most of their social relationships tend to be family-orientated. Visiting cousins, uncles, aunts, staying with them, are an integral part of family life. Even an illness striking a family member tends to get transformed into a family problem (Kakar, 1981; Laungani, 2000b, 2001d; Mandelbaum, 1972; Pandey, 1948/1969), and attempts are made to find a joint solution to the problem.

For instance, in the case of a severe health-related problem affecting one of the family members, the entire family once again 'takes over'. Illness is like a magnet which draws families together. Each member volunteers his or her own diagnosis of the illness, its causal factors, and the cures and remedies which he or she would urge the patient to follow regardless of their appropriateness. The entire family may resort to several conflicting strategies in dealing with the patient's illness. Special prayers are held for the speedy recovery of the patient, acts of piety and generosity, such as feeding the poor and the needy, are performed. The women-folk in the household undertake fasts and prayers, and the family members get together to discuss and assess the patient's condition on a daily basis. The patient is seldom left alone. Neighbours and other relatives are informed of the situation, word spreads, and visitors flock in at all hours to spend time with the patient. The fact that the patient might need to be left alone to rest, regain strength, and recover is not seen as an important consideration. Such overwhelming concern for the patient's health to a large extent needs to be seen within the context of social and cultural expectations and not necessarily in terms of 'overflowing' love and affection for the patient. Not to visit a sick relative – close or distant – is likely to earn social disapprobation.

Interestingly enough, there is a paradox when it comes to a person in the family suffering from a psychological or psychiatric disorder. Attempts are made to conceal the disorder from relatives, friends, and the outside world because of the fear of social stigma befalling upon the entire family (Laungani, 2004a). From a cultural point of view it is worth noting that the fear of social stigma related to mental disorders often leads to a conspiracy of secrecy. Many parents have been known to keep the severely disturbed member of the family 'in hiding', concealed from the outside world, confined to a room. Discovery of such a problem would lead to social censure, which may also have an adverse effect on the marital prospects of the girls in the family.

The onset of a physical illness is often attributed to the workings of the law of karma – whether the patient recovers from, or succumbs to, the illness. It was fated. It was written. It was kismet. It was destined. It was karma. But psychological disorders are often explained in terms of 'bad blood' – the family concerned having inherited 'bad blood' from its ancestors.

The contemporary scene

In the past it might have been possible to describe Indian family life in terms of (a) traditional families, (b) transitional families, and (c) Westernized families. The defining characteristics of traditional families would have been their being rooted to ancient Indian traditions, and their ignorance of or indifference to the changes imposed by modernity. Transitional families are those that are in the process of change and adaptation to modernism. Westernized families are best referred to as those that have acquired Western education, tend to see themselves as being modernized, Westernized, and have imbibed many of the Western values systems, including liberalism, individualism, and so on.

In recent years, due largely to the rapid industrialization and globalization in the country, there have been massive, large-scale migrations of younger people from the rural areas into the urban sectors of India. And as indicated earlier, squatter settlements, shantytowns, and slums have grown and sprawled everywhere and have extended even beyond the recognized urban limits. It has been estimated that about 40 per cent of the urban population lives in slums, or squatter settlements, or on streets, in wretched poverty. Their living arrangements are devoid of the basic amenities such as safe water, electricity, sewerage, and health care. Furthermore, the departure of the young migrants from the rural to the urban areas has created an age-related imbalance in the rural areas of India, with a high percentage of the elderly living in the rural areas, which of course makes it even more difficult for them to survive without the help of their children.

The age-related imbalance between the rural and the urban areas, the economic imbalance in the urban areas between those who live below the poverty line on the streets and in the slums, and those who live in houses, with relative economic and financial security, militates against describing an Indian family in terms of urban and rural differences. The elderly who live in villages feel alienated from their children who have migrated to the urban sectors; in turn, the young migrants live in abject poverty, possess limited levels of literacy, have low and inadequate occupational skills, and hardly any preparation for urban life (United Nations, 1996).

From a philosophical and cultural point of view, all Indian families are the 'inheritors' of the ancient Indian traditions, which are enshrined in the Vedas, the Puranas, the Upanishads, the great Indian epics, including *The Ramayana* and *The Mahabharata*, and of course *The Gita*, which forms an integral part of *The Mahabharata*. The ancient Indian traditions also consist of myths, legends, metaphors, proverbs, and folklore, which over the centuries have become part of the Indian psyche. Plays depicting scenes from *The Ramayana* and other ancients texts are played out all over the country during festive seasons.

Whether one sees crude, hastily put together village performances of *The Ram-Leela* or the Dasera festivals or the ones professionally enacted in the National Centre for Performing Arts in Mumbai, the 'theme' of the plays and the emerging moral messages of the performances remain unchanged. Stories from *The Ramayana, The Mahabharata,* tales from *The Jatakas,* stories of bravery, valour, self-discipline, obedience, performance of austerities, prayer, bravery, revenge, and forgiveness form the basis of socialization of children.

Again, it is difficult fully to understand family life in India without taking into serious consideration the role that religion plays in their daily life. Most Hindu homes have a shrine (which may consist of a framed picture of a Hindu god, or a clearly demarcated sacred place of worship) at which prayers are offered day and night. Whether the entire family joins in the prayers – particularly the *arti* – or is left to the women in the house is related to the importance given by the family members to such daily rituals. Children are generally encouraged to participate in such daily offerings and prayers. On all the days that are considered holy it is expected that all the family members will participate in prayers and offerings. The elders in the family – the grandparents, an aged aunt – often develop a special relationship with the growing children. Since the elders are often seen as the repositories of knowledge, virtue, and wisdom, they often take it upon themselves to read from the scriptures to the children in order to 'inculcate' the desired values of obedience, reverence, honesty, and self-discipline in the young children at home.

In addition to the gods worshipped at home and in the daily or weekly visits to temples, Indians also visit their own gurus – or as a cynic has remarked, their 'designer' gurus. They do so at regular intervals, seeking their blessings in whatever, social, spiritual, economic, commercial, marital, and health-related endeavours they are engaged. It is not at all unusual to see several specially chartered plane loads of Indians from abroad, coming over to India to participate in a religious 'jamboree' arranged by the gurus(s) they all worship. To be looked upon as a guru, who has magical, if not divine powers, is to be accorded the highest accolade. (Many of my own extended family members who live abroad undertake regular organized chartered trips every year, spending weeks on end in an ashram in India.) Asking 'favours' of gods and gurus is a custom hallowed by tradition. It operates on a 'barter' system. One tries to do a deal with God. 'God, if You grant me this favour, I'll do this for You!', which could mean undertaking a long, extensive, and expensive pilgrimage to the holy cities in India, the feeding of hundreds of mendicants, special prayers being performed by a team of Brahmin priests either at home or on the banks of the Ganges, and other acts of piety, all of which form part of the 'barter' system. And given the multiplicity of gods and gurus in India, changing or swapping gods and gurus should the favours go unanswered is also a custom hallowed by tradition. Since heresy is a meaningless concept in Hinduism, it is not at all sacrilegious to swap one set of gods for another.

In recent years, the worship of gurus has become a thriving commercial enterprise (for the gurus, of course). The commercialization (or even more appropriately, the industrialization) of the guru cult and its spread in the West – *à la* Rajneesh and Mahesh Maharishi Yogi (the giggling guru of The Beatles' fame) – will not have gone unnoticed by many a Western reader. Many gurus appear to enjoy a higher status and following than is usually devoted to film stars and other celebrity icons. To Indians, God is not merely a metaphysical abstraction – which to a large extent tends to be the case in the West – on which profound discourses can be held, tomes written, books published. There is within the Indian psyche a staunch, unshakeable belief, impervious to any critical reasoning, in the reality and the benevolent powers of God. The desire to follow gurus, to sit at their feet, and have a *darshan* (the sighting of the guru is seen as a beatific experience) is the desire that drives the rich and the poor alike to wherever their guru holds a religious meeting.

It is now clear that, notwithstanding the urban–rural differences, differences in levels of education and affluence, differences in caste and class, differences in occupations, language, diet, and so on, there are a core set of values that Indians, regardless of which part of India they live in or come from, share in common, and that have a direct bearing on family life in India.

Contemporary influences on family life in India

Colossal changes have taken place in India over the last two decades, as a result of industrialization, massive foreign aid and foreign investments, globalization, and a revolution in information technology. When one sees emails being sent through mobile telephones from impoverished villages, one is apt to believe that the old order has changed and is yielding place to new. But in the next breath one notices that water is still being drawn from a well. One notices that the villagers still plough their fields with their own hands, using antiquated implements, where safe water is an undreamt of luxury, and villagers carry their *lota* (metal pot) into the fields to wash themselves after their early morning ablutions. And only a few miles away, on the outskirts of a small town, one can see workmen using pick-axes to dig up ridges to lay fibre-optic cables for advanced telecommunication systems. When such contradictions assault one's senses, one has to concede that the new order by no means has replaced the old. The old and the new, the ancient and the contemporary, the backward and the advanced, the superstitious and the rational, the religious and the secular, live higgledy-piggledy, in an uneasy relationship. Trying to classify families into traditional families, transitional families, and Westernized families seems a meaningless exercise – an old romantic dream that has no basis in reality.

But cultures are living, breathing organisms, pulsating with life. Like all living organisms, they grow, evolve, change, progress, and a few, like the ancient dinosaurs and mammoths, decay, die, and become extinct. And centuries later their remains are unearthed and displayed as archaeological artefacts in museums around the world. Why some cultures develop, progress, thrive, and assert their will, values, and power over the rest of the world cultures is due to several reasons, not the least of which are those related to economic, political, industrial, technological, literary, artistic, and other considerations. Although a discussion of these factors is well beyond the scope of this chapter, there is one issue – globalization – which needs to be examined because of its dramatic and unpredictable impact on the under-developed and the developing countries around the world. Let us briefly concern ourselves with this issue, but bearing in mind that our main concern is with family life in India.

Globalization

One needs only to consider the impact of industrialization on Western society in the nineteenth century to realize how it radically transformed the very structure of Western society. The post-industrialization period in the West led to dramatic changes in religious beliefs, family structures, family size, work ethic, morals, economics, education, literature, health, politics, human rights, medical and scientific research, and several other areas of human concern.

Changes have also begun to emerge in the developing countries, including India. As to what the long-term impact of these changes will be, what benefits they might confer, or what 'threats' they might forebode, one cannot predict with any degree of accuracy. Whether developing countries will also 'go the Western way' or will adopt their own cultural and indigenous means of coping and adjusting to these changes also remains an unanswered question. Nonetheless, by using broad-based economic, social, and political markers it might become possible to articulate and pre-empt the likely future changes in the country as a whole. Let us first consider some of the probable socio-economic and political changes that might affect India in the near future, and then, in the final section, turn to family life in India.

Several experts in the West (Appadurai, 1990; Parekh, 2000; Stiglitz, 2002) are of the opinion that through the vast financial, communicational, and technological investments offered by the World Bank, the International Monetary Fund (IMF), the World Trade Organization (WTO), and several multi-national organizations, universal globalization will usher in a new era of economic prosperity and affluence in the developing countries. It has also been argued that globalization will lead to a process of Westernization and modernization, and all the developing countries will eventually come to imbibe Western values of *individualism, rationalism, humanism, empiricism,* and *secularism*, and will become indistinguishable from other Western countries. Since the West will set the 'gold standard', all developing countries will aspire to achieve such a standard, thus completing the process of homogenization. The East shall no longer be East, and the West, West, as Rudyard Kipling remarked several years ago; in fact, the twain will meet and become culturally unified and homogenized. The idea underlying homogenization, as Parekh points out, is based on the belief that 'there is only one correct, true or normal way to understand and structure the relevant areas of life' (2000: 1). That *of course* – as the 'experts' never tire of reminding us – is the Western way.

Let us briefly consider the two propositions, that:

- globalization will lead to economic prosperity in developing countries; and
- globalization will eventually lead to a homogenization of cultures.

With regard to the first proposition, Joseph Stiglitz, the Nobel Prize-winning Economist, in his book *Globalization and Its Discontents* (2002), has argued that there is little doubt that foreign aid, which is a major thrust in the process of globalization, has brought benefits to millions of people in the developing countries. But he warns us that in the long-run globalization will have a devastating effect on developing countries, including India.

Let us take just one example. According to the World Bank (2000), there is firm evidence to report that in 1990, about 2.718 billion people were living on less than US$2 a day. In 1998 – nine years on – the number of poor people living on less than $2 a day has increased to 2.801 billion. The intervening nine years have created 100 million more people (which is over one and a half times the population of Great Britain) living below the poverty line. If there is economic prosperity in the developing countries, it is clear that the poor, for a variety of reasons, are certainly being kept out of sharing in its prosperity. To discuss the reasons why the poor are getting poorer would involve us in a detailed economic, administrative, and socio-political analysis of the underlying problems. Such an analysis is beyond the scope of this chapter.

Suffice it to say though that, according to Stiglitz (2002), a large part of the 'blame' rests with the Western bureaucrats involved in negotiations of financial aid, technological 'know-how' and other forms of assistance to developing countries. He argues that mismanagement, highhandedness and insolence of Western bureaucrats, create more problems than they are meant to solve. And this, combined with their lack of adequate understanding of the local, regional, and national problems, customs, and cultures, has a devastating effect on developing countries. Stiglitz is of the opinion that economic prosperity in developing countries, if not exactly a myth, is a failing enterprise. Economic colonialism, in the form of aid, keeps reinventing itself. It is hardly surprising that sociologists scathingly refer to these problems as a form of 'coca-colonization'. These are strong words. But they have been expressed by a person who is not only a Nobel Laureate, but has been actively involved in decision making at the highest inter-governmental, inter-agency levels, including The World Bank and the International Monetary Fund (IMF). One would therefore be loath to dismiss his views, regardless of their negative sentiments.

On the other hand, there are others who believe that globalization during the last decade has conferred colossal economic, technological, informational, social, and political benefits to the developing nations, including India. According to Das (2002), economic prosperity has brought about an upward shift in levels of poverty, general affluence, a change in values, social customs, and a newfound confidence in people all over the country. It is difficult to decide which of the two polarized views will come to prevail in future.

Let us turn briefly to the second proposition, namely that globalization will eventually lead to a homogenization of cultures, in the sense that all cultures will gradually follow and adopt Western attitudes and values and over time will become indistinguishable from Western cultures. The corollary to this argument is the belief that economic development may actually be harmful for a nation because it may result in the erosion of one's cultural traditions and heritage (Das, 1995; Marglin & Marglin, 1993; Sen, 2000).

The proponents of homogenization have pointed out that it is better to be rich and happy than to be poor and traditional. In their simplistic approach they have either ignored or have not taken into account that the last 30 years have seen the emergence, if not recognition and acceptance of cultural diversity, or multiculturalism, in virtually every sphere of life. In Britain, for instance, multi-culturalism is seen as a major issue, and various government initiatives have been put into action to achieve this end, in several sectors of society (Parekh, 2000). Even in the United States, the struggle by the blacks followed a cultural route; the black leaders were vociferous in their claims for recognition and acceptance of their ethnic identity, whose origins they traced to Africa. 'Black is beautiful' was one of the most popular signature tunes of the blacks in America in the 1960s and 1970s, one might recall. From a psychological point of view it needs to be stressed that although all human beings share a variety of common biological, physical, and psychological characteristics and behaviours, they have uniquely different, diverse and idiosyncratic ways of responding to their environment and to their own world. Human beings, regardless of their cultural origins, have the ability to share certain common values and agree to common commitments. It does not therefore follow that such consensual agreements will necessarily lead to a corrosion of one's cultural identity and one's traditional values, leading to the acquisition of a 'universal' Western identity. Despite economic prosperity (or economic deprivation), people do not jettison their own cultural identity. Indians, like chameleons, have the distinct ability to adapt and incorporate the changes within their cultural identity without wrecking their ancient structure. Given the long history of foreign rule over India – the Turks, the Moguls, the Dutch, the Germans, the French, the Portuguese, and last but by no means the least, the

English – extending over a millennium, Indians have still managed to retain their unique caste system, their law of karma, their gods, their languages, their characteristic extended family networks, and to a large extent their ancient values. Even the concerted attempts, initially by the Muslim rulers and a few hundred years later by missionaries, to convert Hindus (particularly from the lowest caste) to Islam and Christianity respectively, did not meet with great success. (To put this in the context of numbers, the present Christian population in India is just over 6 per cent, whereas the Dalits (previously known as untouchables) constitute over 17 per cent of the total Indian population (*Encyclopaedia Britannica*, 2003). Buddhism too, despite its origins in India, has failed to make the same impact in India as it has done in Sri Lanka and China.

Herein lies an interesting paradox. On the one hand there is increasing recognition of multiculturalism in Western cultures, and on the other, a gaining belief in the very same Western countries in the eventual homogenization of cultures the world over. Despite the difficulties in reconciling these two polarized views, it would be unwise to underestimate or ignore the impact of globalization on developing countries in terms of the cultural identity, their pattern of life, and the structure of family life of people in developing countries, including India.

Let us now turn to final section of the chapter

The impact of globalization on family life in India

That certain Western values as a result of globalization will impinge upon the people of Asian cultures is inevitable. In so far as economic affluence is concerned, this is already evident by the significant changes that are noticeable in India. The affluent Indians in the urban sectors of India have begun to adopt Western ways of living, which include living in luxurious high-rise blocks, condominiums with swimming pools and tennis courts, furnishing their homes in modern Westernized styles, membership to exclusive Western-type clubs, Western culinary preferences, modes of dress, artistic and other aesthetic preferences, driving imported luxury cars, increasing use of communication and information technologies, and last but not the least, foreign travel. Conspicuous consumption of 'new' money appears to carry the same hallmark as it does in many Western countries.

The West, in that sense, is certainly making a major commercial and economic impact in developing countries. It is interesting to note that there are over 35 million homes with cable television – more than all of Latin America put together (Das, 2002). English is also fast becoming the language that is spoken in large metropolitan cities of India. However, the spoken English is a curious mixture of Indian languages, particularly, Hindi. The Indian English is referred to as Hinglish (Hindi and English). It has been predicted that by 2010 'India will become the largest English-speaking nation in the world, overtaking the United States' (Das, 2002: 19). Even the Bollywood film industry has turned 'native', in the Western sense of the word. In addition to Western types of sets, Western forms of dancing, English and Hindi dialogues, with a bewildering variety of Indianized English accents continue to assault puritan ears.

As far as the family life of Westernized affluent Indians living in large metropolitan cities is concerned, a change is beginning to become noticeable in young children from the age of six onwards. The major change, to a large extent, is noticeable at a consumer level: preference for fast foods offered by McDonald's and other multinational outlets, designer clothes and footwear, mobile phones, computers, digital televisions, camcorders, and such other consumer goods. To all outward appearances, there are hardly any differences between an Indian child and an American child.

But as soon as one starts to dig deeper and observe the day-to-day lives of families at home, the picture changes; the observable similarities, so easily noticeable from the outside, seem merely cosmetic – not unlike a new, conspicuous patchwork on an ancient family heirloom. The house, although furnished in modern Western style, is still dominated by a temple or a shrine. The family members, one finds, usually eat their meals together, the home-cooked food often conforms to the families' indigenous regional culinary habits, family life still tends to operate on a hierarchical order. Although children 'enjoy' a certain degree of latitude in expressing their views and opinions, and although the children are not any the less indulged than they were in the past, deference to the views of the elders to a large extent is taken for granted and remains unquestioned. Collective activities, in which all family members are expected to participate – visiting and entertaining relatives, performing prayers and 'pujas', participating in all the religious rituals (for example *mundan*, the tonsure ceremony), the sacred thread ceremony, betrothals, marriages, and festivities, are still an integral part of family life.

One of the most important factors which distinguishes Indian families from Western (English or American) families is the fact that children (sons), upon reaching maturity, are *not* expected to leave home and set up their own lives, so to speak. Any departure from this norm causes distress, but over the years, such a departure has come to be accepted with resigned equanimity. The married sons, however, may choose to live separately, but the general trend is to live close to one another – even in the same block of flats, should that be possible. In many such homes, cooking is centralized; meals play a central role in uniting the families.

Indian society, as we have already indicated, has displayed the ability and the tenacity to survive through centuries of foreign invasions and occupations. It is therefore questionable that globalization, in all its magnitude and economic power, will completely transform the ancient value systems of Indian society and lead to a process of 'cloning'. At a superficial level, it might seem as though the East is beginning to become indistinguishable from the West. But the cosmetic changes in India must not lull one into believing that the bell has already started to toll, proclaiming the demise of values in India.

In terms of physical distance, the West has crept closer to the East. But in terms of fundamental cultural values, it remains as distant as it ever was.

Perhaps, a little less so!

Intercultural Perception and Interaction

Seems, madam! Nay, it is; I know not 'seems'.

Hamlet, Act I, ii.

It is possible that a few of you may not have heard of Hermann Rorschach. He was a well-known Swiss psychiatrist (1884–1922) in the early twentieth century. He was a proponent of Freudian psychoanalysis, a theory which argued that a large variety of human problems often lay buried deeply within one's unconscious mind and, for a variety of reasons, were not easily brought to the surface of one's consciousness – certainly not without the help of a trained psychoanalyst. It was only through detailed, systematic, and painstaking analyses of a person's *unconscious* processes that one could 'unlock' the mysteries of the human psyche. But the process of psychoanalysis, as we all know – and Rorschach knew only too well – is long drawn-out; it may take several months, if not several years, to arrive at a clear and authentic understanding of the patients' (as they were referred to in the past) unconscious. To Rorschach this seemed a serious impediment, which he was convinced could be rectified.

Rorschach (1921) set to work. He constructed the 'Rorschach Ink-blot Test', whose judicious usage, he believed, would enable him to 'tap' into the patient's unconscious processes. The test he constructed is very simple, or seemingly so. It consists of ten official ink-blots. Five ink-blots are black ink on white. Two are black and red ink on white. Three are multicoloured. The ink-blots are sufficiently ambiguous and unstructured to enable respondents to interpret them in any way they choose. The test is also easy to administer. It is shown in a particular order and the patient is encouraged to offer the first response that comes to mind. The psychologist writes down everything the patient says or does, no matter how trivial it might sound. The responses are then analysed and interpreted symbolically in terms of the patient's conflicts, negative and positive feelings, and emotions towards the important persons in the patient's life, for example, mother, father, siblings, spouse, children, and such others. On the bases of the projections a trained observer, Rorschach believed, would be able to pinpoint deeper personality traits and impulses in the person taking the test.

Over the years the test's popularity increased. Clinical psychologists and other academics started to use it in the course of their own clinical and research work, designing objective ways of scoring and interpreting the responses given by the patients. Like many psychiatrists of his time, Rorschach was impressed by symbolic associations, and in a paper, *Clock and Time*, he proposed that the love of watches by some neurotics was related to a subconscious longing for the mother's breast with the ticking representing heart beats.

As is often the case with innovative ideas, the objectivity and validity of the Rorschach Ink-blot Test came to be seriously questioned, challenged, and in many instances found wanting. Critics pointed out that the test was flawed because the blots of ink were inherently meaningless and subjective. To evaluate the results of a test it would be necessary for the ink-blots to have some meaning, otherwise the images projected into the patterns are of little value in assessing personality traits. Initially, Rorschach's work was credited with great originality. But the idea underlying the test was not as original as it had appeared at first sight. The roots of these ideas lie elsewhere, buried in the writings of Shakespeare and Plato, as the following two examples demonstrate.

Hamlet's brief encounter with Polonius

Ham: Do you see yonder cloud that's almost in shape of a camel?
Pol: By the mass, and 'tis like a camel indeed,
Ham: Methinks it is like a weasel.
Pol: It is backed like a weasel.
Ham: Or like a whale.
Pol: Very like a whale.

Hamlet, Act III, Scene ii.

Put your mind back and recall the occasions when you, along with your family members and friends, may have spent many a warm and pleasant summer afternoon lying under the sun, looking at the changing shapes of the clouds floating across the blue skies. You interpret and reinterpret the shapes and configurations and even argue over whose interpretations are the correct ones. But you know in your mind and in your heart that there are interpretations and more interpretations – none of which could be identified as being the real, the 'correct' one.

The myth of the cave

A similar but more powerful theme emerges when we consider Plato's philosophical account of the prisoners in a cave. Plato puts into the account in symbolic form his view of the condition of human knowledge in relation to reality as a whole. Imagine, says Plato in his book *Republic (Book VII)*, a group of persons who are chained and sit in a dark cave with their backs to the sunlight. The world passes them by but all they can see are blurs and flickering shadows and reflections that pass by behind them. All they hear are muffled sounds and echoes. As a result they remain ignorant, mistaking appearance for reality, surface for depth, glister for gold. The world of their experience is only a shadow, a reflection of the real world. Plato goes on to say that had one of the prisoners managed to escape from the cave, he or she would still have encountered formidable difficulties in understanding the real world.

Extrapolating from Plato's story it would seem that all of us, not unlike the prisoners in Plato's cave, often tend to perceive ourselves, and the world around us, in an *unseeing, unmeaningful* way. We see and do not see, or are unable to see. We mistake appearance for reality – the 'seems–is' dilemma posed by Hamlet, quoted at the start of the chapter. The longer we remain chained and immobile, the less likely we are to acquire any deep and meaningful understanding of our selves, of our own psyche of others, and of the world around us. Any knowledge that we gain *en passant* is likely to be superficial, stereotypic, and even irrelevant. Misperception may then become our permanent *modus operandi,* leading to our striking out at imaginary windmills, such as the ones portrayed by Cervantes in his magnificent novel, *Don Quixote.*

This, in a broad sense, is what the ink-blot test was designed to achieve, namely, our personalized idiosyncratic responses to a set of ambiguous ink-blots, which are then reinterpreted by analysts in accordance with their theoretical orientations. We saw earlier that the responses of individuals to the Rorschach Ink-blot test were by no means uniform. Despite presenting an identical stimulus to a group of persons, responses vary significantly from person to person. The research studies in this area demonstrate that the responses of an individual can also be inconsistent. They may also change over time. The question is, why? Why one person should see a butterfly with its wings spread out, and another, two women stirring a brew in a cauldron, is difficult to explain. It is difficult too to determine which one of the multiple responses offered is the correct one. What does one mean by a correct response? Does the correct response reflect reality? Does reality in this instance mean objective, phenomenal reality, or the individual's subjective sense of reality? It is clear that in interpreting responses in terms of butterflies, or two women stirring a brew, each respondent has gone *beneath* the surface characteristics of the stimulus object, offering an interpretation from a subjectivist and a relativistic perspective. The psychologist or the psychoanalyst involved in interpreting the respondent's interpretations of the ink-blots takes it a step further. He or she then attempts to interpret the respondent's interpretations in unconscious psychodynamic terms, ranging from Oedipal complexes, oral and anal fixations, to narcissistic anxieties, and so forth.

Here too we encounter another difficulty. There is considerable evidence to show that two psychoanalysts of different theoretical persuasions and allegiances offer interpretations which are more in keeping with their own theoretical attachments. Again, how can we tell which of the psychodynamic interpretations is the valid one? As is well known, Freudian patients have Freudian dreams, and Jungian patients, Jungian dreams (Ellenberger, 1970). Similarly, one psychoanalyst may offer a Freudian interpretation, another a Jungian, and so on.

Having read thus far, you might feel that I am possibly making a mountain of a molehill. You might point out to me that it is not as though the person looking at the ink-blots is unable to see the ink-blots, for they are what they are, clear as daylight: ink-blots! You might even go further and say, black is black and white is white – anyone with any degree of common-sense would see that. You might question the interpretation, but surely you cannot question the truth of the ink-blots? Truth of this kind is self-evident.

So it would seem. But is it? Let us discuss it further.

Popper's views on perception

Let us turn to Karl Popper (1963), one of the greatest philosophers of science of the twentieth century, for an answer. Truth, according to Popper, is *not* self-evident. It is not manifest. He points out that at a philosophical level the doctrine that truth is manifest 'lies at the heart of teaching of both Descartes and Bacon' (p. 7). Descartes put forward a theory of *veracitas dei*, namely that what we clearly see to be true must indeed be true – if it were not true it would imply that God was deceiving us. Bacon, on the other hand, offered a doctrine of *veracitas naturae*. Nature is an open book. He who reads it with a pure mind cannot misread it.

To Popper both doctrines are flawed. He argues that any perception, from the simplest to the most complex, involves a hunch, a guess, a conjecture, even an unverified hypothesis. In other words, all our perceptions are embedded within a conceptual framework. In that sense, therefore, all perception is theory-laden or theory-saturated. Even the simplest of perceptions – for example, perceiving a black dot on a white surface, distinguishing a figure from its background – are not as simple as they appear at first sight. To perceive black against white, to distinguish figure against background, one needs to have acquired a conceptual schema of colour, some understanding of the concept of the superimposition of figure against background. It is this acquired knowledge that enables one to perceive correctly. The errors involved in the perception of physical objects, to a certain extent can be corrected. But interpretations, on the other hand, are often grounded in subjectivity and relativity. From this it is clear that our perceptions are seldom unbiased and hardly ever neutral, and may easily be influenced – consciously or unconsciously – by several other factors.

Before directing the spotlight on the nature of intercultural perception and intercultural communication, it would be useful to focus the spotlight on ourselves and find out how we perceive ourselves. An analysis of how we construe the internal and the external worlds that we inhabit will assist us greatly in understanding the manner in which we perceive others, but also why we perceive others as we do. To ignore the perceiver and concentrate only on the act of perception is unlikely to provide us with a comprehensive understanding of the issues at stake.

Perceiving oneself

Let us start by considering the nature of selfhood by asking ourselves what the *self* that we refer to consists of. In an attempt to understand the nature of selfhood, William James (1890/1983, 1910) distinguished between the 'I' and the 'Me'. To him, 'I' refers to the *self-as-the-subject* and 'Me' to the *self-as-an object*. He then divided the 'Me' into three hierachical constituents, which he referred to as *Spiritual me* at the top, the *Social Me* in the middle, and the *Material Me* at the bottom. The distinction between 'I' and 'Me' can also be explained in terms of 'I' being one's *internal self* and 'Me' one's *external self*. The internal self comprises one's ego. According to William James, the ego, which is the experiencing subject, remains unchanged; the inner world, which it inhabits, is the territory of the stream of consciousness. It is not visible to others; it 'resides' within oneself, part of one's psyche. (The reader must appreciate that what is referred to as 'psyche' is also an abstract construct.) No one other than *you* has direct access to your internal self. But it is possible that another person – a psychoanalyst, for instance – may be able to arrive at an understanding of your internal self.

The external self – the 'Me' – on the other hand, has multifarious manifestations, which include one's body, one's clothes, home, possessions, and the social and professional roles one plays. It creates in one the feelings of pride when one is loved, admired, and appreciated and feelings of shame, mortification, remorse, anger, and guilt when one is not. The external self is the image, the persona that we present to the outside world. James believed it was important to find ways of reconciling the unity of the 'I' with the multiplicity of the 'Me' (Paranjpe, 1998). This to James is the most puzzling problem which psychology has to contend with. How can such a unity be achieved? It is clear that the greater the distance between the 'I' and the 'Me' the greater the conflict within the individual. If one's own perception of oneself should be out of tune it is not inconceivable that one's perception of and interaction with others is also likely to be out of tune. The problems related to understanding the relationship between the 'I' and the 'Me' have been examined by several other psychologists, including Allport (1943, 1955, 1961), Cooley (1902/1968), Mead (1934), Freud (1955/1974) and Erikson (1968, 1982). The importance of finding a unity between the 'I–Me' dichotomy is beyond dispute. Sadly this area of research has not been given its due consideration by most psychologists. The reason for this neglect is not hard to find. Western psychologists, enamoured with the idea of their discipline being a science, have no place in it for abstract, metaphysical, and ontological concepts. To them it would mean putting the clock of progress in reverse. The fact that there may be more things in Heaven and Earth than are dreamt of in their philosophies cuts no ice with contemporary Western psychology.

Be that as it may, the question that concerns us is this: is it possible to create conditions which would bring about the desired reconciliation, even harmony, between the 'I–Me' dichotomy? I venture to say yes, it is possible. To achieve this I need to recount a personal experience, which provided me with the required insight.

A serendipitous 'discovery'

During the summer of 1989, I went to Bombay (now known as Mumbai) on a research assignment. I spent about a fortnight visiting families in Dharavi, which is perhaps the largest slum in India, if not in Asia. Every conceivable disease, hardship, tragedy, misery, misfortune, destitution, which only a febrile mind can conjure up could be found in the slum, which contained over a million people surviving within an area of 4.7 square kilometres. Within a few weeks of my returning home, I fell critically ill and was taken into hospital. Within a couple of days I was admitted into the intensive care unit, where my condition deteriorated dramatically. It took the doctors several weeks to arrive at a firm diagnosis: polymyositis, which I was told was a rare, life-threatening disease of unknown aetiology. It had something to do with the breakdown of protein in one's muscles.

I learnt too that it was an autoimmune disorder and could lead to serious complications. My condition in the intensive care unit deteriorated further, and within a few days I was paralysed. I also learnt to my horror that as the disease was of an autoimmune nature I could easily 'pick up' another 'nasty'. Since misfortunes come not in singles but in battalions, it was hardly surprising that within a few years of my illness I acquired a chronic and degenerative life-threatening illness: pulmonary fibrosis.

Trying to live with one illness is not easy, but having to cope with two is unimaginable. The prognosis, from the understated hints the doctors dropped, was also poor. I was referred to as a 'terminal' patient. At that point I felt my life was over. There was nothing for me to do but sink into a state of despair and hope for the end to be swift and merciful. I felt the noose had been tightened, the black hood had been dropped over my head, and soon – too soon, alas – the trap door would clang open, signalling the end. But as the days went by I assumed in my febrile state that the hangman, for reasons best known to him, had disappeared, giving me temporary reprieve. I brooded over my rapidly deteriorating condition. It did not take me long to realize that the kind of life I had lived prior to my illness was now over. I could no more thump a cricket ball than run a mile. Every activity which a person in normal, robust health takes for granted seemed a Herculean task to me, including walking, climbing stairs, having a bath, squeezing toothpaste out of a tube, getting into my clothes, swallowing food, and such other simple physical activities. The research studies that I had planned to undertake, the books I had been meaning to read (and a few hopefully to write one day), the countries that my wife and I had planned to visit, all seemed unattainable wistful dreams. I soon saw myself in the role of a sad, useless, unkempt invalid, shuffling about in a faded dressing gown, an albatross round my wife's neck. My own perception of myself was totally distorted. I kept wondering how I would live out the rest of my life. The weekly doses of chemotherapy merely confirmed my own miserable state. I realized to my grief and sorrow that I would never become what I wanted to be; instead I would become what I *didn't* want to be – a sad embittered man of no consequence. Prior to my illness I had, luckily, managed to achieve a happy compatibility between the 'I–Me' dichotomy. But with the illness, it all fell apart. There were serious ruptures both within the 'I' and the 'Me' – a bitter animosity had arisen between them.

But as the months went by I began to re-evaluate my condition. In their own understated way the doctors had made it clear that I would never walk again. But my wife had greater faith in my ability to drag myself out of the pool of self-pity in which I wallowed. She persuaded me to relearn to walk. That was the first step. With the help of physiotherapists I relearnt to walk unaided. And since nothing succeeds like success, in less than a year I resumed full-time work at the university. It was within the working environment of the university that I began to realize that it was I, and I alone, who could become the architect of my own fate, the master of my own destiny.

Gradually I worked out a strategy, which brought the 'I' and the 'Me' together. It took a while, months really, but I did it. Even now, the 'I' and the 'Me' do not always work in perfect harmony, but to a large measure peace between the inner core and the outer husk of my self has been restored. My present condition is even more critical than it was 17 years ago, and I am acutely aware that I am living on borrowed time.

When I was fit enough to resume work, I was eager to try out my own strategy on others. I ran a few training courses on stress management, intercultural perception, and communication. Relying on my own experiences, I devised an exercise which I felt would assist a few persons in nurturing reconciliation between the 'I–Me' dichotomies. I should like to make it clear that the technique that I have devised is not as original as I in my delusional fantasies of grandeur might wish to believe. It is a relatively straightforward technique interwoven with cognitive-behavioural, Freudian, and deconstructionist approaches, which combine to create what I refer to as a 'moral dialectical approach'. I have called the exercise *Mirror, Mirror on the Wall*.

The astute reader will have noted the similarity between my choice of the phrase, *Mirror, Mirror, on the Wall,* and Cooley's famous metaphor of *'the looking glass'* (1902/1968). Cooley argued that we often tend to see our reflections in the eyes of others, our parents, our friends, with whom we establish relationships; we are happy and elated when we feel that we have created a warm and positive image and saddened or humiliated when it is the opposite. Cooley believed that our own understanding of ourselves – our character, to use a popular word – is our perceived reflections of ourselves in the eyes of others. Subsequently, Leon Festinger (1954) developed and elaborated Cooley's formulations in his well-known theory of social comparison processes. *My concern is not only how we perceive our reflections in others, but within ourselves,* which is in keeping with the Socratic dictum, *'know thy self'.*

Box 8.1: Mirror, mirror on the wall

Please assume you are one of the participants. This is the scenario. You, on your own, are persuaded to stand before a full-length mirror in a well-lit room. You are encouraged to describe your physical self in detail, starting from the top of your head right down to your heels. As you point to and describe each feature of your face, your body, including your clothes, you are asked to comment on each aspect of your body in some depth and at the end give an impression of your physical and social self in holistic terms. A series of pre-prepared 'leading' questions is put to you at this stage, a few of which are:

(Continued)

- Do you like your body, your build, your face, your teeth, your smile, your hair, and so on?
- Which do you think is your best feature? Why?
- Do people in general find you attractive?
- Do people like you and seek you out?
- Do people trust you?
- Do you trust people?
- Is there anything about your body or about yourself that you find dissatisfying and wish you could change?

A significant amount of time is then spent discussing your assessment of your own body, and other physical and social characteristics, which include your voice, your speech pattern, the clothes you wear, the manner in which you carry yourself, and how you feel you come across to others, and how you feel others see you. Right at the outset, one of the ground rules that we each agree to abide by is our freedom to question, agree, or disagree with each other's evaluations, thereby creating an opportunity to adopt a dialectical approach, which hopefully will lead to a synthesis.

After the 'Me' part of the exercise has been dealt with we turn to the 'I' part of the exercise. You are told that you have been speaking what the mirror has been reflecting. It is now your turn to look inward, focusing on your internal self – a part, which is not visible to others. You and only you are aware of your internal self, your ego and all that resides within your psyche. Those that know you well might guess, but they can never be certain of their guesses being right. You are then persuaded to look inward, reflect on the internal side of your psyche, and respond to a series of pre-prepared questions. The questions that are put to you cover a wide range of themes – ethics, morality, integrity, duty, joy, happiness, goodness, sorrow, pain, suffering, death, and your own existential evaluation of yourself and of other people.

As you can imagine, a great deal of ground is covered. Your responses are then scrutinized very carefully, and the two sets of responses, the 'I' and the 'Me', are compared for conflicts and contradictions, and so on. You and I then hold further discussions to find ways by which the conflicts and the contradictions – the antithesis – can be ironed out, creating genuine synthesis between the 'I' and the 'Me'. A perfect example of such a synthesis is given below:

> *I think it better, my good friend, that my lyre should be discordant and out of tune, and any chorus I might train, and that the majority of mankind should disagree with and oppose me, rather than I, who am but one man, should be out of tune with and contradict myself.*

> Socrates, in Plato's *Gorgias*

At this point I would like to follow in the footsteps of Karl Popper (1963), 'stick' my neck out, as he would no doubt suggest, and offer four bold but risky conjectures or hypotheses:

1   Self-perception of a person with a disjointed 'I' and 'Me' will tend to be biased and irrational.
2   A person's perception of others will also tend to be biased, irrational, and prejudiced.
3   The self-perception of a person with a harmonious 'I' and 'Me' will tend to be objective and rational.
4   A person's perception of others will also tend to be objective and rational.

It is possible to design a research programme to test these conjectures. Since they have not been subjected to a rigorous examination so far, their corroboration or refutation remains unknown. To test the hypotheses, one would have to abide by certain assumptions:

• One's selfhood consists of the external 'Me' and the internal 'I'.
• There is a dialectic between the self and the other – the 'I' and the 'Me'.
• The dialectic in many instances leads to a harmonious synthesis between the 'I' and the 'Me'.
• In many instances, the two selves 'I–Me' do not always work in tandem or in harmony.
• The lack of harmony creates conflict within the individual.
• At a personal level it also distorts one's view of oneself.
• The greater the conflict, the greater the distortion.
• At a general level too it distorts one's view of others and of the world.
• Unresolved distortions are likely to lead to stress, illness, depression, and self-directed aggression.
• They may also lead to other-directed hostility, prejudices, and aggression.

Intercultural perception and interaction

Perception, as we have already seen, is not as straightforward a phenomenon as it seems at first sight. It is influenced by a variety of factors: physical, physiological, neuro-physiological, linguistic, cultural, and psychological, which include our internal mental states, levels of motivation, mental set, past experience, learning, anticipated reinforcement contingencies, personality, and our beliefs, attitudes, and values.

Our cultural upbringing too plays a crucial role in the manner in which we perceive ourselves, others, and even reality. This has been demonstrated by a variety of cross-cultural studies, which cover a wide range of areas: moral reasoning across cultures (Gielen & Markoulis, 2001), language and communication (Beatty, 2001; Lambert, 1972; Osgood, Suci, & Tannenbaum, 1957), culture and emotion (Ekman, 1972, 1973, 1985, 1994; Ekman & Friesen, 1975; Ekman & Heider, 1988; Matsumoto, 1989), culture and stress (Laungani, 1997b, 2001d, 2005a,

2005b, 2005d), mental illness across cultures (Draguns, 2001; Laungani, 1992c, 1999c; Zaman, 1992), death and bereavement across cultures (Laungani, 1999c, 2000a, 2001d; Parkes, Laungani, & Young, 1997; Morgan & Laungani, 2002, 2003, 2004, 2005, in press), child development (Adler & Gielen, 2001), cross-cultural encounters (Brislin, 1981, 2001), family life around the world (Roopnarine & Gielen, 2005), and so on. Several other studies have concentrated on cultural variations in social cognitive processes, emotionality, inter-group relationships, morality, and the process of attribution (Berry, Poortinga, & Pandey, 1996; Gudykunst & Bond, 1997; Markus & Kitayama, 1991; Matsumoto, 1996a; Mishra, 1997; Semin, 1995; Shweder, 1991b; Shweder & Sullivan, 1993; Sinha, Mishra, & Berry, 1996; Triandis, 1994).

Most of the studies demonstrate that we all see the world and ourselves in it through our own cultural prisms, which we acquire and internalize through the process of socialization. This of course does not include certain kinds of experiences such as natural disasters, earthquakes, tornados, volcanic eruptions, flooding, and so forth, which would be universally perceived as being traumatic. However, the manner in which we attempt to explain natural disasters and deal with them tends often to be culture-specific, and explanations may range from 'natural causes' to divine retribution, the workings of the karma, the will of Allah, and so on.

Common sense too confirms the observation that the perception of an event varies from one individual to another, from one group to another, from one time to another, and from one culture to another. One's perception of oneself and of others tends to be kaleidoscopic: a slight tilt and the pattern changes. But unlike the kaleidoscope, where each tilt brings forth a new symmetrical pattern, the patterns one sees in real life are not always symmetrical and by no means harmonious. And even our own evaluation of an event changes over time, stressful or traumatic on one occasion, exciting on another. A person unused to public speaking may find the experience extremely traumatic, but with practice and encouragement, the same experience on another occasion might seem quite exhilarating. Moreover, one individual's trauma might be another individual's thrill. For those living in the Sahara desert, the perception of stressors, for instance, is likely to be significantly different from those living in the rain forests of the Amazon.

To interact meaningfully with others, be they persons from our own cultural background or from different cultures, one needs to acquire a body of objective knowledge about that culture. Equally importantly, one also needs to possess the sensitivity to 'see' the world from the perspective of the other person. Sadly one is not born with such ability. Nor is it acquired overnight. The reverse is often the case. Not surprisingly, it is far easier to misunderstand than to understand. This is because:

- like the prisoners in Plato's cave, one is chained to one's culture and as a result it becomes easier and safer to see the world from one's own cultural perspective;

- one is often unwilling to admit that one does not know, or that one does not understand. Denial of ignorance merely compounds ignorance; and
- ignorance then becomes a breeding ground for stereotypes.

It is important to note that serious misunderstandings can and do occur not just in cross-cultural interactions and encounters but also within one's own culture, among one's own people. Moreover, they can occur even in casual encounters. Let us run through two such encounters, one in London and the other in Bombay (now Mumbai).

Box 8.2: Encounter in London

Past experience tells you that from the moment you leave home until the time you return home you are likely to run into several people: your neighbour, with whom you may exchange a pleasant greeting (or turn away from, pointedly), the person from whom you buy your Underground, or bus ticket, or your petrol, the newspaper vendor who sells you your newspaper, the little café or 'deli' from where you buy your sandwiches and salads, the publican who sells you a thirst-quenching pint, the shop assistant who sells you whatever you may have come to buy, and perhaps the people at the gym where you do your evening work-outs. It is with your work colleagues and associates, however, that your interactions are likely to be more involved. The newspaper vendor expects to be paid for the paper, so does the railway booking clerk and the others. These casual interactions do not include the thousands of other people you walk past on busy streets, railway stations, shopping arcades, and such other crowded arenas, every day. All these interactions – other than the ones with your work colleagues – tend to be brief and are negotiated with minimum effort. Language is the key factor that facilitates such interactions, for the persons you interact with speak the same language, differing accents notwithstanding.

Box 8.3: Encounter in Bombay

Let us replay the same scenario in Bombay, a city you have not been to before (in theory it need not be Bombay, it could be Delhi, Calcutta, Lahore, Karachi, Dacca, Kuala Lumpur, Bangkok, Manila, or any other large city in South East Asia). Let us assume that a large multi-national organization for which you work has sent you on a three-to-six-month assignment. Like most thoughtful, rational, educated persons, you have prepared yourself for this trip. You have read a few recommended books on India, spoken with some of your friends who have been there, even seen a few Indian films, and you feel that you have acquired some knowledge of the people, the culture, and the country which will be your home for the next few months.

(Continued)

You are met by the company chauffeur at the airport and are driven to a flat, which has been arranged for you by the company. You are a bit peeved at not being received by any one of the company executives. (What of course you are not aware of – and there is no reason why you should be – is that the day of your arrival happens to coincide with an important religious holiday in India. It is unlikely that any of the executives would abandon their familial, social, and religious obligations to come to meet you at the airport.) The flat, you notice, is reasonably well furnished; it also offers the services of a resident cook-cum-major-domo, who greets you upon your arrival.

The following day, after your first taste of a spicy Indian breakfast, you leave your flat and stroll down the road – as you would no doubt have done in London. What meets your eye is virtually incomprehensible. All your assumed expectations come to naught. Discordant sounds assail your ears, old dilapidated yellow-and-black taxis rattle past you, red buses, replicas of the London double-deckers, belching poisonous fumes trundle past you, people – and even more people – brush past you, the heat overpowers you, beggars sitting by the roadside accost you, money changers noticing your unmistakable white skin sidle up to you – you feel trapped in a vortex of chaos. Anxious to seek directions, you approach a stranger. To your dismay you learn that the person you have chosen to speak to does not understand a word of English. You have no idea which of the 40-odd languages (not counting the several hundred dialects spoken in India) is spoken by the stranger. You are not aware that in a large metropolitan city like Bombay you are likely to hear a mixture of several languages: Hindi, Urdu, Marathi, Gujarati, Kutchi, Sindhi, Punjabi, Bengali, Konkani, Malyalam, Kannada, Telugu, Bhojpuri, Portuguese, and of course English and Hinglish (a unique combination of Hindi and English). It takes a while to make yourself understood, and eventually you manage to find a taxi that takes you on a long bumpy ride to where you have to go. India, you realize, does not offer you the monolingual security of England. Nor do all the other countries in the world where English is not spoken.

Interpretations of Box 8.2 and 8.3

In the first encounter, you were on your home territory, aware of the rules of communication, experienced in dealing with such necessary but trivial daily situations. Interactions flowed smoothly. In the second encounter, you were in a foreign country, unaware of the rules, customs and norms – and more importantly the language(s) spoken by the people that guide interactions. Besides, you had to compete and ride over the distracting and seemingly distressing stimuli to which you were subjected. All these factors conspired to make your initial interactions frustrating and even quite painful.

An inability to speak or understand any of the local languages increases one's sense of isolation and vulnerability. You suddenly realize that it is not going to be easy to live there for a period of six months, unless of course you decide to 'opt out' of the culture

(Continued)

and live like many other foreigners – join a club, where you swim, play golf, and meet and associate with people who share your visions and values – as members of the British Raj did a century ago. But despite the affinity, you might still feel homesick and share the feelings expressed in the following lines:

I am homesick after my own kind
Oh I know that there are folk about me, friendly faces,
But I am homesick after my own kind

Ezra Pound (1907)

At a personal level too I can testify to such powerful and potentially self-destructive feelings of alienation, as when I first came to England. It was my first experience of a *culture shock* I have stated elsewhere:

England came as a shock! There were as many accents there as there are dialects in India – or almost. Each of them as though spoken in a different tongue, and a few even in forked tongues! I found it difficult to distinguish between levity and seriousness, jest and truth, praise and censure, affection and affectation, between acceptance and rejection. It was exasperating not being able to read correctly their feelings and emotions when, on occasions they chose to express them. In India I had been born into a particular caste and had learnt through childhood what was expected of me in a variety of social situations, which involved a mingling of castes. But with the English it was difficult to place them in their appropriate class categories. On the one hand, the class divisions seemed rigid, and on the other they seemed blurred and not as clearly defined as castes are in India. It was difficult to work out what was expected of one in different situations and of different people. I was distressed that hardly any of the English friends I made, showed any curiosity concerning my own cultural origins and upbringing. They avoided personal exchanges as assiduously as an orthodox Brahmin might avoid an untouchable. Either they were too reticent to ask and find out or disinterested. I chose to believe the latter.

Living in a foreign country was like fighting a lone battle on several fronts: the weather, the climate, the preserved and processed food, the strange customs and conventions, the patterns of day-to-day life, and of course the people. I committed unforgivable social blunders; I was guilty of all sorts of faux pas; I annoyed people without meaning to. I asked questions which the English considered private, personal, and sacrosanct. I volunteered information, which they found difficult to handle. There were people who annoyed me to such an extent that I drove metaphorical stakes through their hearts! Although we spoke the same language, although we had past historical associations, although I had read the books, which I had assumed they would have also read, and although I dressed the way they did, I could tell that a vast ocean of differences separated me from them. I felt alienated. I drowned and died a hundred deaths in the first waves of misunderstandings, which engulfed me. I found that we were divided more by our differences than united by our similarities. Rudyard Kipling's observation that 'The East is East and the West is West – and never the twain shall meet' was made almost a century ago. Yet his words seemed as appropriate then, as they are today!

I soon realized that to relate with the English and thus get on reasonably well with them, it would be I who would be expected to make all the adjustments – not they. In other words, I would have to learn to assimilate into their culture – if I could get round to understanding it. I did not relish the idea of assimilation because of its negative connotations.

At a personal level I was totally opposed to the idea of learning to become like them – in speech, in dress, in conversation, and all such characteristics, which would have enabled me to be 'accepted' by them. I had no desire to become a metaphorical English clone. Even if I tried, I knew that I would only become a two-dollar note – a counterfeit! I could not countenance such a move. For me, it would have meant a serious cultural compromise, an assault on my own notions of my 'self' and my 'identity', which I had developed rightly or wrongly, over the years during the course of living in India. And more importantly, such a compromise would have meant a sad loss of my own moral integrity.

It was then that it became clear to me that culture is an extremely complex and elusive concept (Berry, Poortinga, Segall, and Dasen, 1997). Most of our cross-cultural interactions – particularly when mutually unintelligible languages are involved in the interaction – are often based on superficial stereotypes. Moreover, such 'exchanges' may even succeed in compounding misunderstandings and misperceptions.

I became acutely aware of the powerful influences which my own culture had had on my growth and development, and on the way in which I saw myself, and the world around me. Like the others, I too was handcuffed to my own culture by its past history. (Laungani, 2001d: p.).

The experiences I have narrated, which include the less than favourable judgements, took place about 30 years go. You are of course entitled to ask if over the years I have had any reason to change my views. In 2004 I was invited by the Editor of a British journal to give an interview on my own experiences related to cross-cultural interaction and assimilation, as a result of living in England. Allow me to quote the relevant parts of the interview (West, 2004).

Box 8.4

Pittu Laungani: I came to England, bursting with enthusiasm. I kept reminding myself that I was part of the culture, I spoke English with reasonable fluency and in a naïve sort of way I felt I was reasonably well read. I felt that life in England wouldn't turn out too badly. [However], I found it incredibly difficult to get to know [the English]. I could not befriend them. They seemed 'insular', 'unapproachable' and self-contained. They had no awareness of the languages we spoke, nor were they interested. Luckily, I never expected the English to understand any of the Indian languages.

(Continued)

William West:	Apart from language, are there any other cultural differences which you have noticed and which you would say have affected you personally?
P.L.:	… There are several other differences I have noticed. To my mind they are unbridgeable. I'd be very surprised if they were.
W.W.:	Which are?
P.L.:	Living in this country and engaged in the professional work of an academic, there is an unvoiced expectation among friends and colleagues that one would be reasonably familiar with Western music, Western art, Western literature and such other attributes and acquisitions which go toward distinguishing to a large measure the middle classes from the working classes.
	Although I can with some effort tell the difference, say between Beethoven's *Sixth,* and Mozart's *Jupiter,* or between *The Moonlight Sonata* and the *Requiem*, my knowledge of Western classical music is extremely superficial and my ears, untrained. Yet I have seen sly and 'knowing' looks exchanged whenever I have been unable to identify a piece of music, or tell a Hogarth from a Constable.
W.W.:	If I get you right, what you're saying is that there is only conditional acceptance of you as a colleague and perhaps even as a friend.
P.L.:	So it would seem.
W.W.:	What about the other way round? How do we come up to your cultural expectations?
P.L.:	I think your imperialist past acts as a safety valve. It continues to protect you. It is your talisman. It acts as a shield that virtually guarantees your insularity and disinterest in peoples of other cultures.
W.W.:	I don't think that is strictly true.
P.L.:	Let me give you a few examples: How many English people do you know who have some familiarity with Indian literature, including poetry, drama, fiction, philosophy, religion? The great Urdu, Persian, Hindi, Telugu, and Sanskrit poets of eras past and present remain virtually unknown – other than among scholars. Generally speaking the writers whom the general public may have read are the modern writers whose books have been published in the West and those who have had some impact – people such as Naipaul, Rushdie, Vikram Seth, Gandhi, Vivekanada, Krishnamurthy and a few others. Even Kalidasa, the most famous and illustrious of Indian poets and dramatists remains virtually unknown in the West. And so do the great Urdu poets such as Mirza Ghalib, Bahadur Shah Zafar and others. Find me half a dozen English persons selected at random from British universities, who could distinguish between different forms of Indian music: a thumri from a gazal, a geet from a bhajan, and in dancing, Bharatanatyam from a Kathak, Manipuri from Kahtakali.
W.W.:	What you are suggesting is that cultural changes are a one-way process.

(Continued)

P.L.: No. That is not the impression that I wish to create. What I am trying to say is that there is a one-sided expectation. I will not deny that cultures change.

W.W.: But obviously you've learned to cope.

P.L.: I guess so. I suspect one of the main problems as I see it is their lack of 'openness' – particularly among the kind of persons I know and meet and entertain…. Much to my surprise I found that hardly any of my colleagues at the University ever enquired if I was a Hindu, Muslim, Parsee, or Catholic, Sikh or Buddhist. I just felt they were not interested. They seldom took any interest in my life, hardly ever discussed personal issues, and in general maintained a social distance. I also knew that the onus was upon me to make the right overtures – personal, social, academic, and even philosophical – if I were to learn to understand them and 'get on' with them. But I found that the more I tried to relate to them the less easy it became. I had no wish to become like one of them in order to be 'accepted' by them. I could not countenance such a move. It would have meant a serious cultural compromise, an assault on my own notions of my 'self' and my 'identity', which I had developed over the years in India. More importantly, such a compromise would have meant a sad and irretrievable loss of my personal moral integrity.

Yet, I was at my wit's end. I did not know what to do. I was aware too that one could not easily give up one's cultural roots. My own feeling is that Westerners (and in particular, the British) are even more aware of cultural differences – how can they not be so, having ruled over more than half the world? But they feel decidedly ill at ease with cultural differences. And as you well know, one of the easiest ways of dealing with a painful problem is to ignore it.

W.W.: That's interesting. Why do you say that?

P.L.: Let's turn to history. Britain was an imperialist nation. Britannia ruled the waves. They ruled over several countries, over several diverse cultural groups and over several hundred years. That is a stupendous achievement! Yet they remained aloof, even distant from those over whom they ruled. Barring notable exceptions – and there have been many – the rest made very few attempts to understand their cultures and learn to live with them. You might argue that all this was in the past and it's old history. But sadly, past history 'catches' up with us in the sense we fail to learn the lessons which history teaches us. It is not history that repeats itself; it is we who repeat history.

W.W.: Do you think the British are culture-blind?

P.L.: I'd say, myopic – not blind. Myopia is not incurable. A different pair of culture-sensitive lenses would help.

W.W.: Do you think that one day the lion shall lie with the lamb?

P.L.: I am not so sure that the lamb would consent to lie with the lion! Not unless the lion were disarmed, toothless, and more importantly, a vegetarian. As I said earlier, one can but live in hope.

(West, 2004:)

In recent years, several cross-cultural psychologists (Berry, 1976; Berry & Sam, 1997; Billig, 1976; Brislin, 1993; Tanaka-Matsumi & Draguns, 1997) and others have highlighted the major factors which would need to be taken into serious consideration to facilitate intercultural interaction and thereby establish friendly working relationships. Some of the factors that have been investigated over the years are:

- Words and language (Hayakawa, 1965; Munroe & Munroe, 1994);
- Perception of feelings and emotions (Matsumoto, 1989);
- Non-verbal communication (Argyle, 1982);
- Understanding social customs (Bloom, 1971; Laungani, 2005b);
- Acculturation and adaptation (Berry & Sam, 1997; Ward & Kennedy, 1996b);
- Forms of greeting;
- Cultural adaptation;
- Accepting and offering hospitality (Laungani, 2004d);
- Patterns of relationships (Roopnarine & Gielen, 2005);
- Health and psychopathology (Tanaka-Matsumi & Draguns, 1997);
- Avoidance and resolution of conflict (Taylor & Moghaddam, 1987);
- Dimensions of contact (Triandis & Vasiliou, 1967);
- Caste and class differences (Laungani, 2004a).

This is by no means an exhaustive list. There are other areas of research in which cross-cultural psychologists have also been involved. To discuss the research enterprises in each of the above areas in depth would necessitate writing an entire book on this subject. We shall single out the important role of language in understanding cross-cultural interaction.

Words and language

Imagine a world where no word is spoken. Not a single human sound reaches your ears. You hear nothing. You read nothing. You utter nothing. All you ever hear are the sounds of nature, the cries of birds and animals, the wind rustling through the leaves, and perhaps the gentle beating of your heart. All is silent. Such imagination is inconceivable. For even now, although you may be trying to visualize a soundless world of humanity, you are reading the words that are printed on this page. A wordless world is inconceivable.

Fortunately we live in a world of words, words, and words. More words are exchanged – spoken, written, published, read – than all the currencies of the world put together in any one day. Words surround us and hound us. Words intimidate us and uplift us. Words demean us and ennoble us. Words hurt us and heal us. Even when we are asleep, we know not what dreams may pass over our troubled brows. Our relationships with others are cemented or fractured by words. Words raise us to levels of sublime ecstasy and also plunge us into the innermost regions of hell. Words shape our thoughts, feelings, and our actions. Words allow us to make sense of ourselves, of others, and of the world in which we live.

All the reputable theories of counselling and psychotherapy, ancient, traditional, and modern, share this very powerful feature – the use of words. Freud, you will recall, called his form of therapy the 'talking cure'. Such is also the case with the post-Freudian, neo-Freudian, and other talking therapies: transactional, gestalt, existential, behavioural, cognitive-behavioural, person-centred, to name but a few. They all use words as the basic tool of therapy.

Given the undeniable importance of words in our daily lives, the question is, how accurately do we understand one another, interpret each other's meanings correctly? Do we, through the words we hear, have the ability to 'crawl' into the psyche of the other person and interpret correctly the meanings they assign to words? Why do conversations and interactions with others often lead to misunderstandings, misperceptions, and misrepresentations?

Paradoxically misperceptions occur more easily in situations charged with strong feelings and emotions, such as in a counselling or therapeutic encounter. The situation assumes even greater importance when a therapeutic encounter occurs between counsellors and clients of different cultural backgrounds. This can be compounded by the fact that non-verbal factors too play an important role in interaction.

Darwin, in his famous book, *The Expressions of Emotions in Man and Animals* (1872/1965), demonstrates the means by which animals communicate with members of their own species: through facial expressions, gestures, grunts, noises, sighs, and a variety of other non-verbal physical movements. Subsequent studies by ehtologists, including Lorenz, Hinde, Ekman, and others, made clear that communication, both among animals and humans, is an extremely subtle and complex process. In certain instances, failure to perceive subtle non-verbal and/or bodily cues with accuracy can mean the difference between life and death.

This caveat applies not just to animals but in certain circumstances also to humans. Bruno Bettleheim, in his book, *The Informed Heart* (1986), based on his experiences in the Nazi concentration camps in Dachau and Buchenwald, records in harrowing detail the cues that the inmates of the camp had to perceive with unfailing accuracy to survive the brutality of the guards patrolling the camps. This of course is an extreme example, but it does illustrate the point that regardless of the situation one finds oneself in, one needs to be eternally vigilant in order to make sense of even a casual social encounter.

At an empirical level, though, it is worth asking if therapists do really acquire such astute observational, intuitive, empathetic, and interpretative powers. Or do therapists, given the very nature of their professional work, merely assume that they possess all the highly desirable observational and empathic skills? Or is the world of the client a figment of the therapist's imagination? Such questions are extremely difficult to answer. Do therapists possess 'that something extra' which an ordinary mortal lacks?

As Hayakawa (1965) points out, we each construe words differently, especially those which reverberate with feelings and emotions. Beauty, in that sense, is in the eye of the beholder. And so is ugliness! Given the tyranny of words, it seems a virtual miracle that we are able to communicate with one another reasonably successfully. How many of us would dare explain Freud's concept of 'cathexis of energy' as Freud conceptualized it? Do we really understand what a therapist means when he or she points out that the client's problems can be traced to 'the anal explicative or anal retentive psychic tendencies, which manifest themselves in an overtly hostile but covertly passive unconscious oedipal relationships with his or her significant others'? Is it possible to translate this high-sounding nonsense into words that would make sense to the client? Or is it an art, acquired by many people as Somerset Maugham wrote, of 'speaking nonsense with distinction'? To me, it seems more like a consciously contracted 'disease' from which many academics have no immunity whatever.

The tyranny of words

Words, as Osgood, Suci, and Tannenbaum (1957) in their research into psycho-linguistics have demonstrated, carry two distinct types of meanings which they have identified as *denotative* and *connotative*, or in other words, objective and subjective. Meanings of words according to them can also be perceived along three major dimensions, which they refer to as *evaluative*, *potency*, and *activity*. Even the word 'table', which should arouse little confusion in its objective definition, may inspire different subjective evaluations; a Victorian table, a Chippendale table, old grandma's table, or the table which Eddington visualized in terms of an unpredictable dance of sub-atomic particles, floating in space.

To some, all this might seem an irrelevant digression from the main theme, which is concerned with cross-cultural interaction. But as was stated right at the outset, all our meaningful, rewarding, and enduring interactions depend upon words. For interactions to progress in a 'satisfactory' manner – I shall abandon any attempt at defining the word 'satisfactory' – it would be beneficial for both the parties involved in the interaction to understand the diverse emotive and cognitive meanings which each of them attaches to words. It is only through a close correspondence in understanding the subtle nuances of words, which form the basis of interaction, that some genuine progress can be achieved. A proper use of language also involves the use of metaphors, similes, and proverbs, all of which form an integral part of communication.

Metaphors

Each culture produces its own sets of metaphors. Metaphors help us to articulate, interpret, and reinterpret our own world of experience. Gombrich (1979) argues that a society which fails to embellish its language by reaching out into the sources of metaphor would cease to be a society. Let us consider a few English metaphors: Trojan horse, Draconian laws, stoic endurance, Quixotic, Dionysian, Apollonian, Platonic, Faustian, Kafkaesque, Oedipal, Confucian, Elysian, Darwinian, Epicurean, Freudian slip, the playing fields of Eton, meeting one's Waterloo, being in limbo, the patience of Job, the thin end of the wedge, crossing the Rubicon, and so on. It is of course possible that one may be unfamiliar with the classical origins of metaphors and yet be familiar with their subtle meanings. Metaphors, as one can see from the few examples quoted above, have both negative and positive meanings.

Metaphors to a large measure are also class-related. The above metaphors reflect a certain kind of learning and upbringing and are less likely to be understood by all and sundry. On the other hand, metaphors such as: it's not cricket, he had a good innings, between the devil and the deep blue sea, sour grapes, up the creek without a paddle, thick as two short planks, a lemon, the wrong end of the stick, and so on, are more commonly employed metaphors.

All metaphors have their own historical origins and are culture-specific. Let us consider a few metaphors that are popularly used in India. Metaphors such as: *imaan, bey-imaan badnaseeb, haraam, halal, izzat, shudha, pavitra, apavitra, vairaag, punya joothaa, shubha, dharma, karma, kismet, gyani, chukka, hijra, jaisi-karni-vaisi-bharni, aankh ka noor, be-raham, zaalim*, are part of common lore. Since Indian society is structured along caste divisions, the above metaphors cut across caste boundaries and are used with equal facility by all and sundry. The origins of the above metaphors do not necessarily reflect classical learning. They arise out of the popular stories from the ancient Indian epics, such as *The Mahabharata, The Bhagawad Gita, The Ramayana* and the *Koran*, which are told and retold to children as an integral part of their socialization and upbringing. Through constant exposure, the metaphors get internalized, becoming part of everyday speech. For instance, the word *shudha*, which translated literally means 'pure'. However, the word *shudha* carries with it a host of other meanings, such as: spiritual purity, pure (uncontaminated) food, a pure, truthful, honest, trustworthy person, and so on. Many mythological figures from Hindu religious texts – *Satyavan Savitri, Yudhisthira, Rama, Sita, Laxman Arjuna, Bhim* – also come to be used as metaphors. They arouse special positive feelings when used. At the same time there are a host of metaphors with negative connotations, such as when a person is referred to as a *bhangi* (sweeper), *hajaam,* (barber), *dasu* (demon), *chamaar,* (cobbler) *chandaal* (an untouchable), and so on.

Metaphors are part of everyday speech. A mutual understanding of metaphors facilitates interaction at a fairly deeper and more meaningful level. But an inability to understand metaphors may seriously impede interaction.

To get a 'flavour' of a cross-cultural encounter, let us visualize a scenario. Let us eavesdrop on an encounter between a white English (or American) therapist and a Pakistani (Muslim) client facing him on the other side of the desk. My reason for choosing a therapeutic cross-cultural encounter is based on the assumption that counsellors and therapists, by the very nature of their work, would be (or would need to be) more in tune with cultural differences of their clients, and would have the skill and the ability to understand the client's inner motives far more clearly than a person untrained in the field.

Client:	Well, Doctor *Sahib*, what should I do? *(He rings his hands in a gesture of despair and looks imploringly at the therapist.)*
Therapist:	*(After a long silence.)* What do *you* think you should do?
Client:	*(Rather peeved, even angry.)* Every time I am asking you a question you are throwing the question back at me!
Therapist:	Oh, am I?
Client:	*(Exasperated.)* You have done it again! Look, Doctor *Sahib*, you are the expert. I have come to you for help. If I knew how to help myself, I would surely not come to see you.
Therapist:	Mr Ahmed, it is really for you to decide what you should do. I cannot decide for you.
Client:	*(Acutely disturbed and even bewildered.)* But why not! I don't understand. I am coming to you for help. You should be guiding me, helping me. But you want *me* to decide what I should do. When I go to see my GP, he tells me what I should do, what medicines I should take – and then leaves it to me to decide. But you don't tell me what I *should* do! *(Looks at the therapist.)* If you were a brain surgeon, would you be *asking me to perform my own operation?*
Therapist:	*(In spite of himself.)* Of course not!
Client:	So you would perform brain surgery, if you could. But you will not perform psychosurgery – which you can!
Therapist:	*(Refuses to be drawn into an argument.)*
Client:	You know what I think, doctor? *(Pointing his index finger to his forehead.)* It is fate. It is Allah's will. It is my kismet, my 'taqdeer'. What was to happen has happened. Who can fight against one's fate, against what is written! *(Here he quotes the well-known couplet from the Persian poet Omar Khayyam, (translated by Edward Fitzgerald, 1859/1972)):*

> The Moving Finger writes; and having writ,
> Moves on: nor all thy Piety nor Wit,
> Shall lure it back to cancel half a Line
> Nor all thy Tears wash out a Word of it.

Therapist:	*(Totally at a loss as he hears the poem, which his client has recited in Persian. Sits in embarrassed silence, unable to decide what he should say.)*

Let us now analyse the above encounter in psycho-cultural terms. Even without any specific knowledge as to the nature of the problem, one can see that there is a gulf between the client and the therapist. Both of them are locked into their own private cultural worlds. They are either unable or unwilling to step out of it.

The client's worldview

The client lives in a world where one's life appears to be preordained. There is in him a belief that one needs to submit unconditionally to the will of Allah, and hope that the almighty Allah will take mercy upon his lost soul. At the same time, he looks upon the therapist, albeit in a minor sort of way, as an 'intermediary' who might intercede on his behalf and bring him succour. Second, seeking *uncon-ditional* guidance from one's healer is seen as an integral part of Islamic and Hindu culture. The client's belief in the ability of the therapist to 'solve' his problems arises out of the unswerving faith which people from Eastern cultures have for therapists, healers, gurus, and shamans (Hoch, 1974; Kakar, 1982; Roland, 1988). He sees his therapist as a spiritual guide, even as a guru whose magico-spiritual powers will cure him of his problems. He fails to understand why the therapist remains so distant, aloof – and even quite cold. The failure or the unwill-ingness on the part of the therapist to offer such specific guidance is a source of acute disappointment for the client.

The therapist's worldview

As far as the therapist is concerned, one might argue that the therapist has some awareness of the client's subjective world. But for him to accommodate the client's world into his own schema would mean an abandonment of his own beliefs and values, which are at variance with those of his client. His personal philosophy (into which he has been socialized since childhood) has little room in it for a deterministic formulation. Life to the therapist is not ordained or preordained. One has control. One has free will. One has choice. It is through the exercise of one's free will that one is able to bring about the desired changes in one's life. In adopting a stance of neutrality, the therapist is 'playing out' his own internalized value systems to which, without being wholly aware, he is handcuffed. In the famous words of Sartre, he is *condemned to his freedom.* In keeping with his non-directive, non-judgmental theoretical orientations he is unwilling to play a didac-tive role in the therapeutic encounter, while the client expects of him. While he is willing to play the role of an empathetic but dispassionate observer, and even a 'sounding board', he is unwilling to guide and direct the client in terms of the kind of decisions the client should or ought to take.

Even the manner in which they relate to one another reveals their unique cultural biases. The therapist operates on a 'horizontal' model, which posits a non-hierarchical but formal interpersonal relationship. The client, on the other hand, prefers (or would prefer) to adopt a 'vertical' model, which posits a hierarchical but informal relationship between him and the therapist. The client is eager to seek guidance (and succour) from the therapist, which the therapist is unwilling to offer. This is not an unusual therapeutic situation; and one can see that there is a genuine clash of cultural values between the therapist and the client.

What can be done? The question is this: can the clash of cultural values be overcome? Are there legitimate ways by which one might transcend cultural boundaries and perhaps even formulate a super-structure that would digest all the cultural variations and anomalies? This question is by no means easy to answer.

Conclusion

Is there a way by which we might transcend cultural boundaries and learn to understand and interact meaningfully with people of other cultures? The answer is a cautious yes. How shall this grand aim be achieved?

It is only when the East and the West meet as joint partners and agree to learn from one another, thereby ushering in a new era in which people shall live in peace and harmony. Please permit me to end this chapter in the form of a brief sermon:

Ask not what the West can teach the East.
Ask instead, what the west might learn from the East.
Ask not why Nietzsche announced the death of God in the West.
Ask instead, why Gods are alive and well in the East.
Ask not why families in the West are disunited.
Ask instead, why families in the East remain united.
Ask not about the whys of modern-day terrorism.
Ask instead about the whys of Western militarism.
Ask not if the wolf will continue to kill the lamb.
Ask instead if the wolf might learn to lie with the lamb.
Ask not if white will glister and black will fade.
Ask instead if the two will form a glorious pattern of light and shade.

Cross-Cultural Considerations in Health, Happiness, and Illness

Doctors put drugs of which they know little, in bodies of which they
  know less, to cure diseases of which they know nothing at all.

                    François-Marie Arouet (Voltaire)

He jests at scars that never felt a wound.

                    Romeo and Juliet, II.11.1

L et us start by examining the two views quoted above. It is clear from the first quote by François-Marie Arouet – better known as Voltaire – that he did not take kindly to the medical profession. Whether his contempt at the perceived ignorance of doctors was based on personal experience or that he was simply stating a hyperbole, one cannot say without going into Voltaire's lifestyle and his involvement with the medical profession. But despite his exaggerations, it would be useful at a general level to inquire if there is any substance to his accusations. The second quote, which is from Shakespeare's *Romeo and Juliet*, displays the 'arrogance' of a person who has never felt ill. This would suggest that most healthy people take their health for granted and may even be insensitive to the sufferings of others.

The question is, how shall health and illness be defined? At a common-sense level we all have our own personal, intuitive, idiosyncratic, and experiential conceptions of health and illness. Based on our own knowledge and experience, we often tend to see health and illness in multi-factorial terms, namely in physical (organic), mental, cultural, religious, existential, and spiritual terms. We are also aware that health and disease are not dichotomous terms. They lie along a continuum without a single cut-off point. The lowest point on the continuum signifies death and the highest corresponds to what might be referred to as 'positive health'. It is clear that health fluctuates within an optimum level of wellbeing to various levels of dysfunctions, at the extreme end of which is death.

Our own notions of health and illness are not acquired in isolation, nor are they formed in a social vacuum. They are moulded by the culture into which we are born and into which we are socialized. Culture exercises a powerful and enduring influence on virtually all the major areas of our lives, including religion, beliefs, values, our familial and social and relationships, our psyche, on our worldviews, and of course on our health. However, as we all know, there are significant differences in cultures in terms of beliefs, attitudes, values, and levels of scientific, bio-medical, psychological, and psychiatric knowledge. Therefore our understanding and our conceptions of health and illness are likely to vary accordingly.

What also adds to the difficulty is the conflict between subjective evaluations and objective definitions of health and illness. At a subjective level, conceptions of health and illness may be seen as shared social constructions. They arise partly through the individual's personal experience. However, for the experience to be construed as disease, or an illness, or whatever, it needs to be located within the larger context of social values, which are an integral part of the cognitive and emotional structure of the individual's culture. Once the experience finds acceptance within the individual's social milieu, it can then be appropriately labelled, not otherwise. Let us sample a few *popular* definitions:

- Health is the condition of being sound in body, mind, or spirit.
- Health is an absence of disorder and distress.
- Health is freedom from physical diseases or pain.
- Health is a state of complete physical, mental, and social wellbeing and not merely an absence of disease or infirmity (WHO, 1984).

- Health is the ability to lead a socially and economically productive life (WHO, 1984).
- Health is *an ideal* to which we all aspire.
- Health is a state of equilibrium between mind and body, a balance between yin and yang.
- Some see health and illness in dichotomous terms; others construe them as extending along a continuum.
- Some see health as a unitary concept, others as a multi-factorial one.
- Tillich (1961) sees health and illness as existential concepts: one does not exist without the possibility of the other.
- Health is also seen as an ability to cope with stressful events and the ability to maintain a strong social support network (Bowling, 1992).

The above definitions seem reasonably adequate, but they run into a few problems, particularly when we move from the abstract to the concrete, for instance:

- Is a healthy person one who has been *insufficiently diagnosed?*
- Would a person with a well-toned body of a young Schwarzenegger with the mind of Peter Sutcliffe (the serial killer better known as The Yorkshire Ripper) be considered a healthy person?
- Can one be free of diseases and yet see oneself as being sick and unhealthy?
- Would an elderly person in his or her seventies construe health in the same way as a strapping youth?
- Would a person pronounced as unhealthy in one culture be seen as being relatively healthy in another culture? Arthur Koestler (1967) cites an example of how a person diagnosed as a schizophrenic in America, upon flying back to England may be diagnosed as suffering from a mild personality disorder.
- Do women see health differently from men?

No easy answers to the above questions are forthcoming. Let us take an imaginative leap and ask if the following people – people who in amazing and wonderful ways have enriched our lives – would be considered healthy or ill:

> Socrates, Plato, Sophocles, Buddha, Dante, Galileo, Newton, Martin Luther, Leonardo da Vinci, Beethoven, Nietzsche, Freud, Tolstoy, Dostoevsky, Proust, Gaugin, Van Gogh, Lincoln, Darwin, Picasso, Hemingway, Scott-Fitzgerald, Primo Levi, James Joyce, George Orwell, William Blake, Churchill, Gandhi, Stephen Hawking.

How many of the persons named above would have been diagnosed as suffering from serious physical (organic) and/or mental disorders? According to Simonton (1999) they all, without exception would have been diagnosed as suffering from extremely serious psychotic disorders, ranging from depression and manic-depressive psychosis to schizophrenia. Simple though it might seem at first sight, it is by no means easy to define health and illness with calibrated precision.

Let us explore these problems further by considering the following four interrelated issues.

1 *The 'freedom from' model of health in medicine;*
2 *The 'freedom from' model of health in psychology;*
3 *The 'freedom to' model of health and happiness in psychology;*
4 *The cross-cultural model of health, happiness, and illness.*

The 'freedom from' model of health in medicine

Health is seen as *freedom from* disease. It is seen in biological terms, where every cell, every organ continues to function in perfect harmony with the rest of the body. This biomedical or the disease model of health had its basis in the 'germ theory of disease', which dominated medical thinking at the turn of the twentieth century (Park & Park, 1991). Even today, the main concern of the medical profession appears to be with the human body. The body is seen as a piece of machinery, which with the use of scientific technology can be repaired, replaced, or restored to its original state. In a metaphorical sense modern medicine sees illness as a chess game, where the armoury of modern medicine prepares to battle against the army of bacteria and other noxious and life-threatening viruses, allergens, fungi, and so on, ready to invade, capture, and destroy the body. With skill and expertise, the 'grand master', namely the consultant and his or her team of 'disciples', may move, repair, or replace each piece to achieve the desired result, namely the eradication of the disease. That they do not always succeed in their 'game' is stating the obvious. Sadly, patients do die.

Medical science appears to pay far greater attention to differences among diseases but hardly any to differences among people (Chopra, 1991). Their disease-oriented ethos leaves little room to consider the role the patient might be expected to play. In fact, hardly any room at all. Even more importantly, hardly any consideration is given to the patient's subjective evaluations concerning his or her illness.

In ancient times the situation was different. Lessons from ancient Greek civilization clearly point to the *'freedom to'* model of health and illness. Most of the ancient Greek and Roman philosophers, from Socrates onwards, were concerned about human growth and development. They argued that we have the desire, the willingness and the ability to grow, develop, mature, to be happy and shower happiness, to form loving and caring long-lasting relationships with ourselves and with others, to respect and be respected, to engage in acts of kindness, benevolence, and charity, to do our duty, to live in peace and harmony with others, to appreciate nature, art, beauty, and music, to be responsible citizens, to realize our potential, to 'self-actualize', to be rational, self-directing, autonomous individuals, to lead a good, noble, and honourable life, such as the kind envisioned by Socrates, Plato, Aristotle, Seneca, Cicero, Protagoras, and several other Greek philosophers of the past. Cicero argued that all human beings possessed a divine spark of reason in them, which conferred on them a duty to develop themselves to the full as civilized educated individuals and to treat each other with respect and generosity (Grayling, 2003; Johnson, 2000).

The *'freedom to'*, or the growth model, thesis suffered a gradual setback during the pre-Renaissance period. Christianity exercised a powerful influence on the day-to-day lives of people. Illnesses, both physical and mental, were often explained in terms of the wrath of God, divine retribution, sin, the workings of the devil, and so on. People were cowed into obedience by their fears of purgatory, hell, and eternal damnation. Those who had the audacity to question the teachings of the Bible were branded as heretics and were dealt dire punishments, which in extreme cases led to their being burnt at the stake. One could envisage the fate that would have befallen Galileo had he not recanted his heliocentric theory and accepted the geocentric theory, namely that the Earth moved round the Sun, which of course was in keeping with the tenets of the Bible.

The Renaissance period followed by the period of Enlightenment and Humanism in Europe ushered in a new era of progress in science, medicine and technology, bringing about a 'paradigm shift'. Old theories were questioned; some were put to the sword. God was ex-communicated by the secular papacy. Religious dogma – the main adversary of the humanists and the rationalists – was increasingly relegated to a position of lesser importance. Illnesses, it was proclaimed, were *not* brought about by God's wrath, or by other supernatural forces. Nor were they due to loss of virtue, or by colluding with the devil and other malevolent forces. Supernatural explanations of illness gave way to natural, scientific explanations. The rise in empirical research led to a gradual decline in metaphysical reflections. Faith was dethroned. Reason and science were enthroned (Grayling, 2003; Paranjpe, 1998). Gradually, Western medicine hitched its wagon to the shining star of science and ignored, underplayed, and disregarded the *'freedom to'* idea. Even the patients' subjective evaluations of their own condition were thrust aside. They were of no relevance to the outcome of their illness. The patient was often seen as an object, a compliant and malleable object of the doctor's expertise.

'Doctor knows best' became the clarion call of the medical profession. It still is.

I can testify to this based on my own experiences of having languished as a patient in an intensive care unit and subsequently in a high-dependency ward of a hospital in London for several months (Laungani, 1992c, 2004a, 2005a). I have no desire to be the centrepiece of this chapter, however, I feel it is important to describe at least one such experience (out of several) which convinced me that the medical profession to a considerable extent subscribes to the view that *'doctor knows best'*.

Box 9.1

Within a day or two of being admitted into hospital in London, the doctors carried out a bewildering variety of tests. There was no stone left unturned. There was hardly a test I was not subjected to. But before they could arrive at a firm diagnosis, my condition deteriorated and I was transferred into the intensive care unit (ICU). Eventually I was diagnosed as having contracted a rare disease called 'polymyositis'. I was told that polymyositis had something to do with the breakdown of protein in my muscles. It also had an adverse effect on one's immune system. Although rare, it was a serious disorder. All this of course made no sense to me; all I knew was that I had acquired a rare disease, which was critical and could result in death. The ICU became my temporary home. I made myself aware of the mortality rates related to polymyositis by badgering the nurses in the ICU. I wanted to know what my chances of survival were; they were grim. Grim statistics brought up images of the Grim Reaper. Within a few days my condition deteriorated even further. My body turned into a sculptor's mould; it was 'stiff' – but not quite in the sense of the American slang! I was paralysed. My heart muscles were functioning, but in a painful, dilatory fashion. I spoke in whispers, barely able to hear myself. I kept wondering if I'd ever regain the use of my muscles, be able to stand, walk, and even run. It seemed hopeless. There was some cold comfort in the knowledge that if I were to die – which seemed very likely – it would all happen quickly and I'd die with the full knowledge of what I was going to die of.

High doses of steroids (occasionally exceeding 140 mg per day) along with other forms of medication flowed into my system intravenously. When after a few days the doctors discovered that the steroids appeared not to being doing the 'trick', I was given another form of treatment: plasma exchange. After a course of 15 plasma exchanges – one every other day – my condition began to show mild improvement. For the first time since my admission into the ICU, I was able to twiddle my thumbs and move my fingers. Four weeks later, I was moved out of the ICU into a high-dependency ward.

The next day the Consultant came to see me, accompanied as ever by his deferential junior doctors.

'It's a miracle, you've pulled through. You aren't quite out of the woods, yet, though.'

I smiled and said nothing.

'You must be prepared for the fact that your muscles have been very severely bruised and damaged. You've lost a lot of weight too.' He waited to see my expression. 'It will be a long while before you are able to stand and walk again – if at all.' He added gently. 'You might have to use a wheelchair for the rest of your life.'

So saying, he and his entourage flocked out.

I was devastated! My wife came to see me in the afternoon. I could tell by looking at her face that she knew. We sat looking at one another, each unwilling to articulate the 'death sentence' that had been passed upon me. I drowned in waves of despair. However, my wife was unwilling to give up so easily.

A few days later I agreed that, with the help of physiotherapists, I would do my utmost to try to learn to stand. I knew the crucial test lay in my being able to stand. If I were able to stand up unaided, I was confident that the rest – my ability to walk – would follow. Of that I had no doubt, whatever. Were that to happen, I knew that I would need neither

(Continued)

a wheelchair, nor a pair of crutches. I pinned all my hopes, all my dreams on my ability to stand.

Never could the physiotherapists have been pestered more! Not a day went by without their coming to see me once, twice, sometimes even three times a day, to assist me in my attempts to stand on my two feet. And then one day, I felt the hardness of the ground beneath my feet. I could actually stand! Without crutches. Unaided.

That was the start. After several days of such sustained efforts I tried to walk. I failed. I could not raise my feet off the ground. It was impossible. I tried dragging my feet instead; one foot following the other, in awkward, jerky movements. My inflamed muscles protested as I dragged one foot behind the other. After great efforts, I took two shaky, wobbly steps. Gradually I was able to walk about ten steps during the course of the day. On one of his daily rounds, accompanied as he always was by his junior doctors, trailing respectfully and deferentially behind him, I demonstrated to the Consultant my newfound ability to walk a few steps, unaided. He was surprised and elated – but his emotions soon gave way to acute embarrassment when I reminded him that only a week or two ago he had warned me that I would never walk again. He neither apologised nor attempted to defend himself. Clenching and unclenching his fists (which I took to be a sign of controlled aggression), he walked away without a word. Chuckling to myself and with malice aforethought, I winked at the junior doctors as they sheepishly followed him out of the room.

Interpretation of Box 9.1

There is an important point, that we need to take into serious consideration. It is not often realized how frequently doctors with varying levels of expertise and experiences err in their diagnosis and prognosis of illnesses. Erroneous prognostications, needless to say, can lead to serious complications and even fatal consequences. The attitude of deference, trust, and respect bordering on unquestioning faith in the doctor's infallibility is so deeply ingrained in the human psyche that it has given rise to the subtle but cynical joke:

What is the difference between God and a doctor?
God knows he (or she) is not a doctor.

Like the rest of us, doctors are human – despite a few who haven't realized it or haven't quite come to terms with it! My own belief, harnessed by my wife, in my willingness to learn to stand and walk, was obviously *not* shared by the consultant in whose care I was. Had I but accepted and 'given in' to the medical judgment, I may have become a victim of the 'self-fulfilling prophecy' which Sophocles prophesized in his great play, *King Oedipus*.

Sadly, medical science has ignored Hippocrates' wise dictum:

It is more important to know what sort of a person has a disease than to know what sort of a disease a person has.

The present *scientific biomedical model of disease asserts a materialist, disease-based framework*. Most diseases, it is argued, are treatable – although their aetiology may remain elusive. Thus, science and its technology serves as the ruling paradigm in Western medicine. There is an assumption that if science has not been able to find definite cures for some particular disease, sustained research sooner or later will find a cure. Although the *'freedom from'* model is popular within the medical profession, it suffers from the following weaknesses:

1   Since the main focus of medical science has been on organic (the disease) factors, it has tended to pay increasingly less attention to the subjective or the mental side of illness. With the staggering progress of science and technology in the twentieth century, the very existence of the mind has come to be seriously questioned and even denied. Why talk of the mind when we cannot empirically demonstrate its existence? It is as futile as talking about the soul and such other metaphysical concepts – this is the general thinking among contemporary medical scientists. The word 'mind' has become a meaningless philosophical appendage of little use to medical scientists, but of continued concern to philosophers, counsellors, psychotherapists (of certain types), and healers from different parts of the world. To dismiss the relevance of the mind–body problem in medicine and in psychology is unwise and counter-productive. Let us follow René Descartes and admit to the Cartesian notion of mind–body dualism and leave it at that. We know from our own knowledge and experience that our body can have serious repercussions on our mental state, and similarly, our mental worries and our anxieties can wreak havoc on our bodies.

2   At a common-sense level, the meaning underlying *'freedom from'* includes, in addition to organic factors, freedom from stresses and strains, from anxieties, worries, sorrow, unhappiness, depression, poverty, insomnia, loneliness, social isolation, alienation, old age, ill luck, misfortune, and so on. Clearly, our interpretation of *'freedom from'* is far more comprehensive, for it goes beyond the disease model and weaves its way into social, religious, cultural, familial and ethical areas.

    However, common-sense evaluations can be misleading. One may be unaware of one's illness; one may underestimate it, or even deny its severity; or one may invent an illness where none exists – which of course is not difficult to do. Besides, common-sense formulations often include concepts such as poverty, old age, misfortunes, ill luck, as indicators of illness; strictly speaking, they would not conform to medical evaluations.

3   Conceptualizing health and illness from a *'freedom from'* model is a *narrow and negative way of understanding health and illness*. The approach ignores vast areas of human beliefs, behaviours, and values that involve growth and development, kindness, autonomy, and courage, which lend existential and spiritual meaning and poignancy to one's life.

Such a narrow view has not gone unnoticed. There are increasing voices of dissent. There are medical practitioners – both among GPs and among consultants – who question the hegemony (and in some instances, even the validity) of the scientific model. Many of them have moved away from the biomedical model and have proposed, supported, and adopted alternative forms of medicine, which include homoeopaths, acupuncturists, herbalists nutritionists, dieticians, ayurveds, yogis, indigenous healers, and several others. But despite their growing numbers, their voices are feeble. It is too early to tell what impact, if any, their dissent will have on the present hegemony of the medical scientists.

Having discussed health and illness from a biomedical perspective, let us now discuss it from a psychological perspective. Are psychological approaches to health and illness and their treatment in any way different from those of biomedical science? Let us once again adopt a historical approach to understand the problems involved.

The 'freedom from' model of health in psychology

Psychology, as Herman Ebbinghaus had remarked, has a short past but a long history, which can be traced to the early writings and speculations of the ancient Greek philosophers from the sixth century BCE. Philosophy was seen as the prime discipline or the parent subject of all disciplines (Kenny, 1994; Leahey, 1997; Magee, 1997; Russell, 1946/1961). For over 2000 years psychology remained an integral part of philosophy. The ancient philosophers of Greece, Italy and Egypt, from around the seventh century BCE onwards, raised the perennial questions concerning the nature of nature, the nature of human nature, the mind, the soul, purpose, will, freedom, determinism, beliefs, values, happiness, hope, sorrow, despair, good, bad, moral, immoral, sin, virtue, beauty, ugliness, health, illness, life and death, and of course the nature of the human soul. Their thinking was also influenced by the religious mythology, which played a significant role in their day-to-day lives (Kirk, 1974; Onians, 1951). Gradually, the theo-centric models gave way to non-theistic and rational considerations in their quest for answers to cosmological and human problems. The Greeks laid the intellectual foundations on which future ideas and theories were constructed. It is fascinating to note that most of the issues of concern to ancient philosophers are as relevant today as they were in the past.

It was only in the latter part of the nineteenth century that several psychologists in America and in Europe began to question what they felt were the constraints of philosophy upon their fledgling discipline and started to consider the possibility of transforming psychology into a scientific discipline. Their emphasis was on the study of overt, observable, measurable behaviours. John B. Watson took his cues from the pioneering work of the Russian physiologist Ivan Pavlov. Watson was critical of concepts such as introspection, unconsciousness, mind, and all the metaphysical concepts which could not be observed and investigated objectively. Although he conceded that people displayed anxiety, depression, joy, happiness, and so on, all these concepts acquired meaning only when one was able to observe their precise behavioural correlates.

In their eagerness to turn psychology into a science, they espoused the natural science paradigm (Barnes, 1979; Laungani, 1996c) and Western psychology came to be defined as the science of human and animal behaviour. It was believed that the laws of the natural science would apply not only to the American people but also to the rest of the world. Metaphysical abstractions were ignored and in many instances thrown overboard. They were replaced by concepts such as positivism, operationism, empiricism, environmentalism, secularism, radicalism (a la Skinner), behaviourism, scientism, and a few other-isms, such as humanism, individualism, and cognitivism.

Western psychologists came to look upon their discipline as being scientific. Human behaviour, they believed, could be altered, modified, changed by the use of a variety of techniques, including cognitive and behavioural techniques, the use of reinforcement contingencies, and other behavioural techniques.

Their present emphasis is on behavioural and neurological processes, which they believe hold the key to understanding and modifying human behaviour. In recent years many neuro-physiologists, neuroscientists, psycho-pharmacologists, psychologists, psychiatrists, and the promoters of the human genome project have undertaken investigations to establish precise relationships between brain, genes, drugs, and behaviour.

But several eminent psychologists have rebelled against the very idea of a scientific psychology. Sigmund Koch remarked that he would 'prefer a defective understanding of something of value over a safely defended description of something trite' (in Robinson, 2001: 420). William James, one of the greatest of the American psychologists, refused to accept a psychology that won 'system' at the price of reality itself (Robinson, 2001). Paranjpe (1998) is critical of the scientific attitude adopted by contemporary Western psychology. He points out that 'contemporary [Western] psychology tends to favour a Newtonian conception of causality and lawfulness as a matter of empirical generalization' (p. 344). Paranjpe points out that Newton's laws lend themselves to empirical verification on the basis of repeatable observations. They can be stated as universal generalizations to which exceptions are virtually non-existent. But despite their astonishing predictive powers, even Newton's laws may fail to meet the criteria imposed by David Hume, namely that empirical generalizations about natural phenomena cannot be guaranteed to perpetuate forever. But despite the epistemological criticisms, American psychologists and to a large extent Western European psychologists are wedded to a scientific *zeitgeist*.

The 'freedom to' model of health and happiness in psychology

In the past, the therapeutic approaches used were in keeping with the *'freedom from'* format. The patients – as they were referred to then – were 'treated' for their psychological disorders, ranging from anxieties and phobias to fears and panic attacks, from delusions and persecutions to aggressive and psychopathic impulses, from obsessions and amnesias to depressions and other drug-related disorders, and so on. The aim of the therapist was to *free* the patient from such debilitating, traumatic, and destructive behaviours. There were also the traumatized war veterans of the Second World War who needed care and treatment. Soon after the War, in 1949, clinical psychology was formally inaugurated as a discipline within the American Psychological Association (APA). However, not all psychologists worked within the cloistered arbours of academia. Many opted out and elected to go public.

Until about the 1960s, the *'freedom from' health model* was the accepted approach within clinical psychology and psychotherapy in the United States. During the early 1960s, America got involved in the Vietnam War. Young Americans, many of whom did not even know where Vietnam was, let alone have any tangible ideas why America had got embroiled in a war which was not of their making, were being drafted into the army and sent to Vietnam. They were being forced to fight a war which was not their war. Not surprisingly, this was a period of acute unrest, uncertainty, dissension, and disenchantment among the American youth with the prevalent value systems. There was an acutely felt need for psychological help and succour. The availability of insurance reimbursements for psychological services, namely therapy and counselling, made it easier for many academics to opt out of academia and choose specialities outside their old core areas of experimental psychology. They moved into the applied areas such as health, stress, trauma, counselling, psychotherapy, clinical psychology, child development, advertising, marketing, motivation, and management, among others. Many of them entered into private practice and consultancy. Others attempted to promote self-help groups, do-it-yourself groups, encounter groups, ran workshops of a similar nature, produced manuals ranging from training in positive growth and health to creating a 'feel good' factor among individuals in search of a *personalized* existential meaning in their lives (Zilbergeld, 1983). Psychology, as Leahey (1997) pointed out, had gone public.

Such has been the impact of psychology going public that one would be right in referring to the existence of two types of psychologies: psychology as it is taught, researched, and applied in universities, and psychology as it is offered to the general public through books, magazines, CDs, video-cassettes, DVDs, workshops, lectures, residential courses, on the Internet, and on certain television channels.

The picture that presents itself *outside* academic corridors is one of infinite variety. If today you were to leave the cloistered arbours of academia and stroll along with Babbit – the central character in one of Sinclair Lewis's great novels – and transport him into Sinclair Lewis's *Main Street,* lo and behold, an extraordinary scene unfolds before your disbelieving eyes! Counsellors and therapists, healers and homeopaths, nutritionists and naturalists, dieticians, ayurveds and acupuncturists, spiritualists and séance masters, mediums and mystics, confidence boosters and confidence tricksters of every description are ready to offer their services – for a price, of course. You are in a consumer's paradise! Every conceivable type of therapy, treatment, counselling is on offer. Bespoke therapies. Exclusive therapies. Individual therapies. Group therapies. Weekend therapies. Long, elaborate residential therapies. Transcendental therapies. Yogic therapies. Primal-scream therapies. EST therapies. Self-disclosure therapies. Health therapies. Meditational therapies. Sex therapies. Religious therapies. Verily, you feel like Ali Baba, dazzled by all the undreamt of treasures on display. Here you can meditate, engage in yogic pranayamas, shout, get shouted at, abuse, get abused, scream, get screamed at, massage, get massaged, sing and dance, watch others do the same, work yourself into a frenzy, throw tantrums, rest, sleep, dream, have nightmares – in such a godless world, all is permitted. Here you are King, Caliph, Pasha and Sultan (Laungani, 1995a). The world is your oyster. Given the vast storehouse of treasures which lie within your easy reach, you are dazzled by all that is on offer, including the inexhaustible number of books which would easily decorate the entire Wall of China.

It is here that you encounter a variety of competing theories related to treatment, therapy and growth. It is here more so than in academia that you come across the *'freedom to'* notion of health. Even the words such as 'treatment' and 'therapy' have slowly given way to words such as: empowerment, autonomy, independence, assertiveness, realization of one's personality, realization of one's potential, self-actualization, inner growth, fulfilment, positive development, to become a 'better' person, and so on. The emphasis is on growth and positive change. Happiness, so the belief goes, is not a pot of gold at the end of a rainbow; it is within each individual's easy reach. A few sessions with the 'streetwise' therapists and Cinderella turns into a princess. The ugly duckling into a beautiful swan. Depression into ecstasy. Sorrow into joy. Quasimodo into Adonis or Narcissus. The inflated optimism and their bubbling champagne-like confidence draws clients in by their droves, keeping their cash registers singing and ringing. You may find the above rhetoric harsh. But I believe that the use of rhetoric, as Petrarch and several other Renaissance poets and writers have pointed out, allows one to present a case with force and elegance. The ancient Greeks, and in particular Protagoras, the pre-Socratic Sophist philosopher, ran courses in rhetoric, extolling its virtues as an excellent learning device. Let me share with you a counselling experience that I witnessed about 25 years ago at an international conference in England.

Box 9.2

The encounter took place at a prestigious university in Britain where, accompanied by a colleague, I had gone to present a paper at the conference. On the second evening of our stay at the university, after the day's papers had been presented, we were all invited to participate in a group counselling/therapeutic session that was being run by two Americans from California. The session was being held in a large room, on the third or fourth floor of the university building. Since dinner was also to be served in the same room at the end of the session, many of the delegates decided to stay and observe the two therapists in action. About 50 people decided to participate in the group session. The others sat around, smoking, talking, and watching the session that was beginning to unfold before us.

The two American counsellors/therapists/healers – it was difficult to find out what their professional training and qualifications were – were young, vibrant, and full of verve and charisma. Since most people are familiar with the 'warm-up' strategies that are used to get the crowd of strangers to form a cohesive group, there is little need to describe them. They were applied with great skill and aplomb. The participants did their bidding, and from time to time turned to their neighbours, looked into their eyes, shook hands, and spoke a few words about what they liked about them, and so on.

Being rather shy to participate in the sessions, I sat with my colleague. We sat at some distance, sipping our soft drinks, watching the session as it began to gain some momentum. It was a pleasant, warm summer evening. The setting sun cast its glow in the Western sky. About 20 minutes later, my colleague noticed one of the delegates quietly slipping away from the group session that was by then in full swing. He went and stood by the open window, looking out into the distance. No one took any notice. Suddenly, the young man clambered up the window ledge, holding the sashes for support. He swayed a bit but managed to check himself from falling out of the window. My colleague, who in his younger days had been a rugby player, without as much as by your leave, dived towards the window, grabbed hold of the person just as he was about to let go of the sashes, and brought him to the ground.

As one can imagine, the group session came to an abrupt end. The delegates were horrified. The delegate who had tried to throw himself out of the window was comforted and led away by some of the other delegates. The two Americans running the show tried to talk their way out of a potential suicide, but were not given a chance to explain themselves. Unceremoniously, and with venom aforethought, they were asked to leave – not just the room, but the building.

No one saw them again.

Interpretation of Box 9.2

I have deliberately kept the name of the university and the year of the event concealed. Little point would be served in raking up old wounds. However, I feel that I need to make my own position clear. The episode that I have described briefly affected me quite

(Continued)

deeply. I have written this not out of spite or malice. I neither knew the American mavericks nor the unhappy delegate who may have died but for the great presence of mind of my friend and colleague.

My concern is with *what might have happened. That is the fundamental moral problem.* It raises a host of terrifying dilemmas to which no conscience-calming, guilt-reducing answers are forthcoming. Could the suicide have been justified in any morally acceptable way? Could it have been explained away as an unfortunate accident? Would the person concerned have committed suicide in any case? In addition to the moral dilemmas, there are a number of practical questions that would need answering. What kind of training and qualifications did the two encounter-group therapists have in running such groups? Did they hold a legitimate, recognized training qualification? Did they have any awareness of how a situation seemingly tranquil could suddenly become turbulent, leading to the possible death of a person? Did they have the experience to anticipate the potential risks in running such training sessions? Had they taken into serious consideration the moral issues underlying their work? Alas, we shall never know. It is of course possible that the entire session may have gone smoothly, receiving flattering accolades from the participants. But the point is, it didn't!

This form of ignorance is dangerous. It raises several major issues: the training of such types of counsellors, their knowledge of human understanding, their experience in handling large groups, a clear understanding of the theoretical model (if any) on which their training was founded, and so on. I have searched the field and have been unable to get a clear account of the *testable* theoretical basis of this form of work. Nor have I been able to obtain any clear, unequivocal evidence concerning its validity. Over the years, I have become extremely wary, even partly hostile to popular approaches to solving deep-rooted human problems. Such forms of therapies (if they can be called as such) can inadvertently damage one's health, not cure it. Sadly, in a free-market economy, where 'consumer is king', there does not appear to be a way by which such untested and potentially dangerous therapies can be put to flames, as David Hume, the Scottish philosopher, would have suggested.

In the last 20 years or so, the course of counselling, psychotherapy, and other forms of treatment of psychological disorders has undergone a change. The *'freedom from'* model to a large extent has changed into a *'freedom to'* model. The impetus to construe health from a genuine *'freedom to'* or the growth model of health has come from a movement within psychology, best referred to as positive psychology.

One of the pioneers who has ushered in the *'freedom to'* approach in health is Martin Seligman, who has formulated what is grandiosely referred to as the *'new science of positive psychology'*. Martin Seligman's initial research interests were in the field of what he referred to as *'learned helplessness'* (Seligman, 1975, 1991, 1993).

In keeping with the behaviourist paradigm, he argued that stress produces feelings of helplessness. His theory rests on three interlocking factors: (1) when a predicted outcome in the environment is beyond one's control; (2) the cessation of those responses, which do not produce the desired reinforcements; and (3) the generalized cognitive belief that no voluntary action can control the outcome. He suggests that the theory of learned helplessness is also a theory of achievement. When repeated attempts to achieve the desired reinforcements fail, one begins to see oneself as being helpless. This feeling of helplessness impedes progress. People achieve less – in school, in sports, in work and in physical health. He believes that pessimists who experience helplessness become sick and may perhaps die earlier than optimists.

Furthermore, learned helplessness creates three deficits. The first is motivational, when a person in a state of helplessness makes no effort to change the outcome. Second, helpless persons fail to learn new responses. And third, helplessness leads to feelings of depression (Seligman, Klein, & Miller, 1974). He carried out several remarkable studies on dogs – in the Skinnerian behaviourist tradition – and demonstrated how, through the use of carefully monitored positive and negative reinforcements, the behaviours of the dogs could be changed in predicted directions. Seligman's theoretical orientations too were not dissimilar to Skinner's notions of environmental determinism, although he did concede that cognitive factors and the role of genetic inheritance could not be ruled out in bringing about (or failing to bring about) behavioural changes.

Seligman's theory, as was stated above, springs from a behaviourist paradigm. It is not as unique as it appears to sound at first sight. When one turns away from a behaviourist paradigm and examines the construct from a cognitive social psychological perspective, one can trace its similarity to the idea of the 'self-fulfilling prophecy', which was first propounded by Sophocles in his great play, *Oedipus*, and subsequently over the centuries by others. Karl Popper refers to this as the 'Oedipus effect'. In the 1950s, several social psychologists, including Gordon Allport (1954), promoted similar ideas, the central theme of which was that 'expectations often determine outcomes'. If one expects to fail, one often does, and one often succeeds when one expects to succeed. Rosenthal and Jacobson's classic study (1968) on school children – and their fluctuating scores on intelligence tests – demonstrated the validity of the notion of the self-fulfilling prophecy.

Seligman has argued that for the past 50 years or so professional psychology had been obsessed with examining *what was wrong with people* – their emotional life, their relationships, their feelings of sorrow, despair, loneliness, and unhappiness. The *'freedom from'* model of health and illness was the norm to which virtually all psychiatrists clinical psychologists, psychotherapists, counsellors, and 'healers' subscribed. What was ignored and not given serious consideration was the reverse side of human unhappiness: namely, happiness. He felt that it was important for psychologists to study the nature of human happiness – what it means to be happy, what makes for good, healthy, and happy persons (how they differ from persons who are sad, depressed, and unhappy), the manner in which they function, their styles of relating to themselves and to the world, and how such happiness can be achieved. His pioneering research endeavours in the field of positive psychology have had a sizeable impact on research within this area, creating a small industry of adherents who have followed his lead and have written on a variety of subjects, which in some way or other are related to positive psychology.

His present work in positive psychology has by no means gone unchallenged. The challenges, as is to be expected, have come from familiar sources: humanistic psychologists, followers of Rogerian client-centred therapy, supporters of Abraham Maslow, Rollo May, and other existential therapists who claim that they had been involved in this kind of work well before Seligman came into the frame. There is a feeling among many therapists that what is important in his work is not new, and what is new in his work is not important. In addition to the humanistic critics, there are others from within academic psychology who have argued that positive psychology, despite its grandiose claims, can hardly be referred to as a scientific discipline. They are critical of the empirical strategies which the researchers have employed – their over-concern with questionnaires, rating scales, personality tests, and such other measuring devices.

They are also critical of the rather ambiguous and indefinite meanings that the researchers have assigned to terms and concepts of positive psychology. And finally, because a large number of Seligman's followers have jumped on the 'positive psychology bandwagon', their research interests, their theoretical assumptions, methodological approaches are extremely diverse and hence not easily commensurable. Although they all refer to the general concept *positive psychology* with its several variants, for example, optimism, happiness, authentic happiness, autonomy, assertiveness, and so on, one is left wondering if they are all engaged in a unified research enterprise and are in any way talking about similar issues. (One hardly needs reminding that a rose by any other name does *not* smell as sweet – despite what the romantic poet Gertrude Stein might have had to say!)

The current *'freedom to'* health type of research can be criticized from four epistemological perspectives:

1   Lack of a unified research paradigm.
2   Misplaced emphasis on empirical research.
3   Falsification – the ideal goal of scientific research.
4   Conflating reliability with validity.

Let us discuss each of them briefly.

Lack of a unified research paradigm

One of the major criticisms of research into positive psychology is that *it suffers from a lack of a clearly formulated, clearly defined research paradigm to which all research workers would willingly subscribe* – such as the one proposed by Thomas Kuhn (1996, 1998). Research in positive psychology has not acquired the status of what the late Thomas Kuhn referred to as 'normal science'. Progress in the chosen field of investigation occurs when scientists work within the paradigm. Conflicts arise when serious anomalies begin to appear in the research findings of the scientists, leading to a crisis of confidence in the paradigm. The crisis gradually gets resolved when a paradigm shift – a 'gestalt switch' – occurs. This then leads to the inception of a new paradigm, and the scientists once again begin to work within the parameters of the new paradigm. Working outside a clearly formulated unified paradigm, according to Kuhn, militates against any form of commensurability and leads to a state of epistemological anarchy. The field of positive psychology – interesting and even in many ways exciting – lacks a unified research paradigm. It is not surprising that research in this area tends to be ad hoc idiosyncratic, and bitty. And one knows from the research of the earlier post-war gestalt psychologists (Kohler, Koffka, and Wertheimer) that the 'whole' is always greater than the sum of its parts, suggesting that all bits and pieces of research added together rarely, if ever, present a comprehensive meaningful picture.

Misplaced emphasis on empirical research

Popper (1963) points out that empirical investigations in the absence of clearly formulated theoretical constructs need to be tempered with intuitions, hunches, guesses, and conjectures, which may subsequently help in formulating a more rigorous theory. It is clear therefore that all methodologies – from the crudest, involving a simple head-count, to the most sophisticated, namely the use of advanced measuring instruments currently used in experimental research – need to assume a conceptual framework of some kind or other. One needs to ensure that one does not construct complex methodological systems without having some awareness of the reasons underlying their usage and their feasibility.

Blind empiricism, regardless of how accurately and perfectly the accumulated facts and data may have been gathered, does not lead to objective scientific knowledge (the tail, as we know, does not wag the dog.) The telephone directory is an empirically gathered factual, precise document. It offers the most precise information. So is a railway timetable. But by no stretch of imagination can they be referred as being scientific. There are several areas of empirical investigations which lie completely outside the realms of science (Gjertsen, 1989).

Falsification – the ideal goal of scientific research

In contradistinction to popular thinking, Karl Popper (1972) argues that *our confidence in a theory increases when we fail to disconfirm our hypothesis.* Researchers, in general, shy away from seeking *disconfirmations.* They are all concerned with seeking confirmations of their hypotheses – or what is grandiosely referred to as 'evidence-based research'. But as Popper has pointed out, it is not so much the confirmation of hypotheses that matters in terms of establishing the validity of a theory. *It is failure to disconfirm a hypothesis that lends greater support to the validity of a hypothesis.* In other words, one should be actively engaged in trying to falsify our hypotheses instead of finding confirming evidence to our hypotheses. Confirmatory evidence is largely correlational, seldom causal, as several epistemologists have argued.

Paradoxically, confirmatory evidence of a hypothesis is not difficult to obtain. One can cite several Freudian theoretical concepts (for example, reaction formation, introjection, denial) which can be interpreted in mutually contradictory ways. But there is a serious flaw with such an approach.

First, as David Hume the great Scottish philosopher pointed out, even an unequivocal verification of a given hypotheses does not allow one to go 'beyond' the finding and make statements of a general nature. One can never be certain that *a* leads to *b*, or that *b* follows from *a*. All one has established is an observed relationship between *a* and *b*, and not that *b* is caused by *a*. Equally importantly, there is no guarantee that the same finding would be replicated on subsequent occasions, ad infinitum. To expect that is to expect a continuity of consistency – that tomorrow will be an exact replication of today, and today is the same as yesterday. There are no logical grounds for making such a prediction. Such an expectation or prediction leads us into an inductive trap, which David Hume drew the world's attention to. There appears to be no way of getting out of the inductive fallacy. Bertrand Russell (1912, 1946/1961) defends induction, but he does so by shifting from the high ground of timeless certainty to the low ground of probability, for example, it is highly probable that the sun will rise tomorrow, but it is by no means *certain* that the sun will rise tomorrow. Several unknown factors could intervene – a hurtling meteor, which could upset the operation of the laws of motion, for example.

Second, logically there may be an infinite number of hypotheses which could explain the prediction. One might argue that the practice of Indian forms of meditation 'lead to' beneficial consequences – lowering of one's blood pressure, a slowing down of one's heart rate, feelings of wellbeing, tranquillity, and so on. However, similar responses may also be obtained by other variables. There is also a reverse feature to this side of the argument. Instead of obtaining the expected or predicted relationship, one may actually obtain an *unpredicted* or *unintended* relationship. A meditating person may experience fear, claustrophobia, boredom, aches and pains, and so on.

It is clear, therefore, that an unwillingness to consider the fundamental episte-mological problems related to scientific research leaves the researcher vulnerable to indefensible criticisms. Many of the research studies within this area are ad hoc, idiosyncratic, naïve and so ill-conceived that to refer to them as 'theories' is to insult the divine origin of the Greek term *Theo* from which the term 'theory' is derived.

Conflating reliability with validity

I believe it is important not to forget the very important lesson which Imre Lakatos (1978), the eminent philosopher, taught us several years ago, namely that neither the popularity of a theory nor a high degree of consensus among its prac-titioners guarantees its value or validity. He points out that a theory may be valu-able even if no one believes in it, and it may be without any value even if everyone believes in it. Consensus, as we know, is a measure of reliability and not of valid-ity. A thousand-year consensual belief in Ptolmey's geocentric model of the Universe was struck a fatal blow by Galileo, and was replaced by the heliocentric model of the Universe, first articulated by Copernicus. In other words, the value or the validity of a theory is independent of its popularity and its reliability – and even more importantly, independent of the mind that created the theory. Let us now leave behind the epistemological issues related to the testing of theories and their role in generating objective knowledge and consider the nature of positive psychology from a cross-cultural perspective.

The cross-cultural model of health, happiness, and illness

Western conceptions of happiness

Do the salient concepts of positive psychology, for example, happiness, feeling good, optimism, freedom, autonomy, confidence, assertiveness, self-expression, and so on, share the same meanings and values when examined from a non-Western perspective? Can the meanings of the concepts be interchanged, transferred from one culture to another? Many concepts, which form part of the Seligman band-wagon are of little relevance when seen from an Eastern cultural perspective. In the West, happiness is generally construed in behavioural terms. It is seen in terms of individual effort and achievement. As the common phrase goes, 'one works towards being happy'. Happiness is seen as an acquisition. One acquires it through effort, as a person might a fortune, or a skill. Western psychologists as we know, in their desire to turn psychology into a science, discarded notions of internal mental states, consciousness, from their research vocabularies. In so doing they also got rid of concepts such as an inner state of quiescence, tranquillity, a sense of inner peace, and so on. Happiness in Western society is also perceived from an individualistic perspective, which emphasizes gaining self-esteem, which is then related to self-confidence, one's ability 'to express and assert oneself', being 'materially and financially comfortable', being 'successful', being 'attractive', being independent, having friends with whom one can share one's joys and happiness, being equal (if not more equal) to others, being treated with respect and courtesy, being able to exercise one's inalienable rights, being able to enjoy the pleasures which life has to offer, being able to travel, take holidays, afford luxuries, and so forth. A happy person needs also to be seen as being happy – akin to conspicuous consumption. The danger with such an approach is that happiness, like wealth, turns into a consumable commodity. How different the cotemporary Western conception of happiness is from the ancient Greek approach to happiness, as the last lines of the chorus in Oedipus The King, demonstrate:

> Therefore, while our eyes wait to see the destined final day,
> We must call no one happy who is of mortal race,
> Until he hath crossed life's border, free from pain.

Sophocles: Oedipus the King

Eastern conceptions of happiness

Happiness in Eastern cultures including India, Pakistan, Bangladesh, Sri Lanka, Tibet, Nepal, and South East Asia, and even in parts of China, is best understood as an internal state of mind, a state of peace and quiescence. How is such a peaceful internal state of mind achieved? The following factors cohere to create this mental state.

Religious beliefs and practices

Easterners in general tend to see the vicissitudes of life in religious and cosmic terms (Herman, 1976). At a spiritual level their daily life is seen as a continuous struggle between good and evil, purity and pollution, duty and desire, and sin and atonement. In one's relationship to God, the spiritual duties one is expected to perform include a vast number of rites and rituals, which include prayers, devotion to God, doing one's expected duty, ensuring the welfare of one's children, and so on. Among Hindus and Buddhists for instance, it is important to live one's life in accordance with one's dharma (which loosely translated, means 'duty'). One needs to perform one's duty with complete detachment. Duty needs to be performed for its own sake. Even young children are socialized into and expected to participate in all the religious ceremonies that are performed at home and in temples and on days of festivity.

One of the unique features of Hinduism (see Chapter 5) is the impact that the Hindu belief in the law of karma has on the development and formation of the Hindu psyche. The law of karma allows a Hindu to accept with passivity and fortitude the vicissitudes of *life as part of one's karmic reactions to one's actions in one's past birth(s)*. Thus, sorrow, suffering, illness, health, misfortune are explained in the inexorable workings of the law of karma.

To Muslims, happiness results from submitting to the will of Allah. One learns from childhood to obey the will of Allah by following the teachings of the Koran. In obedience lies happiness, in disobedience, pain, suffering, and sorrow. All devout Muslims are also expected to observe and perform all the required rites and rituals found in the Koran (Esposito, 1998; Farah, 1994).

Among the Buddhists too there is a strong belief that suffering is part of the human condition. No one is free from suffering. The reasons for human suffering are articulated in Buddha's exposition of the Four Noble Truths. But suffering, although part of the human condition, is avoidable by following the eight-fold path (*ashtha-marga*) which, when pursued with faith, diligence, and non-attachment, leads to an inner state of wellbeing and also enables the person to transcend the sorrows and sufferings of life and eventually attain a state of nirvana (Batchelor, 1994; Eckel, 2003; Klostermaier, 1999; Rahula, 1997). At a material, physical level too their daily life is an unceasing struggle for survival. Religion provides some comfort. Religion to the Hindus, the Muslims, and the Buddhists acts as their protective shield.

We have seen that the pursuit of happiness in Eastern cultures is intimately entwined with religious beliefs and practices. One of the rare exceptions is to be found in the ancient Chinese philosophy of Confucianism. Let us spend a few exciting moments understanding the main tenets of Confucianism, which along with Taoism and Buddhism has been the most influential systems of thought in China for centuries and remain even today an important part of Chinese civilization (Finagrette, 1972; Oldstone-Moore, 2003; Wei-Ming, 1985). The main focus of Confucianism is on creating social harmony and responsibility in human society, ordered along hierarchical lines. The need for harmony is seen to be of greater importance than individual freedom and rights. Confucius observed that for a society to live in harmony, peace, and in happiness, it was necessary that the relationship between the parent and child were founded on obligations of filial piety – honour, respect, love, and service owed between parent and child. The parent–child relationship is the template for all other relationships – even that of the government to its polity in creating a harmonious society, a virtuous, ethical, and benevolent state. An ordered, harmonious society could only come into being when each member of society played his or her part appropriately and with good intent.

The concept of *yin* and *yang* plays a key role in understanding Confucian philosophy. According to ancient Chinese cosmology, everything that exists in the cosmos is made up of *qi* (vital matter, life energy, or life force), which is manifest in two complementary forces – *yin and yang*. Yin denotes that which is dark, moist, and feminine and yang denotes that which is bright, dry, and masculine. It was believed that all things consist of yin and yang in varying proportions.

In the last two or three decades there has been a resurgence of interest in Confucian teachings, which has now spread to other countries including Japan, Korea, Vietnam, Taiwan, Singapore, and several other countries in East Asia. Oldstone-Moore (2003), points out that 'Confucianism has been identified as the vital part of the mixture that has contributed to the booming economies of East Asia in recent decades' (p. 21).

Familial and communal factors

Eastern cultures to a large extent are family oriented. Since life revolves round one's family, one's extended family, and one's community, there is an expectation that the performance of familial, social, religious, and caste-related duties leads to an inner spiritual growth. To see one's children grow and develop into responsible beings, to have one's children handsomely married, to take upon oneself to impart the teachings of the scriptures to one's children and grandchildren, to relinquish the reins of one's control as head of family to one's children and withdraw from material aspirations, to lead a life of detachment from worldly materialism, to look after and care for the elderly at home, to achieve a mental state of peace, tranquillity, and harmony through meditation, yogic exercises and non-involvement – all such activities are sources of great joy and happiness and health. Failure to live one's life in accordance with the Hindu scriptures or the dictates of the Koran and the Buddhist teachings may lead to sorrow, grief, and illness.

Several factors may account for the onset of illnesses. One of them is caste contamination. Illness and misfortune may occur due to caste contamination (marrying outside one's caste), through spiritual pollution, through the workings of the law of karma, by the vengeance of the gods for evils perpetrated, planetary perturbations, and so on. In addition to the law of karma, there is among Asians a strong belief in magical or supernatural explanations of illness, which can be brought about by the influence of malevolent demons and spirits acting upon one's life for real or imagined misdemeanours.

When contrasting the Hindu, Buddhist, and Islamic views with those of the ancient Greeks and Romans and Christians, and with contemporary Western approaches, one notices a startling difference. All the above religions adopt, each in its unique way, a holistic approach to health and illness. They have never sought to see the human body as a thing apart. As Hippocrates had proclaimed, 'it is more important to know what sort of a person has a disease than to know what sort of a disease a person has'. In treating the person suffering from a disease, every attempt is also made to take the impact of one's culture on understanding the nature of the illness and the indigenous methods that are used to bring about a cure. The attitudes of Western countries to indigenous methods of treatment was, at best, one of condescension, and at worst, of dismissal. But the tide, though slow, appears to be turning. It is refreshing to note that many enlightened therapists and counsellors in the West have sought to promote a dialogue between the two groups, and it is hoped that the West and the East over time will come closer and start to learn from one another's theoretical approaches and therapeutic strategies, which also include shamans, witch doctors, priests, faith-healers, palmists, fortune-tellers, exorcists, *pirs*, *bhagats*, and a variety of other indigenous healers all over the world (Al-Issa & Al-Subaie, 2004; Launagani, 2005c; Moodley, 2005; Smith, 2005; Pankhania, 2005; Rubin, 2004).

I do not wish to convey that Eastern and Western cultures are sharply divided on all issues. There are a vast areas of commonalities shared by all cultures all over the world. Human beings are not only divided by their differences but are also united by many of their similarities. All cultures are living organisms. They grow, develop, change, decay, and some, like the Hellenic cultures and the Roman Empire of the past centuries, die. All cultures inherit their own unique philosophical, religious, social, and spiritual legacies of the past, which they weave into their contemporary way of life. All cultures create their own social ecological, political, legal, ethical, moral, and religious systems. All cultures have valuable lessons to learn from and teach other cultures. It is through such interchange of differences and diversities, common cares and concerns, that life around the world as a whole becomes meaningful and is enriched.

Although human beings learn to live in relative peace and harmony with peoples of other cultures, they also rebel and take arms against other cultures. Past and present history points out that human beings are perhaps the only species that finds it difficult to live not only with themselves, but also with one another. Human beings to a large extent are the only species that kills for fun, pleasure, and profit. Human beings are perhaps the only species that imprisons, incarcerates, tortures, and executes people in their millions, who hold beliefs and worship gods that are different from those of their captors.

One of the greatest 'levellers' of humanity is the fact that we *all* experience illness, both physical and mental, pain, distress, loss, sorrow, bereavement, and so on. No culture has ever been successful in eliminating such conditions permanently. Each culture also acquires its own traditions, which enable them to formulate their own culture-specific, health-related systems that explain health and illness in all its forms.

Each cultural 'cookie' crumbles in its own way and therefore strikes a blow at universal or etic constructions of health, illness and happiness. Western psychologists, eager to turn their discipline into a science of psychology, have always been keen to discover *universalistic patterns of behaviours in people across the world*. But their attempts in a large number of cases have resulted in constructing emic (culture-specific) measures, which subsequently by sleight of hand are passed off or imposed as etic (universal) measures (Paranjpe, 1998). Some Western psychologists engaged in this kind of research will perhaps be the last to recognize the emperor without clothes.

In broad terms the divergent approaches to health, happiness, and illness between Eastern and Western cultures can be explained in terms of two major factors: individualism and communalism; and the age-old conflict between faith (religion) and reason. Although the conflict between individualism and communalism has been explained at length in Chapter 5, let us consider it from a different perspective and then examine the factor related to faith and reason.

The foundations of the philosophy of individualism, as we know, were laid during the fifteenth, sixteenth and seventeenth centuries, which ushered in the glorious Enlightenment era in Europe. Individualism legitimized the relationship between the individual and the state, which recognized and guaranteed to uphold the rights (and duties) of individuals to pursue their own interests that included free speech, occupation, ambitions, religious and/or secular beliefs, acquiring property, free trade, and other interests, not to mention the exploration, exploitation, and the conquest of other nations. Philosophers such as Locke, Hume, Adam Smith, and others promoted the view that human beings had a natural right to independent existence, free speech, and pursuit of their self-interests. Kant saw the Enlightenment period as man's emergence from his self-incurred immaturity. Individualism brought about liberation from the constraints imposed by what until then had been a traditional society. There are several other virtues one could catalogue, which thrust Europe from its medieval state to one of great progress in the arts, literature, sciences, medicine, trade, and economic competition, and of course military warfare. Unfettered greed and the desire for wealth and power led to warfare and conquests of other countries. Even human personality came to be defined by personal choice, desire, and ambition and the capacity of self-transformation (Laungani, 2005a).

However, despite the fresh air of freedom which the Enlightenment era brought in, there were problems: Adam Smith pointed out that the pursuit of power, wealth, and free trade was unlikely to *immunize* people against fear, sorrow, disease, and death. If anything, individualism created its own monsters: it alienated people from one another, it weakened and in many instances destroyed traditions.

Conflict between faith and reason

The conflict between faith and reason came to a head during the later Enlightenment period in eighteenth century, when the hegemony of religion came to be questioned (Grayling, 2003). Lives, it was argued, could be bettered by applying the lessons of science. Several philosophers, scientists, writers, poets, literary figures, painters, artists, and musicians and other intellectuals including Fermat,

Spinoza, Locke, Shakespeare, Cervantes, Milton, Rubens, Vivaldi, and several others endorsed this view that religion was a barrier to intellectual development.

Secularism gradually came to be recognized and accepted as the ruling philosophy in most Western democracies. Among many of its splendid attributes, it extols the virtues of human rationality. At a personal level, I must confess I have reservations about the proclaimed virtues of rationality. Consequently, I am critical of the condescending manner in which the notion of faith in human affairs is dismissed by the rationalists and the secularists in the West. Coming as I do from an Eastern Hindu culture, brought up as I was with more than a lukewarm belief in the powers of faith, I find it hard to give up one for the other. There is, in my own philosophy, room for a rapprochement between faith and reason. Let me explain.

Human rationality is eminently desirable. It is prized greatly. Rationality enables us to understand and make sense of our lives, of the lives of others and of the world around us in a logical, ordered, and a relatively predictable way. Rationality allows us to differentiate between right and wrong, good and bad, fact and fiction, myth and reality, and so on. Rationality helps to solve a variety of scientific, technological, social, economic, and human problems. Human rationality presents us with choice. It embodies within it the notion of free will. We are free to choose. In fact Jean Paul Sartre (1966), the existential philosopher, points out that human beings are *condemned* to be free. He warns us, though, that the freedom to choose comes at a heavy price. Our ability to choose freely gives us an edge over fate. Rationality thus serves as a strong guide to lead the 'good life'. When used judiciously it prevents us from engaging in behaviours and actions which are injurious to ourselves, to others, and in extreme cases to societies and cultures as a whole. Rationality also teaches us tolerance, respect and acceptance of others. The virtues of rationality are virtually endless. All the major philosophers in the world from the pre-Socratic, the rationalists, including Descartes, Kant, and others, right up to the present, have extolled the virtues of rationalism.

However, the question is, do human beings live by reason alone? This is an important question and merits a detailed answer.

1   It is not being suggested that human beings are incapable of living by reason – they most certainly are! But to live by reason, to put reason at the forefront of all one's thoughts, and actions – from the trivial to the profound – would require the kind of eternal vigilance which most people would find difficult, if not impossible, to sustain. This type of exclusivity, which the proponents of rationality hark after, although grandiose in its conceptualization, is a myth.

2   The other interesting conundrum which rationalists may find difficult to resolve is how they would attempt to bring their emotions under rational control, or bring about reconciliation between the two.

3   Even among those who claim to be rationalists, one would be more than likely
    to find several persons who are faith-driven, 'believers', regular church goers and
    those who perform sacraments, observe Lent, and participate in all the Christian
    rites and rituals related to birth, marriage, and death. Such beliefs and practices
    undoubtedly create some cognitive dissonance between reason and faith.

   Let us now speculate on what would happen if the Western world were to
operate on a strict Kantian philosophy of secular rationalism:

i   The superstructure of Freudian psychoanalysis with all the additional wings
     which have been added to it by the untiring efforts of its ardent disciples over the
     last 100 years would, like the walls of Jericho, come crashing down to the ground!
     It was Freud, one might recall, who shattered the myth of rationality in human
     affairs, and emphasized the ubiquitous power – creative and destructive – of
     irrational forces, buried within one's unconscious! Although Freudian theories
     to a certain extent have been ignored and even discarded by the 'scientifically
     orientated psychologists' they have, by no means died a death or become
     extinct like the dodo or the dinosaur. No one thus far, not even Eysenck in his
     book, *Decline and Fall of the Freudian Empire* (1985), succeeded in bringing
     down the Freudian Empire! Freud made it clear that human irrationality,
     which may also include faith, plays as important a part in our lives, as does
     rationality. Arthur Koestier, in his book, *The Lotus and the Robot* (1966), had
     remarked that no man remains a saint for 24 hours of the day. Similarly, it
     seems 'reasonable' to suggest that no man (or woman) remains a rationalist for
     24 hours of the day.
ii   It would be difficult, even impossible, to explain behaviours such as violence,
     crime, murder, corruption, greed, child abuse, suicide, mental illness, depres-
     sion, alcoholism, teenage pregnancies, drug addiction, AIDS, obesity and
     several other ills which plague Western society. Surely rationality ought to be
     able to combat these destructive forces in their own societies! Even more to
     the point, it is impossible to explain why countries, which pride themselves on
     their models of rationality, would drop atomic bombs on Hiroshima and
     Nagasaki, vaporizing more than a quarter of a million innocent people!
     Or those who would carry out mass cremations in specially constructed gas
     chambers of millions of *living beings* in Europe!
iii Although this sounds like hyperbole, one does wonder what alternative occu-
     pations counsellors, psychotherapists, psychiatrists, healers, mystics, fortune-
     tellers, astrologers, hypnotists, gurus, and others would need to find in the
     absence of clients.

   Human life is a curious mixture of rationality, and irrationality, logic and intuition, whims and wishes. In fact a large number of the beliefs and behaviours that

we live by are untested and unverified, and if they were to be put to a critical test they would turn out to be non-rational, even irrational.

Is there a 'rational' answer to explain such irrationalities? The term rationality when examined searchingly often seems like a meaningless *mantra*. Perhaps a more rational way of understanding rationality in human affairs is to see it as an *ideal,* which people attempt to aspire to. An ideal, not unlike a utopia, is not easily attainable, if at all. An attempt to achieve the ideal, it must be stated, notwithstanding the above criticisms, is far more visible in Western nations than in the developing countries at present.

What about faith, you might ask. Does it fare better? Does it fulfil the promises which rationality has failed to deliver? Once again the answer is no. Faith, as we know, is understood in religious and supernatural terms (Ahmed, 1993; Esposito, 1998). Hindus explain it in terms of the law of karma, the Muslims in terms of the will of Allah, and so on. Fate is a strongly held belief that both the intended and the unintended consequences of our actions are determined by fate. I personally do not share the divine and supernatural meanings attached to faith. I disown such explanations.

Faith, without invoking its mystical and religious connotations, may be construed as a firm belief held by an individual in his or her ability to succeed in a chosen activity despite the odds against them. While reason may prompt caution, a person driven by faith heeds not such promptings and goes ahead regardless of the consequences. A few examples from literature might convey the meaning more clearly. George Orwell, who was dying of tuberculosis, completed his novel *1984* from his deathbed. Had he but listened to the voice of reason, the chances are the world would have been deprived of a great piece of literature. There have been writers and artists, musicians and composers, warriors and conquerors, explorers and mountaineers, who have gone far, far beyond the bounds of rationality and proceeded to accomplish their chosen goals. Many of the great works of fiction – *The Old Man and the Sea, Moby Dick, Robinson Crusoe, Sidharatha, The Divine Comedy, Faust, The Iliad, Anna Karenina, King Oedipus, Prometheus Bound, Don Quixote* to name but a few, deal with characters who despite the insurmountable odds against them have achieved – or died in their attempts to achieve – their chosen goals. Such persons are never defeated. They may be destroyed, but they are never defeated. Their achievements are frighteningly awe-inspiring. There is nobility and grandeur in their actions. Faith mocks at reason. It cuts across time. It scoffs at cultural boundaries and barriers. It unites them with others of their kind across the world. The world is eternally beholden to them. Their legacies never die.

To highlight the influence of faith on our understanding of health and illness, let me present you with a vignette.

Box 9.3

Let us imagine that you and I have come to India to visit the major holy cities of India, not as pilgrims but as 'seekers of knowledge' of Eastern cultures. We are now in Varanasi (or Banaras, as it was known during the days of the British Raj). It is winter. Our warm jumpers, anoraks, and scarves notwithstanding, it is bitterly cold. As we stroll along the ghats whose steps lead down to the river Ganges, we see the first rays of the sun painting the river with its wondrous red glow. Despite the piercing cold we notice hundreds of worshippers – men, women, and children, and even infants in arms – offering their pre-dawn prayers to the pantheon of Hindu gods. They appear to be unperturbed and unaffected by the cold and the vagrant wind ruffling the waves of the river.

As we stand there watching the worshippers, the smell of burning flesh from an early morning cremation assails our nostrils. In the distance, at the bottom of the steps, stands a group of mourners, all dressed in their funereal white. The entire panoply of life in its myriad forms – from infancy to youth, from old age to death – confronts our disbelieving eyes. Presently we notice an extremely frail and aged man being led by two youngsters down the steep stone steps of the ghats to the river. They pause at each step for the old man to regain his breath. On reaching the edge of the river, the youngsters help the old man to remove his clothes. His body shivers uncontrollably as he wades his way gingerly into the river. The old man scoops up the water in the palm of his hands, looks up 'heavenwards', offers a prayer, recites a few verses, and pours the water back into the river. The youngsters offer him a garland of marigolds, which he offers to the gods; the garland floats away with the tide. Gradually, they make their way back to the foot of the ghat, where they help the old man to dress. With slow, measured, painful steps they help him to climb the stone steps until they reach the top of the ghat.

Interpretation of Box 9.3

Observing the above scene, one would be tempted to inquire: are the people not aware that they could catch their death of cold and even contract pneumonia? Have they no concept of what their exposure could do to their health? How could they take such insane risks? How could they 'tempt' fate? Are they not aware too that the Ganges, like many other rivers in India, is polluted and one could easily pick up serious and even life-threatening illnesses?

I have witnessed this scene on several different occasions in several holy cities of India. On each occasion, like you, I have never ceased to wonder what motivates people to perform such arduous austerities and religious rituals with a contemptuous disregard of the inherent dangers to which they expose themselves. What is it that drives them? Examining this form of behaviour from a rationalist philosophical perspective, one would be inclined to concede that this form of behaviour is irrational and even self-destructive. *But to dismiss this behaviour as a form of irrationality, without endeavouring to understand*

(Continued)

the philosophical, spiritual, and the socio-cultural issues that underlie and guide such actions, is to resort to sterile stereotypes which impede our genuine understanding of cross-cultural differences. Such ill-informed prejudgements are not in keeping with the open and free mind of scientific and Socratic inquiry.

The above vignette gives us a brief glimpse into the way in which people from India and other Eastern countries construe problems of health and illness. Dunking one's body in ice-cold waters, which by all accounts are polluted, is not seen as a health hazard. It is seen as a spiritually cleansing and uplifting activity. Unless one's life was guided and governed by fate it would be impossible to imagine the old, the weak, the frail, and the infirm, waking up in the early hours of the morning in the bitter, piercing cold, climbing down the steps of the ghats and plunging into the icy waters of the Ganges to offer their prayers to the gods. It is their unshakeable faith that keeps them going. But for the power of faith, it would be impossible to understand the daily austerities, the daily rituals, the daily sacrifices they perform with unfailing regularity. Ganges, although seen as a holy river, is polluted. One cannot imagine that a person guided by rationality would wish to undertake such arduous austerities.

Conclusion

We have travelled a long way and have covered a vast territory. We have seen that the West and the East are separated not just by oceans but also by vast stretches of religious, cultural, and philosophical landscapes. It would seem that Westerners have discarded faith in preference to secular rationality. But the galloping resurgence of religious teachings, the concerted opposition to Darwinian theory, the implementation of creationist policies in many states in America, would suggest that God and religion have not been completely abandoned. People from Eastern cultures, in hedging their bets, have arrived at a compromise. Faith plays a major role in the their daily lives and reason allows them to understand, engage, and share in all the scientific, technological, and economic developments around the world. Faith and reason, like *dooa* (prayer), and *dava* (medicine) appear to go together, creating not the slightest dissonance in their lives. At a day-to-day level they are guided more by reason. But at a familial, communal, and social level they tend to entrust themselves to the workings of fate.

Reason without faith inhibits action, and, like Hamlet's conscience, may make cowards of us of all. Faith without reason can become tyrannical. Faith and reason together are the two sides of the coin of life. There is great power in faith, just as there is in reason. Reason may solve problems but faith may go a step further and conquer what reason forbids. The question that for the present remains unanswered is this: can faith and reason be reconciled to form a synthesis? This is the heart-rending dilemma that faces the world.

Death and Bereavement: Cross-Cultural Perspectives

I don't mind dying, but I don't want to be there when it happens!

Woody Allen

Death is so easy we can all do it lying down!

Woody Allen

Imagine you were commissioned to undertake a large-scale survey of people all over the world as to what they feared most. Would it surprise you if you found that the fear of death would win comprehensively over all other fears? Woody Allen has certainly got it right in the above quotes, both of which are wickedly funny. Be not deceived, though. On probing deeply – particularly into the first quote – one notices a dark, sombre and even a sinister side to it. It re-echoes a common universal attitude to death. Fear. Terrifying, paralysing, bone-marrow-freezing fear. Its very utterance unleashes its own demons – demons, which one can neither vanquish nor flee from. The demons haunt us. The demons taunt us. They will not let us be. There is no avoiding them, no escaping them. Wisdom lies in accepting and coming to terms with their inexorable merciless power, and when the time comes, submitting to it with dignity and fortitude.

Death is a universal phenomenon. As a wit has remarked, life is a terminal disease. Death comes to us all. And as Woody Allen has remarked, hardly anyone ever dies standing up. When it comes, it is final, irreversible. The dead cannot be brought back to life although each religion offers its own hopes of an after-life. On the day of judgment, proclaim the Christians, the dead shall rise from their graves. The Muslims too believe in the day of judgement – *qauamat*. The Hindus, in accordance with the law of karma, believe that death marks the end of one life and the beginning of another, thus forming a part of a series of lives and deaths, births and rebirths. Ideas of rebirth and after-life are abstract notions. Although such notions offer some hope of an after-life, they do not necessarily help us to accept our own mortality. Yet death is around us everywhere. But we see it with unseeing eyes. Hardly a day passes without our reading about it, seeing it on television, in the cinema, hearing about it, talking about it as it slips in and out of the caverns of our consciousness. None of us – at least at a cognitive level – is a stranger to death. All that lives must one day die. We know in our heads and even in our hearts that death occurs. Our neighbours die, our pets die, animals, birds, insects, bacteria die. Our friends die, even our loved ones die, societies get wiped out, bombs dropped from the skies obliterate cities, killing people in their thousands; tempests, typhoons, tornados, earthquakes, eruptions, explosions destroy communities in their thousands and thousands. Entire civilizations are erased. Even the stoutest of will, the greatest of the Caesars and the Pharaohs, kings and monarchs, heroes and conquerors, dictators and despots, saints and sinners submit to death's implacable command – its insatiable demand. No one is immune from death. It triumphs over us all.

Death also puts to an end all human pretensions to fame, health, wealth, success, happiness, immortality, and so on. William James (1902/1958), in his inimitable style, referred to death as 'the worm at the core'. Yet we all dearly wish to remain permanently estranged from its hold.

Given the indisputable certainty of death, is it not strange that the heart denies what the head affirms and knows to be true? Like the proverbial drowning man grasping at a straw, we too cling to the duplicitous belief that we shall not die. Somehow we shall survive, we say to ourselves. We shall live – and who knows – even forever! We continue to believe that others die, whereas we – that is, you and I – shall continue to live forever. This is one of our greatest self-delusional duplicities.

Paradoxically, we can even imagine what it is to die, what being dead means. We can even role-play at being dead. We can visualize being laid in a dark, suffocating, airless coffin, even hear the clods of earth dropping on the coffin as it is lowered into the ground. We can, if we put our mind to it, even smell the stench of our own body as it decays, turns rotten, and is feasted upon by armies of maggots crawling out of the damp earth, nibbling into our nostrils, eyes, ears, and other orifices. At some point, however, our imagination falters and reality takes over. We realize we are playing a morbid, grotesque game. For we know that not only are we not dead but, try as we might, we would be unable to *experience* being dead while still alive. Imagine it we can, experience it we can't. To *'experience'* death leads to an irreconcilable logical contradiction. With death all awareness ceases. One cannot be dead and alive at the same time. We can experience the process of dying: the pain, the suffering, the gradual shutting down of our bodily systems, but are unable to experience the final event, namely, our death.

The one question the world has never ceased to ask is, *why? Why, why, why* do we fear death? Why do we it push it aside, thrust it into the closeted layers of our unconscious? Why the idea of one's death should strike such universal terror is a universal mystery. All one can do is speculate – as many have done – and yet fail to come up with a valid answer. *We'd rather death died a permanent death and life went on forever.* According to Kubler-Ross (1969), the fear of death is a universal emotional experience. According to her, one can never prepare enough for one's death. People seldom talk about it, other than in hushed undertones. She felt that it was important to lift the 'shroud' off death and bring it out into the open so that people would not shy away from talking about it and contemplating on it. The mystique and the fear surrounding death would then decrease, if not disappear altogether. But would they, really?

One needs to look beyond the fact of dying to understand our fears of death. An analogy would help. Imagine dropping a tiny pebble into a pond. A ripple appears and in less than the blink of an eye it vanishes. Death too is like a pebble, which finally drops into a pond creating a ripple. How soon it vanishes depends on the size of the pebble, the force with which it drops, the height from which it drops, the depth, the calmness, or the turbulence of the pond. Some pebbles skim over the waters, creating a burst of short ripples before they too disappear and sink to the bottom. A few deaths leave their mark, the ripples creating their own waves; but all others disappear without trace. It is the disappearance that the human psyche is unable to comprehend and therefore unable to accept and come to terms with. Why should their death pass unnoticed, unrecognized, unsung, goes the lament. As though one had never existed. One does not wish to be forgotten. One wants to leave one's mark, one's 'footprints, on the sands of time'. One wants to be remembered not just by a few friends and relatives but by posterity and, hopefully, forever. We refuse to recognize and accept the fact that although we are part of the world in which we live, the world itself is indifferent, disinterested, and uncaring of our private wishes and desires of immortality. Not everyone can be a Shakespeare, a Michaelangelo, a Leonardo da Vinci, an Einstein, a Beethoven, a Tolstoy, or a Darwin. Such persons were 'blessed' with what Plato referred to as 'divine madness'. Why do *we* 'lesser mortals' (if I might be permitted to use the self-deprecating phrase) consider ourselves to be special beings? What is so precious about our lives?

In fact, the range of human suffering around the world – destitution, disease, infirmity, old age, poverty, sorrow, depression – is so vast and so terrifying that one might find reasons *not to want to live in the world*. Like the lemmings, one might wish to leap off mountaintops, bridges, spires, and buildings and put an end to all our suffering. But no, we continue to live and suffer. Whatever for, if for what lies at the end is nothing but nothingness?

Here, I feel a compelling need to share with you an experience I had several years ago in Madurai in the state of Tamil Nadu in India, which illustrates the above point.

Box 10.1

It was an extremely warm, airless, suffocating, sweltering summer afternoon. In slow measured steps, my wife and I ambled through the temple streets of Madurai in South India. We had spent the morning visiting the famous temples of Madurai, and were exhausted by the effort. We were in search of a restaurant where we could rest in air-conditioned bliss and order a few soft drinks to quench our thirst. The street along which we walked was crowded. Hawkers lining the pavements beckoned us with their wares. Taxi-drivers leaning on their horns solicited our custom. Pie dogs, overcome by heat, lay in the shade of trees. Beggars whined and pestered us. Cyclists dodged in and out of our path as we picked our way through the morass of humanity around us.

At some distance we noticed a small group of people that had gathered round, forming a closed semi-circle. My first thought was that of a snake charmer. My wife had never seen a snake charmer or a cobra in her life; we hurriedly joined the group. What met us was an astonishing sight.

A frail, wizened old man of indeterminate age lay on the road. He was caked in mud and dirt and bits of excrement, a strong unpleasant stench hung around him. Flies buzzed over his face, entering the cavity of his nostrils. His sun-blackened body, lean, emaciated, his rib bones sticking out of his skin wrapping, shook uncontrollably. Sweat poured off him in rivulets. But for a loincloth he was naked. He had no legs; they ended in raw, red, ugly stumps above his knees. He had no hands either. His arms ended just below his shoulders. It was clear that he had been a victim of a horrendous accident at some point in his life. He was not a stranger to the place. I wondered why the crowd had gathered to watch him.

(Continued)

It soon became clear: he had acquired a new form of transport. His back, bruised and calloused, rested on a wooden board, which was screwed on to four rusty wheels of a roller skate – presumably a gift from a kindly soul. He could move neither forward nor backward without taking a wide parabolic turn. He could only move to his right or left, by jerking first one shoulder, then the other, then again the first and so on until he made progress in the direction of his choice. Amid great merriment, the crowd that had gathered round him, teased him, taunted him, made fun of him, some threw a few coins at him, which he was unable to retrieve. The crowd soon tired of the novelty of his new mode of travel, and slowly dispersed. A few intrepid street urchins, who had followed the trajectory of the coins, rushed to collect them and disappeared with their meagre trophies. My wife and I stood there, looking down at him in wonder.

On an impulse I bent down to talk with him. It took me a while to get him to talk. He had, I learnt, lost his arms and legs in two separate train accidents, one over 16 years ago and the other over 11 years ago. He had been turned down by the Municipal Hospital, which claimed not to have the resources to provide him with the required prosthesis. His wife – he had been married then – taking their two children with her, had left him after his second accident (which resulted in his losing his legs) and returned to her own village where she lived with her parents. He had been living on his own for the past 11 years, surviving on charity, and on the occasional help he received from other dispossessed persons. Unbeknown to his wife, one of his sons came to see him every two to three days and attended to his needs as best he could. His visit was a source of great comfort to Kara Baba, as he was known in the area.

How he had managed to survive for as long as he had was nothing short of a miracle of ingenuity. I was humbled by his ability to survive, also revolted by his senseless suffering. Why, I asked myself, my emotions getting the better of me, does he continue to live under the most appalling, inhuman, unchanging circumstances? Why does he not his quietus make with a bare bodkin? But what interested me more than his incredible ability at survival was the question, why? Why did he continue living? What purpose did his life serve – to himself, to the world? I felt it would be naïve to assume that there was a desirable quality to his life that remained unaffected. Having survived for as long as he had, it was clear that he was unwilling to die, unwilling to put an end to all his earthly sufferings, which he could have done with relative ease.

Very gently, I questioned him on this point. His replies were a catalogue of religious clichés. It was God's will. His life was in the hands of God. He would die when God willed it. It was his karma; he was paying for his past sins. God might suddenly decide to cure him. He would be born a better soul in his next birth. Suicide was a venal, unforgivable sin. The meaningless clichés tripped off his tongue with practised ease. Was he frightened of dying, I asked?

'*Arre* Sahib, we are all going to die. If not today, then tomorrow. Better the hell I know than the one I might get into.'

I was deeply touched and impressed by his remark.

> **Interpretation of Box 10.1**
>
> The earlier case study establishes clearly the stubbornness with which Kara Baba clung to his life. At an objective level, one might question the purpose of such a life. Was there any meaning, any purpose to it?
>
> Kara Baba chose to see his life from a Hindu religious perspective, simple though his understanding of Hinduism was. He strongly believed that he was being punished for his sins and misdeeds performed in his past birth. He believed that if he bore his miseries uncomplainingly and with fortitude, there was a possibility that God would forgive him and hopefully find a miracle cure for him, or failing which, he would in his next birth be born into a noble, high-caste family.

The dread of death in the undeniable certainty of death remains an unresolved universal mystery. We *know* we are going to die. Yet we are terrified at the idea of our death. Shakespeare encapsulates this mystery in the following lines:

> Of all the wonders that I have yet heard,
> It seems to me most strange that men should fear,
> Seeing that death, a necessary end,
> Will come when it will come.
>
> *Julius Caesar*, II, 2

He also provides a tentative answer, which is not really an answer but an assertion of our ignorance concerning what follows death:

> But that the dread of something after death, –
> The undiscover'd country, from whose bourn
> No traveller returns, – puzzles the will,
> And makes us rather bear those ills we have
> Than fly to others than we know not of?
>
> *Hamlet*, III,1

Denial of death

The theme underlying the denial of death has nowhere been so poignantly portrayed than in the Pulitzer Prize-winning book, *The Denial of Death*, written by Ernest Becker in 1973, when he was critically ill, dying of cancer. Luckily he was able to see his book in print before he died.

Our fear of death is non-combative. We are unable to take arms against it, unable to conquer it, unwilling to submit to it. We can neither cheat death, nor hoodwink it. We play the oldest psychological trick on ourselves. *We deny it.* It can't happen. It won't happen. Certainly not to me, you say to yourself! In the process of denying it, we feel able to overcome it. Even in situations such as war, natural disasters and calamities, where a hypothetical possibility may be transformed into an imminent reality, we still cling to the belief that 'no, this will not happen to me, others may die, not me'. There is in Becker's thesis the total unwillingness of the human psyche to accept the ultimate finality of its existence.

Why do we deny the inevitability of our death? What are the terrors that lurk within our psyche, which make us shrink in horror? He points out that 'the idea of death, the fear of it, haunts the human animal like nothing else. It is the mainspring of human activity – activity designed largely to avoid the fatality of death, to overcome it by denying in some way that it is the final destiny for man' (Becker, 1973: xvii). We are, Becker says, powerless to cope and come to terms with the idea of death and total extinction (or non-existence). It is unbearable and, at a personal, subjective level even unimaginable.

The certainty of death raises a variety of fundamental questions. Is there a purpose to human life? The question is by no means easy to answer; in fact, it leads to further questions, such as: does human life need to have a purpose? How do we define purpose? Do we refer to purpose in religious, philosophical, and teleological terms, in familial and social terms, or in the qualitative meanings individuals assign to their own life? One does not know if human life serves any purpose, since all life eventually ends in death. These questions have disturbed several existentialist philosophers over the years, and each in their own way, including Soren Kierkegaard (1940), Carl Jaspers, Martin Heidegger, Jean Paul Sartre (1956), Albert Camus, and others, have tried to find answers to these fundamental questions. For instance, Albert Camus (1955) points out that the world in which we live is unreasonable and consequently it is impossible to find any clarity and significance in it other than the meanings which *we* desperately attempt to assign to the irrational. Were we to contemplate on our daily life, we could not but be overwhelmed by the absurdity of our existence (Camus, 1955). Perhaps one lives, in spite of oneself, unthinkingly, mechanically, out of habit.

Take an example of a severely brain-damaged patient in a prolonged state of coma, kept 'alive' at great cost on a life-support machine for years on end, with hardly any hope of recovery. Is there any purpose in the patient being kept alive? There are no easy solutions to these ethical conundrums.

In our terror we take refuge in *denial*. Denial fosters the belief that we shall somehow, by some means (fair or foul and as yet unknown) give death a slip and live forever. How easily are our nightmares of mortality vanquished by our narcissistic dreams of immortality! Such dreams assume various forms of beliefs: eternal life in terms of rebirth and reincarnation, some form of life after death, resurrection, the day of reckoning, the Armageddon, and such other comforting palliatives. The scientifically oriented individuals might pin their hopes on heart, kidney, and liver transplants and other forms of spare-part surgery, including cloning, and the handing over of one's body to a new breed of scientists known as 'cryonicists', until such time the *elixir of life* is discovered and the body is restored to life.

Denial of death has haunted humanity from ancient times to the present. It is not inborn, nor instinctive, nor is it located in the unconscious at birth. *The unconscious, as Freud remarked, has no conception of death*. Death is an abstract concept. Animals never acquire this concept. They live. They die, unaware of their own existence, unaware of any purpose in their lives. Newborn babies, infants, and toddlers too have no awareness of death. The concept filters into our consciousness through the process of socialization. As we grow up we realize that we are all destined to occupy but a limited number of years of our life on earth, and then like our forefathers we too shall die – *and be forgotten,* or in the classic words of Hemingway, *descend into nothingness*. As the idea takes firm root in our mind it becomes too painful to bear and is repressed into our unconscious.

The question that intrigues us all is this: do people all over the world, from primitive societies to advanced technological societies regardless of the culture they come from, regardless of their beliefs and values, their social, religious, and spiritual practices, fear and deny death? Becker seems to believe so. But anthropological evidence does not support such a claim. There are, as Rosenblatt (1997/2003) points out, several small societies dotted around the world where the passing away of a person is celebrated. There are other notable exceptions too to the universal fear and denial of death: suicides, euthanasia, martyrdom, and a willingness to kill and even die for one's beliefs.

Western approaches to death

Medicalization of death

In the past, common law defined death as 'a moment when life had ceased'. Physicians defined death as 'a total stoppage of circulation of the blood and a cessation of the vital functions such as respiration, pulsation, and so on. From a clinical point of view, the organism upon death ceased to function, that is, the person who had died had lost the capacity to breathe and to sustain a spontaneous heartbeat. Death, as Capron and Cass (1980) points out, marked the cessation of integrative action between all organ systems of the body. The established medico-legal system demanded that a person's death was recorded and documented in terms of time, place, and cause.

In the last two to three decades, even the definition of death appears to have undergone a dramatic change. Staggering advances in medical research have cast doubts on how death shall be defined. Capron and Cass (1980) point out that the courts and physicians can no longer assume that defining death is a relatively simple matter. When exactly is a person deemed to be dead? This question is difficult to answer. The development and use of complicated machinery to maintain circulation and respiration adds to the difficulty in defining death.

It is clear that the notion of life and death being an 'either/or' in recent years has come to be questioned (Aries, 1981; Kastenbaum, 2000; Loffland, 1978). First, the increasing ability of medicine to resuscitate dying patients and keep them alive on sophisticated machinery, and second, the ability of modern medicine to transplant organs from one person to another, has led to a soul-searching re-evaluation of the definition of death (Horan & Mall, 1980). As a result, death is seen not in terms of an 'either/or' but as extending along the points of a continuum. As Moller (1996) points out, death is seen as a medical failure, and 'saving life at all costs' has become the guiding philosophy of Western medical science, which in turn has brought about different sets of expectations, many of which are as unrealistic as they are unrealizable. The reliance on technology has had the effect of shifting the values of society from a moral and social order to a technical order.

As soon as one construes death from an exclusively medical perspective, all the other factors on which one depended in the past and which gave meaning and comfort to the dying individual, the grieving relatives, and society, cease to be of importance (Laungani, 2001a, 2001b). If the medical profession is unable to help the dying patient – so the argument runs – there is little that society or the relatives or the clergy can do to help the dying person. Even the word 'death' appears to have fallen into disuse and euphemisms such as the patient has 'passed on', 'passed away', 'has gone to meet his or her maker', and so on are substituted instead. In the case of the death of an elderly person, a sporting analogy borrowed from cricket is used: he or she had a good innings. At my father-in-law's funeral – he was 92 when he died – over a dozen people who offered their condolences said *what a wonderful innings he had had*. It was with some effort that I restrained my impulse to blurt out, '*Another eight years and he would have scored a century!*' My own experience of having lectured in several hospices in England confirmed my observations. I was surprised to note that neither the physicians nor the psychiatrists and not even the palliative care nurses used the word 'death' in the presence of their patients. Death was a taboo word, as though given greater lease of life by its very denial. Hospitals too take great pains to keep death closeted. Ingenious techniques are used to remove the corpse from the hospital bed to the morgue. Such swift, secretive measures merely add to the feeling of alienation and depersonalization of death in modern Western society. The hasty removal of the body prevents the bereaved relatives from seeing the body and expressing their grief and sorrow openly on the ward, thereby causing undue distress to other patients. Thus are the living protected from the dead!

Even within the medical profession there is a reluctance to 'accept' death. There is a growing body of research literature on a variety of death-related subjects, which include:

- Past-life therapy;
- The elixir of human immortality (Reyes, 1986);
- Communication with the dead (Almeder, 1987);

- Cryonic suspension (Kasterbaum & Kasterbaum, 1989);
- Death-bed visions (Barrett, 1926; Moore, 1981);
- Déjà vu (Wolman, 1977);
- Recall of past incarnations (Wambach, 1978);
- Conscious dying, out-of-body experiences, near-death experiences;
- Return from the dead;
- Reincarnation.

Reports of near-death and after-death experiences contain all the ingredients of high drama. They often tend to get sensationalized. Different versions of the story begin to circulate, each clamouring for attention. The accounts of such experiences are fascinating, but establishing their validity has been problematic, to say the least.

As an example, let us take a case of a patient on a life-support machine. There are no clear guidelines as to the appropriate action that would need to be taken in the case of a long-comatose patient who shows every prospect of 'living' indefinitely with artificial means of support. Should one look upon the patient as being alive or dead? Is such a 'life' worth living? The poor patient, lying in a coma, lost, by all accounts, to the world, has no awareness of his or her condition and is not in a position to say aye or nay about the termination or continuation of his or her life. Should one wait and live in the hope that one day, perhaps either as a result of scientific advances, or by an unexplained miracle, the patient will recover, or should one accept the finality of death, and request the life-support machine be turned off? How shall such a decision be taken? On what grounds are such vital decisions to be taken? Are there established guidelines, which would permit an acceptable and a rational decision? These questions raise serious issues: legal, ethical, financial, social, psychological, and practical – issues on which there does not appear to be a great deal of consensus.

Sanitization of death

In the West, death in general is regarded as a private family affair. Although the distant relatives and friends may be involved, their role tends to be marginal. From the moment of death until the funeral, even the family members of the deceased have no important role to play. As soon as death occurs, by common consent the body is removed by the undertakers and placed in their parlour or chapel, where it is kept until the day and the time of the funeral. Although it would be within the rights of the family members to take the body home from where they could initiate all the funeral arrangements, very few do: inexperience, inability to cope with a cadaver, inhibition, fear, may explain such attitudes and behaviours. It is the undertaker who is entrusted with the delicate and sensitive details related to the washing, anointing, bathing, dressing, the laying out of the body, its placement in the coffin, and the eventual transportation to the cemetery or the crematorium. All these activities, which in the past were undertaken by the deceased's family, are now delegated to paid outsiders. In keeping the involvement of the family members to a bare minimum, they are 'protected' from such painful and distressing details. The ugliness of death is left outside; it does not enter one's house – *at least not through the front door!* One is thus able to dissociate oneself from death. Children, in particular, are not 'exposed' to death. They are shielded and are kept away and are hardly ever given the opportunity of 'confronting' death. There is among Westerners a misplaced belief that children being children would not be able to cope with the sight of death, the effects of which could be extremely traumatic and long lasting.

The undertakers and the embalmers spare no effort in the process of what is referred to as the 'sanitization' of the body. The body is carefully washed, dried, and perfumed, all the gases and other foul and smelly remains are carefully removed from the body, any disfigurements that may have occurred prior to death are smoothed over, the pale bloodless face is painted and made up to look pink and rosy, the body is dressed up in fine clothes and placed in an expensive mahogany casket with soft silk linings – the illusion is complete! Such illusions have given rise to several 'sick' jokes, of which the following is one of my favourites:

> The widow of a deceased husband walks into the undertaker's and asks to see her husband. She is astounded when she sees him in his coffin. He is dressed in his dark grey elegant suit, his hair neatly combed, his face painted pink, his lips parted in a beautiful endearing smile. Unable to take her eyes off him she stares at him for a long time, and finally remarks 'Oh, look at the beautiful smile on his face. The silly fool still hasn't realized he is dead!'

The ugliness of death is transformed into the beauty of life. One might even venture to suggest that some 'life' is injected into death in order to make it more *'acceptable'*. The dead are made to resemble the living – denial carried to its last final detail.

Secularization of death

Right from the beginning of Christianity to the period of Enlightenment, religion (with a capital R) played a dominant role in the lives of most people in the West. From birth to death, people were guided by Christian teachings. God created the world, God created human beings, God who was in heaven, was omniscient, omnipotent, all merciful, all kind and all forgiving. God saw to it that the virtuous, the obedient, and the faithful upon their death went to heaven. The disobedient, the unrepentant sinners, and those lacking in faith were consigned into the darkest layers of hell. (For a chilling, gory picture of what it must feel like to pass through the nether regions of hell, the reader is invited to follow Dante's stupendous epic poem, *Inferno*.)

Religion enshrined custom, guided behaviour, promoted ritual, perpetuated tradition, and assailed doubts – thus creating a certain degree of stability in society. Influenced by the teachings of religion, people remained unperturbed by some of the questions that are of concern to them today. One was as certain of heaven and hell as one was of one's own shadow – despite its lack of substance. But the sixteenth century witnessed a spectacular rise in the growth of science, and as a result engendered a 'paradigm shift' in the beliefs, values, and behaviours of people. Developments in other fields, such as biology, medicine, anatomy, cosmology, and other relevant areas, added to the growing disenchantment with religion. The truthfulness of divine revelations came to be questioned and doubts, with wily stealth, began to creep into the European psyche. The belief in Christian ethics (*God's will be done*) gradually yielded place to human ethics. Man himself became the reference point, and as Protagoras, the pre-Socratic philosopher, had remarked several centuries earlier, '*Man is the measure of all things*' (*anthropos metron panton*). There is no great decisive force beyond humanity.

God, as Walter (1997) points out, is no longer the reference point in life and in death but man himself, and any role played by religion becomes redundant. In recent years such views have been promoted with great vigour by Richard Dawkins. It thus makes sense to see death and its final disposal in secular terms, the central thesis of which is that life ends at death. Since death means a total cessation of bodily and mental processes and functions, how can one know what lies beyond death? Thus, there is nothing to fear. The humanists too assert that such fears are meaningless because none of us knows what lies beyond the grave (Kurtz, 1983). There is no point in worrying about what we do not know and, by all accounts, never shall. This universal ignorance ought to insulate us from these unfounded terrors and make us look upon our impending death and that of our loved ones with equanimity.

Walter (1997) argues that there is merit in the acceptance of the humanist and secular philosophy. It prepares an adherent to face death without fear. What matters to them most is how one lives one's life; their concern is more with life and living than with dying and death. One cannot but admire the refreshing rationality that the humanists and the secularists bring into the field, which has troubled and tormented humanity for several thousand years. Such a view portrays human beings as rational beings who are capable of making the most profound decisions on objective, rational, and scientific grounds. But before siding with the angels of rationality, let us consider a few counter-arguments.

1   Humanists assume that human beings, having arrived at such conclusions, can rationally will themselves to overcome all the primeval fears, which have been part of the human psyche since time immemorial. One does not live by reason alone, as the humanists and the secularists in their naiveté would have us believe. People feed off their emotions, display anger, fear, sorrow, depression, engage in irrational behaviours, display dark moods (remember Churchill's mad dog syndrome?), respond to impulse, and at a more intense level, hurt others, hurt themselves, and even put an end to their lives. Feelings and emotions form an integral part of being human; they cannot always be brought under rational control. Even if it were possible to do so, imagine the colossal loss of creative contributions in the field of music, the arts, literature, drama, poetry, all of which involve an intricate interplay of emotions and rationality – as was discussed at some length in the Chapter 8. But a secularist view allows no room for a free play of emotions even in the final and most profound event of our life – death. The role of emotions – fear, dread, terror, denial, and other equally powerful feelings – has been written out of the secularist 'manifesto'. In denying the startling power of emotions – both constructive and destructive – which may (and often do) have far reaching consequences on people's lives, the secularists have created a sad caricature of human behaviour. However hard one tries, it is not always possible to bring one's turbulent feelings and emotions under rational control all the time. Nor indeed is it easy to tame and subjugate the dynamic powers of the unconscious mind, which knows no boundaries related to time and death. The majority of the people, not just in Western societies but all over the world, are unlikely to acquire the immunity from all their primeval dreads and terrors associated with death and extinction. It is in the nether regions of our unconscious that reason battles with emotions – and often loses.

2   In their evangelical enthusiasm to proselytize the desirability of rationality in human affairs, they become guilty of irrationalism themselves by preaching rationality as the universal standard against which all forms of discourses ought to be judged. One does not wish to decry the importance of rationality in human affairs, but one needs to give serious consideration to vast tracts of anthropological and cross-cultural research literature, which clearly points to different conceptions of reality and rationality across cultures.

At a philosophical level too the supremacy of reason over intuition, faith, and so on comes into question. '*Reason*,' as Kant argued in his *Critique of Pure Reason*, '*leads us into self-contradiction and impasse, for reality does not correspond to reason, therefore it cannot be possible even in principle for us to understand reality by the use of reason alone*' (cited in Magee, 2002).

3 If a group of epistemologists subscribing to an objective scientific approach were questioned on the issue of what follows (or does not follow) death, they would point out that the question is unanswerable with any degree of certainty. They would be unwilling to become drawn into metaphysical and ontological arguments related to the nature of being, existence, appearance, and reality. When pressed for an answer the response would be one of healthy scepticism, which, in a sense, would allow the epistemologists to 'hedge their bets' should future scientific discoveries lead to more conclusive answers on this vital problem.

The reader must bear in mind that the above critical comments are concerned not with the philosophy of secularism, which, as a philosophy and even as a 'way of life', has a lot to commend it. Our concern is with the prevalent belief among secularists that one does not have to fear death because one has either no knowledge of what follows death or that death is extinction – and there is nothing more to be said. It seems as though the secularists in their over-eagerness to extol the virtues of rationalism in human affairs both in life and in death have adopted a holier-than-thou approach, built on the motto that reason triumphs over all. It doesn't – certainly not in all situations and in all conditions.

Secularist funerals

In the course of my research into death and bereavement I took every opportunity to attend funerals: secular, humanistic, and religious funerals, which included Christian, Islamic, and Hindu funerals in England and in India. (I didn't actually 'haunt' the cremation grounds in Bombay, but I seldom missed the opportunity of attending funerals whenever an opportunity presented itself.) Given our vast extended family, communal, and social network, a visit to a crematorium about half a dozen times a year was always within the bounds of possibility. Lest the Western reader assumes – wrongly – that I had a morbid fascination with death, I need to make it clear that unlike children in Western countries, children in India and in many other developing countries are seldom shielded from witnessing a dead body, nor are they discouraged from going to the crematorium and observing the entire funeral ceremony. Of secular funerals I knew nothing until I came to England.

Secular funerals, I gradually learnt, fell into a predictable pattern. The grieving members would gather round and take it in turns to speak of the life of the deceased, focusing on their personal reminiscences of the deceased they knew, loved, and admired. Allow me to recount one of my recent experiences of a secular funeral.

Box 10.2

It was the funeral of a young 15-year-old lad who had committed suicide by throwing himself off the roof of a tall building in London. (Details have been changed to safeguard and protect the identity and the anonymity of the deceased and his family members.) It appears, as I learnt subsequently, that he had been passing through some sort of crises, and being unable to cope and unwilling to confide in anyone, had taken his own life. Although I had met the young lad only once, his parents were great friends of mine, and I felt that it was my moral duty to attend the funeral. It was secular funeral. There were about 20 mourners, including the deceased's parents and their two remaining children. We sat in a room in chairs arranged in a circle. Of the 20-odd people sitting there, only two were dressed in black, an elderly gentleman, who it turned out was the deceased's grandfather, and myself. The rest were in casual clothes – jeans, slacks, jumpers, and overcoats. It was a cold, biting winter morning. Presently, the father of the deceased started to speak. He expressed his deep sorrow at the tragic death of his son and wished it could have been avoided. A life of great potential had lain ahead of his son; if only he had known, had some inkling, some clue of the 'whys', he would have moved heaven and earth to prevent the tragedy. He controlled the tears, which had welled up to his eyes, and fell silent. The boy's mother kept taking off her glasses, polishing them and putting them back on again. She said not a word. Others started to speak: in between moments of silence, some extemporized, a few read from prepared texts, one or two recited poems, and some narrated their accounts of how well they knew the young boy. A few remained silent. They all spoke highly of the dead boy. Unlike Mark Anthony, who came to bury Caesar and not to praise him, the secularists had come with an inverted motive: to praise the deceased for a life lived well. There was no coffin in the room; the dead had been removed from the living.

Presently, the boy's father, regaining his courage, said that they had gathered not in order to pass judgement, point a finger, apportion blame, but to accept the death of their son, whose life though short had been not without purpose. What the purpose of the boy's life had been remained unsaid. One could sense that the mourners who had gathered there wanted to know why the young lad had taken his life; they exchanged glances, but the fatal question remained unvoiced. Looking at his wife, my friend said that they missed their son dearly and hoped that soon they would set up a Trust of some kind in his memory.

At this point one of the mourners who had brought with him a guitar, strummed on it for a while and then sang an old song, which he explained was the boy's favourite. No hymns were read. No prayers were offered. There were no readings from the Bible. One of the mourners produced a battered baseball cap, and said that that was the cap which the boy had loved wearing, and he had decided to wear it as a mark of honour. So saying he put it on. We all smiled. A few clapped their hands. After another song, the ceremony ended. We rose, shook hands, embraced one another and offered our condolences to my friend and his wife. With slow, measured steps we walked out of the room. The entire ceremony lasted for just 45 minutes.

Interpretation of Box 10.2

This particular experience made a deep and painful impression upon me. For a life lived for 15 years to be disposed off in less than an hour with a few homilies, a badly sung song, a prepared text or two, the use of a battered baseball cap, poor attempts at levity, was not what I had expected. A young lad, in the prime of his youth, had put an end to his life; what demons had terrorized him, what nightmares had haunted him, what layers of hell he must have travelled through, what ultimately drove him to his irrevocable fatal decision was beyond imagination. I found it difficult and painful to accept the casual manner in which the last rites – if they can be referred to as such – of the dead lad were performed. There was not even the coffin to remind us of the lad who had died. Apart from an occasional sniffle, a blowing of a nose, a break in voice, the use of a handkerchief to wipe off tears, there were no expressions of grief and sorrow. The English, particularly the middle-classes, pride themselves on their ability to maintain strict control over their emotional feelings in such situations (Hockey, 1993; Laungani, 1997b). Dignity lies in restraint. What distressed me was not just the steely control all the mourners exercised over their feelings and emotions, but also *the lack of any rituals* they might have performed which would have lent depth and dignity, purpose and poignancy to the sad occasion. Symbols and rituals play an indispensable role in human life, and even more so in death. What I observed instead was in complete contrast to what one would have seen in Pakistan, India, Bangladesh, Malaysia, Indonesia, Thailand, China, Taiwan, and in Japan, and in all small-scale societies dotted around the world (Rosenblatt, 1997/2003). The funeral reminded me of a doggerel that I had read in a book of humour several years ago:

Here lies a man,
Who was once alive,
And is now dead.
There's nothing more to be said.

The diminishing role of rituals in secular funerals

Rituals do not play an important role in secular funerals, and in that sense are 'cut and dried'. The secularists, having freed themselves from the 'trappings' of the Church, its sermons, its blessings of reunion with God, in heaven, dangers of purgatory, the fires of hell, have also dispensed with the rites and rituals, including the wearing of black from their funerals. One wonders where the secularists would stand with regard to the cryptic remark of Professor Jaraslav Pelikan (1974) when he said that *tradition is the living faith of the dead; traditionalism is the dead faith of the living.*

Smith (in press) warns us of the dangers of underestimating or ignoring rituals and symbols. He points out that if the trend continues it will in all likelihood lead to our rapidly becoming a *ritual impoverished society*. Rando (1984) points out that funeral rituals are means by which the community attempts to maintain its symbolic connection with the dead and reap therapeutic opportunities to complete unfinished mourning.

According to the great poet, T. S. Eliot (1948), it is important to visualize a continuing relationship of the living with the dead. This can only be attained through a pattern of rituals, which are extensions into the modern world of dogmas that remain unaltered from the past. Eliot believed that when these rituals were disrupted, there would be no connection of the living with the dead, of the present with the past. He laments the fact that the past rituals have been destroyed and have been replaced by ones which are mockeries of the old rituals. In *The Love Song of Alfred Prufrock*, Eliot portrays a society where lives are measured out not by sacraments but with 'coffee spoons'.

Rituals serve extremely important functions, a few of which may be summarized as under:

- To ensure that the dead are in fact dead; to ensure that they stay dead; and to 'carry the members of the family through their dealings with grief' (Hatchett, 1995: 477).
- Rituals grant society and to survivor-friends grief rights (Sklar, 1991/1992).
- Rituals assist mourners in beginning to accommodate to the changed relationship between themselves and the deceased (Mosca, 2002).
- The funeral ritual is a public, traditional, and symbolic means of expressing our beliefs, thoughts, and feelings about the death of someone loved – or, for that matter, someone unloved.
- Rituals confirm and reinforce the reality of death. There is nothing like a corpse to 'drive home' the reality of death. Historically, that was one reason family and friends prepared the body for rituals (Rando, 1984).
- Rites and rituals legitimize social order and uphold social institutions.
- The mentality that discourages viewing the corpse may divert attention from grief issues.
- Rituals assist in the acknowledgment and expression of feelings and offer survivors a vehicle for expressing their feelings.
- Rituals stimulate the recollection of the deceased, a necessary aspect of decathexis. It is common to overhear at visitations, 'Oh, I had forgotten about *that*,' or 'Now that you mention it...'.
- A publicly expressed memory functions as a magnet in drawing out other, often supportive, recollections. In a gathering of grievers, one individual's recollection can 'jump-start' the memories of others. Adapting a liturgical term, the eulogist 're-collects' the words and memories of the assembled grievers (Smith, in press).
- Ritual action anchors people in a sense of deeper identity and belonging (Flood, 1996).

- American society prefers to privatize grief rather than offer safe spaces for mourning. Giving grief a voice through ritualizing is an invitation to others to audition emotions, particularly lament. Rituals have the potential, if well done and paced, to provide *mekom hanekama*, 'a place of comfort'.
- Rituals assist mourners to accommodate to the changed relationship between themselves and the deceased.
- Rituals allow the community to provide social support to mourners.
- Rituals offer occasions to revisit old griefs (Quindlen, 1994).
- Rituals allow the grieving to say their 'goodbyes' in their own unique, idiosyncratic ways (Laungani, in press).

Conquest of death (cryogenics)

In recent years, doubts concerning the finality of death have spurred several enterprizing, scientists, referred to as 'cryonicists', to plan for the future. They are convinced that one day, scientific advances will make it possible to revive the dead, who will then live forever. The lure of immortality has persuaded several persons of affluence to volunteer their bodies to the cryonicists. But for the extortionist costs involved, such an enterprise would probably attract more persons seeking immortality than is true at present. Upon the death of the volunteer, the cryonicists take possession of the corpse, sever the head from the body, drain it of all its blood and other vital fluids, and freeze the cadaver in hermitically sealed concrete vats of liquid nitrogen at a temperature of −196°C. The body will remain frozen for an indefinite period, or until such time the scientists have found a way of bringing the patients back to life. Whether the scientists who have arranged to freeze the bodies will one day – assuming, of course, that they themselves are alive and are able to perform the specialized surgery – be able to revive the bodies and offer the resurrected immortal life, remains a futuristic issue.

Eastern approaches to death

Family and communal considerations

Death among Hindus is seen as a family and communal affair. Most Hindus die at home. Those that die in hospitals are generally brought home. Given the extended family network, the lack of privacy, limited space, the blurring of 'self–other' boundaries, it is not surprising that children are hardly ever shielded from seeing and even touching the dead at home. Quite often, the children are also taken to the crematorium, thereby acquiring an early acquaintance with death. (I can still recall very clearly being taken along with one or two of my cousins to the crematorium by my family members to witness the cremation of my aged aunt, my father's sister. I was then five or six years old.)

Hindu funerals

Undertakers have no role to play in the funeral arrangements of Hindus. Only family members and close relatives are permitted to perform such activities. Under the guidance of the family priest, the family members perform all the rites and rituals related to the handling of the corpse. A Hindu, as is common knowledge, is not placed in a coffin; he or she is carried on a bier, which is often assembled at home by experienced relatives and family members. After the body has been washed, anointed, scented, dressed in a white cotton shroud, it is placed on the bier.

The body is fastened with coir rope and is bedecked with seasonal flowers. The family priest performs the required rites and rituals. At his signal, the male family members invoking in unison the names of the Hindu gods, lift the bier, and gingerly make their way out of the house, where the rest of the mourners await them. The women watch, cry, weep, wail, but do not generally participate either in the washing and the anointing of the corpse or in its transportation.

Women part from their loved one at the threshold of their house. In the past, women were prohibited from entering a crematorium, but in recent years the situation has changed and women are permitted to enter, although the final rites, namely lighting the sacred flame with which the body is set alight, the sacred perambulations around the corpse, are still performed by men. The funeral procession, led by the family priest and the chief mourners, wends its way to the crematorium. It is only in exceptional cases – monsoons and/or vast distances to the crematorium – that the body is transported in a hired van or an ambulance.

There are a variety of social and religious customs surrounding death and bereavement in Eastern cultures. It is expected that the relatives – close or distant – regardless of how far away they may live from the family of the deceased, upon being notified will turn up for the funeral. It is an integral part of Hindu and Islamic religion that funerals take place within 24-hours after death. Only in exceptional cases – when post-mortems are involved, or when mourning relatives live abroad and are unable to arrive on time – that funerals can be delayed. After the funeral, the close relatives are expected to stay with the bereaved family until the final religious ceremony as dictated by custom is performed (Laungani, 1997b). It is of course incumbent upon the family members to make all the living-in arrangements for their funeral guests. In addition to the house-guests, a stream of daily visitors flocks in to offer their support. Mourning and bereavement, as can be seen, is not a private and exclusive family affair as it is in the West. It is communal. For a family of moderate or less than moderate means, it can also be very expensive.

Grief and sorrow are expressed openly, publicly, without embarrassment. Not only one must grieve, but one must be seen and heard to grieve. During the 12 (or 13) days of mourning, grieving, crying, and wailing occurs with unfailing regularity. With each passing day, the wailing becomes less intense, and by the 12th or 13th day, the crying is reduced to sniffs and whimpers.

This is an ancient custom, hallowed by tradition. At a social level, the post-funeral period serves an important function. It provides a source of intense security for the bereaved, and in so doing it also reinforces a sense of communal unity. At a psychological level, the daily communal crying, although it might seem bewildering to Westerners, serves as a necessary catharsis for the entire family. It hastens the process of recovery from the traumatic experience, enabling the family to make the necessary positive adjustments to their altered lives.

Dying a good death

The idea underlying 'a good death' is easy to grasp but quite difficult to internalize. Good death in Hinduism is seen as a voluntary renunciation of life, and the cremation serves as a sacrificial offering of the self to the gods (Ghosh, 1989; Pandey, 1948/1969; Parry, 1994). Death, to many people in Eastern cultures, is often seen as a period of transition. There is a shared belief that upon death although the human body, if left unattended, will rot, decompose, and decay *the spirit or the soul of the deceased will remain free, unfettered and unaffected.* One goes, according to one's beliefs and *(karmic)* actions, to heaven, to an everlasting after-life, or to hell.

In the developing countries – the Middle East, Pakistan, India, Sri Lanka, Bangladesh, and countries in South East Asia, the guiding philosophy concerning life and death is the belief that as one gets older one becomes weak and infirm and eventually, as one's time approaches, one will die. Death is seen as a legitimate *but by no means the final end to one's life.* To die in one's old age, *without undue pain and suffering,* after one has discharged honourably one's duties towards one's family members, one's community, and towards society, is construed 'as a good death'.

In India it is not uncommon for the old and the infirm to express the open wish to die in one of the holy cities such as Varanasi and Hardwar. To die in a holy city, to be cremated along the banks of the river Ganges, to have one's ashes immersed in the river after all the appropriate prayers, rites, and rituals have been performed, to have given alms and fed the needy and the dispossessed, ensures the swift and peaceful repose of the deceased's soul. Such sentiments might sound strange to Westerners, but not so to people from Eastern cultures (Aguilar, 1976; Firth, 1993; Justice, 1997; Laungani, in press; Madan, 1987; Pandey, 1948/1969; Parry, 1994). They are often given serious consideration by the relatives and the sons of the person who expresses the wish to die in a holy city.

It needs to be made clear – unequivocally clear – that the desire of an aged parent to wish to die must not be seen as a form of euthanasia. Nor must it be construed as a suicide. There is in the aged parent a strong desire to give up his or her life, and through cremation, make a sacrificial offering of the self to the gods. The relatives of the aged parent may initially attempt to dissuade the person from embarking on this final journey, and when that fails they then make arrangements to take their aged parent to Varanasi or wherever he or she has expressed the wish to die. The person concerned is then placed in an *ashram* – a holy sanctuary or hermitage. (In recent years, privately funded hospices have also come into being in some of the major cities in India.)

The aged parent often refuses medication and ignores any advice given by the physician who examines him or her upon arrival at the *ashram*. The person has come to die, not to be treated. Justice (1997), in his investigations, found that the person soon after arrival stops eating, and within a few days, nature, as it were, takes its own course and the person dies. No guilt, no shame, no stigma is attached to the relatives of the person who has chosen to die in this manner. This form of death is seen as 'a good death' – a fitting end to one's life. Attempts to keep death at bay, to conquer death, to keeping-alive-at-all-costs, are ideas which are as alien to Hindus as the above Hindu beliefs and practices would seem to most people in the West (Lynn and Childress, 1986).

A good death also occurs when a Hindu dies at the 'right' time *(kal mrityu)* and at the right place. To determine the auspicious time of death, Hindus often seek guidance from astrologers. Although astrological predictions from a strict scientific perspective may be questionable, there is a strongly held belief that there is within each individual a predetermined maximum life span. The fact that a person may die before his or her predetermined life span may be due to the person's bad karmic actions. A bad death is referred to as *akal mrtyu* (Filippi, 1996).

Near-death experiences

From time to time one reads of instances where the dead have come to life, or been brought to life by resuscitation, or in ways which defy rational explanations. The mysteries surrounding such accounts have fascinated people from all over the world, from times ancient to times present. Several researchers working in this area have gathered reports of people who were resuscitated after having been pronounced clinically dead by their doctors (Gallup, 1982; Moody, 1975, 1989). How much credence ought one to pay to such claims, one cannot say with any degree of certainty. Nonetheless, the research studies are quite thorough, although they tend to be anecdotal. Let me recount a 'return from the dead' experience that I witnessed several years ago in Pakistan.

Box 10.3: A Near-Death Experience

This incident took place several years ago: late-1950s in a sleepy little town, Tando Adam in Sind, Pakistan. My father had inherited some ancestral property and we came there every year from Bombay. For me, it was exciting coming to Tando Adam where I met my cousins, many of whom lived there. Around four o'clock every afternoon, the familiar and welcome face of Kalia would pass by our house. Kalia was not his real name, but since he was pitch black in complexion, we all called him Kalia, which means 'black'. His real name, as we found out later, was Satyavan. Although Kalia might seem a derogatory term, it is also a term affectionately used when referring to the Hindu god Krishna. He didn't seem to mind – everyone called him Kalia. Kalia was a hawker. He sold hot and spicy Indian savoury snacks, made from potatoes, chick peas, flour and onions fried in batter; they were garnished with chutney made with mint, tamarind, chillies, lime, and fresh coriander. No sooner did we hear his familiar cries, than we all – my cousins, and I – rushed out of the house to buy the snacks. Each of us clamoured for attention, wanting to be served first. By the time Kalia reached the end of our street, our snacks had disappeared and we had started to lick our fingers, bitterly regretting the fact that we did not have any more money on us.

As usual, we waited for Kalia every day. But the following morning, we all heard that Kalia had died. We were heart-broken. Not for him, though, but for the snacks which we would never eat again. My cousin, who was the oldest of the kids at home, suggested that we should all attend Kalia's funeral – as a mark of respect for the hawker who had given us such untold joy. My father was pleased and surprised that we all wanted to attend Kalia's funeral. Within our family and our community, no one had any qualms about taking young children to the crematorium. It seemed perfectly natural.

Since Kalia was a well-known and well-liked hawker in our area, virtually every one in the neighbourhood (Muslims and Hindus) turned out for his funeral. By six o' clock in the evening, the crematorium was crowded with mourners. Kalia lay in his bier, which was placed on the floor for all to see. His face was left uncovered, his body wrapped in a white shroud, bedecked with flowers. I had a glimpse of Kalia and was surprised and frightened to see how stiff and waxen he seemed.

Like the others, I too bent down before the body to offer my final prayers. I almost jumped out of my skin when I thought I saw his nostrils twitch. But there were flies buzzing round his face.

Presently, the Brahmin priest, in charge of the funeral ceremony, took over. He recited the sacred texts in Sanskrit, and asked for the body to be lifted on to the pile of logs that had been assembled for the funeral pyre.

Kalia's eldest son, his head shaven, dressed in a white dhoti and kurta, who could not have been much older than me, was expected to perform the final funeral rites. This of course was in keeping with ancient Hindu traditions, which decree that it is the sacred duty of the eldest son to perform all the funeral rites of his deceased father – for this ensures the peaceful repose of the father's soul. A flame was lit. It was handed to Kalia's son. He was instructed to hold the flame near the logs. The logs took. Smoke began to rise from the logs.

(Continued)

And then, suddenly, to everyone's total astonishment, there was a piercing cry from the logs. Before the people could even gather their wits about them, the Brahmin priest rushed towards the pile of logs, and with his hands and feet, started to dislodge the logs that had been piled on top of Kalia. Others joined in. Within a few seconds, the logs were removed, and Kalia was lifted from the funeral pyre. They placed him on the floor. His chest heaved. He coughed. He choked. He sputtered. It was clear that he was breathing. He was alive!

'A miracle! A miracle!' people shouted.

Messengers were sent rushing to Kalia's house to inform his grieving wife, his two daughters, his mother, and all the other female relatives who custom forbade their coming to the crematorium. The women, as befitting custom, had parted from their departed loved one at the threshold of Kalia's house.

While Kalia was being revived, rumours wilder than the funeral pyre spread through the crematorium. People looked at the dazed Kalia, shook their heads and laughed. Everyone knew – it was common knowledge in their area – that Kalia and his wife did not get on well with each other. In fact, they hated each other. Divorce was a taboo word, unheard of among Hindus (to a large extent it still is). Kalia's death had seemed a god-sent deliverance for his wife. They all knew that she would go through the motions of crying and mourning. And now he would be returning home once again. The taunts, the torments, the quarrels, and the fights would continue.

When Kalia had recovered sufficiently and was able to stand and walk, someone suggested that Kalia should once again be placed on the bier and brought home. But the bier had got burnt. A huge procession of laughing, joking, cheerful 'mourners' carried Kalia on their shoulders and brought him home. As children, we were allowed to enter the house and slip into the quarters where the women had, until a few moments ago, been wailing and mourning.

Kalia's wife, upon seeing Kalia, burst into genuine tears. She cried, she wailed, she beat her breast, and finally turned to her husband with fury: 'You *shaitaan!* You tormented me while you were alive, and now as a black, evil *shaitaan* you have returned to torment me after your death.' Her screams rang through the house. They were greeted by laughter by all the people who had gathered round the house.

At home, we debated whether Kalia had really died and had returned from the dead. Can people come back from the dead, we wondered? The only doctor – Dr Gurudas – who lived in our neighbourhood, who would have examined Kalia, had gone to Hyderabad for a few days. It is possible that Kalia may have taken ill and slipped into a coma. Being unable to revive him, his family members and his neighbours may have concluded that he had died. We'd never know. Our neighbourhood, however, buzzed with all kinds of fantastic speculations.

We wondered if Kalia would ever return to selling his savoury snacks. A week later, Kalia's familiar cries had us all rushing out of the house to buy the spicy snacks, which we all craved. But by now we had also imbued him with supernatural powers and were not a little frightened of him. We stopped calling him Kalia – as, indeed, did the rest of the people in our neighbourhood – and referred to him by his real name, Satyavan.

(Continued)

Different versions of Kalia's supernatural powers began to circulate and gain currency. Some saw Kalia as a person of immense saintly powers, who had seen God and had returned from the dead to preach the word of God. Others saw him in more malevolent terms, as though he had been in league with the *shaitaan*, the devil. Evil gossip, like poisonous vapour, polluted the atmosphere, affecting all. Kalia had been seen dancing in the crematorium in the middle of the night, eating the flesh of corpses; Kalia could speak in tongues, Kalia could cast spells, bewitch people; Kalia could summon evil spirits from his nostrils; the rumours were as phantasmagoric as they were absurd. Evil triumphed. Gradually, people began to avoid him. Kalia, a poor, humble, uneducated peasant could not cope with the fear, the anger, and the contempt he aroused in the people in the neighbourhood.

He felt rejected by the very people he had served for several years. Less than a year later he threw himself into the well outside their house. A few days later, his bloated body was fished out of the well into which he jumped. Hardly anyone – with the exception of his family members – attended his second funeral.

It should be pointed out that although the above event is quite unique, it is not significantly different from many other 'near-death' experiences described by people all over the world. Such fascinating 'near-death' and 'after-death' experiences have been recorded and discussed at length by Moody (1975, 1977). Reports of 'near-death' and 'after-death' experiences contain all the ingredients of high drama. They tend to attract the attention of the media, and soon different versions of the story begin to circulate, each version clamouring for attention, each asserting its own truth. The above incident, which occurred in a small town and took place over 50 years ago, probably went unnoticed.

Interpretation of Box 10.3

Several questions come to mind with regard to Kalia's death. Did Kalia actually die? If so, how did he return from the dead? While he remained 'dead', so to speak, did he have any experiences? If so, what kind of experiences? Was he actually aware that he had died? (This question leads to a fascinating conundrum: if death means cessation of all awareness, how can one be aware of one's lack of awareness?) Would he have recovered had his 'lifeless' body been brought out into the courtyard and left to warm in the afternoon sun instead of being taken directly to the crematorium? Would he have recovered had the funeral been delayed by a day? Was Kalia incorrectly diagnosed by his family members and pronounced dead? Would he have been diagnosed correctly had the doctor not gone away from the town on the day of his 'death'?

Such incidents, although dramatic are rare; one is not quite sure how one interprets them. From a scientific point of view, it is impossible to provide an unequivocal answer. But that is not our main concern. Our main concern here is not whether Kalia died or

(Continued)

did not die. Our concern is to tease out the underlying notions of religion and spirituality embedded in the important social customs, the rites, rituals and the ceremonies which followed Kalia's death and 'resurrection'. Hindu spirituality can seldom be understood without a close examination of rituals. As Flood points out, 'it is ritual action which anchors people in a sense of deeper identity and belonging. While Hindus have questioned the meanings of ritual and interpreted rituals in a variety of ways, ritual has seldom been abandoned within Hindu traditions' (1996).

Several interesting points emerge from the Kalia episode:

1   Death among Hindus is not a private family affair, as it is in the West. Death is a communal event. Any person or persons who knew the deceased in any way may attend the funeral. This became evident at Kalia's death.
2   One does not need an invitation to attend a funeral. Acquaintance with the deceased or the deceased's family is sufficient ground to attend the funeral.
3   To attend a funeral is considered to be holy, an act of supreme piety. It is a an act of impiety – sin – to miss a funeral.
4   The funeral is performed swiftly and efficiently, within 24-hours following death: (a) because of matters of hygiene; and (b) because of the strongly held belief that upon death the dead – referred to as *preta* – undertake a voyage, a journey which takes them through several kingdoms of Yama, King of the underworld, until a year later they reach an abode referred to as *pitr-loka*. It is a temporary abode of the ancestors, and it is here that it is decided by Yama, Lord of Death, whether the deceased shall go to *svarga* (heaven) or to *narka* (hell) (Bhattacharyya, 1975; Borman, 1990; Filippi, 1996).
5   All the rites (*samskaras*) related to the funeral are ritualistically performed.
6   Death does not mark the end of life. It signals the beginning of a new one. Belief in the unending cycle of birth and rebirth, expounded in the law of karma, forms the cornerstone of Hindu spirituality. (Please refer to Chapter 6 for a detailed exposition of the law of karma.)
7   Death is not seen as an accidental event which occurs by 'chance'. It is determined when and where a person shall die. Destiny plays a hand in one's death.

Several attitudes surrounding the 'near-death' or 'after-death' experiences emerged from the episode. They eventually led to Kalia's suicide. Let us list a few of them:

1   The initial opinion of the mourners was one of wonder.
2   Kalia's 'return' to life was seen as an act of divine providence.
3   Kalia was imbued with benevolent, saintly powers.
4   His 'fame' spread. People from all over the town came to see him, seeking his blessings.
5   A gradual split in attitudes divided opinions in the town. What brought that about?
6   Kalia also came to be imbued with malevolent powers. He was seen as being in league with the devil and other evil and malevolent spirits.

(Continued)

7   The 'malevolent' side of Kalia's metamorphosis gained ascendance and people started to avoid him.
8   Finally, Kalia committed suicide.

Given that there was little or nothing in Kalia's daily life to suggest that he was 'touched' by divinity or saintliness, why did Kalia come to be imbued with divine, saintly powers? Why did the attitudes change? How did the 'saint' turn 'satan'? What brought about the cruel metamorphosis? Did he jump or was he pushed into committing suicide? Sadly, we shall never know.

Religion, disease and death

The Kalia incident took place over 40 years ago. The question is, would such attitudes prevail today? The answer is a cautious yes. Why should this be so, considering that India is a technologically advanced country? But despite the technological advancements, India has a population of over 1 billion, of which 70 to 75 per cent live in rural areas of the country, in villages, where the levels of literacy are low, and where almost 35 to 40 per cent of the people subsist below the poverty line. In many villages, a death certificate is not mandatory for funeral rites to be initiated. It is sufficient that the village *panchayat* – the elected members of the village council – certify that natural death has occurred.

Illness, disease, and death are explained not only in medico-legal terms in large metropolitan cities, but also in religious and spiritual terms. The two sets of explanations – religious and scientific – reside side-by-side, impervious to logical contradictions. Thus, a disease may be construed in terms of sorcery, bewitchment and the malevolent influences of evil spirits, and yet would not be averse to seeking allopathic, homeopathic, ayurvedic, and herbal medication. Belief in the evil eye – commonly referred to as *najar* or *dishti* – is also quite strong and widespread among Indians. A child who meets with an accident or falls seriously ill or dies might be the victim of an evil eye (Fuller, 1992; Laungani, 2005f). Social acceptance of such attributions has served to legitimize the belief in the evil eye, in other evil spirits, and their malevolent variants. All over India one finds an army of faith healers, mystics, shamans, *pirs* (holy men), *bhagats* (religious persons), gurus, astrologers, and palmists, who are often accorded greater respect and reverence than the medically trained doctors and psychiatrists (Kakar, 1982).

Beliefs in astrology and the malevolent influence of planets on one's life (and death) are strongly ingrained in the Indian psyche. That one's life is influenced by the nine planets, referred to as *grahas*, headed by the Sun, is widely prevalent in

India (Madan, 1987). The heavenly configuration of planets at the moment of birth is seen as a determinant of one's life chances. Such astrological formulations permit explanations and the acceptance of untimely deaths, sudden deaths, including suicides. So too might Kalia's death have been explained by all and sundry: 'It was in his stars'.

Conclusion

It is time to bring this chapter to a close. Let us summarize the main lessons that we have learnt from the chapter.

Common universal attitudes to dying and death

1 The fear of dying and death tends to be universal.
2 Paradoxically, it is the one fear that we all share in varying degrees with the rest of humanity.
3 Animals have no awareness of life and death. They just are. They live. They hunt. They eat. They breed. They fight. They die.
4 Although aware of our mortality, we often adopt self-duplicitous tricks to deny its eventual occurrence.

Western attitudes to dying and death

1 Unable to countenance the idea of death and extinction, there is a search for magical solutions, for example, cryogenics – which will resuscitate the dead and keep them alive – hopefully forever.
2 Westerners, having deposed God from heaven, have put their faith in the miracles of science.
3 Religious beliefs concerning heaven, hell, and an after-life have declined, and have given way to secular and humanistic beliefs.
4 The nature, the structure, and the 'style' of funerals have changed dramatically in the last two to three decade.
5 Funerals tend largely to be private, family affairs.
6 Performance of rites and rituals is kept to a minimum.

Eastern attitudes to dying and death

1 Religious beliefs play a dominant role in the acceptance of the inevitability of death.

2   It is the sacred duty of the family members and close relatives to prepare the body of the deceased for its final journey to the crematorium.

3   Great care is taken to ensure that all the rites and rituals related to a funeral are performed sincerely and correctly.

4   Belief in an after-life, rebirth, heaven, and hell are reinforced by the acceptance of the workings of the law of karma.

5   There is a strong desire among people to die 'a good death'. To die in one's old age after one has fulfilled all one's familial duties is seen as a good death.

6   The attainment of *moksha*, or *nirvana*, is the cherished aim of Hindus and Buddhists, for that is the only way to conquer death.

The final word

Death does not discriminate. Whether you are white or black, brown or pink, young or old, rich or poor, monarch or subject, male or female, you can rest assured it will not forget you, nor will it ignore you. Sooner or later (always sooner, it seems to us all) it seeks you out. We all fail to realize that death is but a breath away. We carry it around with us wherever we are, wherever we go. Lock yourself behind steel doors, take whatever precautions you can manage, as Howard Hughes tried to do; it still gets you. Others before you have tried to escape from its clutches. They have all failed. Wisdom lies in learning to accept its visit, which will come when it comes – often announced, but sometimes unannounced.

The secret is to be prepared.

Meet it when it comes. Not grudgingly, but with noble acceptance. Where it shall lead us we know not. Nor should we care. But until its shadow darkens your doorstep, you are free. Free to live each day of your life to its full. In fact, it is this profound awareness of the closeness of death that transforms each living moment into a gift. Harbour no regrets for the morrow, which if death strikes today, you shall never see.

Bibliography

AAA (American Anthropological Association) (1973). *Professional ethics*. Washington, DC: Author.

Abd al Ali, H. (1977). *The family structure in Islam*. Washington, DC: American Trust Publications.

Adair, J. G. (1973). *The human subject: The social psychology of the psychological experiment*. Boston, MD: Little, Brown.

Adair, J. G., Dushenko, T. W., & Lindsay, R. C. L. (1985). Ethical regulations and their impact on research practice. *American Psychologist, 40*(1), 59–72.

Adler, L. L., & Gielen, U. P. (Eds.). (2001). *Cross-cultural topics in psychology* (pp. 213–228). Westport, CT: Praeger

Aguilar, H. (1976). *The sacrifice in the Rg Veda*. Delhi: Bharatiya Vidya Prakashan.

Ahmed A. S. (1993). *From Samarkand to Stornoway: Living Islam*. London: BBC Books.

Al-Issa, I., & Al-Subaie, A. (2004). Native healing in Arab-Islamic societies. In Uwe P. Gielen, Jefferson M. Fish, & Juris G. Draguns (Eds.), *Handbook of culture, therapy, and healing*, (pp. 343–365). Mahwah, NJ: Erlbaum.

Allport, G. W. (1943). The ego in contemporry psychology. *Psychological Review, 50*, 451–478.

Allport, G. W. (1954). *The nature of prejudice*. Garden City, NY: Doubleday.

Allport, G. W. (1955). *Becoming: Basic considerations for a psychology of personality*. New Haven, CT: Yale University Press.

Allport, G. W. (1961). *Pattern and growth in personality*. New York: Holt, Rinehart & Winston.

Almeder, R. (1987). *Beyond death: Evidence for life after death*. Springfield, IL: Charles Thomas.

Altman, J., & Ginat, J. (1996). *Polygamous families in contemporary society*. Cambridge: Cambridge University Press.

APA (American Psychological Association) (1973). *Ethical principles in the conduct of research with human participants*. Washington, DC: Author.

APA (American Psychological Association) (1992). *Ethics code*. Washington, DC: Author.

Appadurai, A. (1990). Disjuncture and difference in the global cultural economy. *Theory, Culture and Society, 7*, 295–310.

APSA (American Political Science Asociation Comittee on Professional Standards and Responsibilities) (1968). Ethical problems of academic political scientists. *PS*, Newsletter of the American Political Science Association.

Argyle, M. (1982). Inter-cultural communication. In S. Bochner (Ed.), *Cultures in ccntact: Studies in cross-cultural interaction* (pp. 61–80). Oxford: Pergamon.

Aries, P. (1981). *The hour of our death*. New York: Knopf.

Aronson, E. (1992). *The social animal* (6th ed.). New York: Freeman.

ASA (American Sociological Association) (1971). *Code of ethics*. Washington, DC: Author.

Baldwin, J. (1964). *Nobody knows my name*. London: Corgi.

Bannister, D. (1966). Psychology as an exercise in paradox. *Bulletin of the British Psychological Society, 19*, 21–26.

Barber, T. X. (1976). *Pitfalls in human research: Ten pivotal points*. London: Pergamon.

Barnes, J. A. (1979). *Who should know what? Social science, privacy and ethics*. New York: Cambridge University Press.

Barnlund, D. C., & Araki, S. (1985). Intercultural encounters: The management of compliments by Japanese and Americans. *Journal of Cross-Cultural Psychology, 16*, 9–26.

Barrett, W. (1926). *Death-bed visions: The psychical experience of the dying*. Reprint. Northamptonshire: Aquarian.

Bartlett, F.C. (1923). *Psychology and primitive culture*. Cambridge: Cambridge University Press.

Bartlett, F. C. (1937). Psychological methods and anthropological problems. *Africa, 10*, 410–419.

Basham, A. L. (1966). *The wonder that was India*. Bombay: Rupa.

Batchelor, S. (1994). *The awakening of the West: The encounter of Buddhism and western culture*. London: Aquarian.

Baumrind, D. (1964). Some thoughts on ethics of research: After reading Milgram's 'Behavioral study of obedience.' *American Psychologist, 19*, 421–423.

Baumrin, B. H. (1970). The immorality of irrelevance: The social role of science. In F. F. Korten, S. W. Cook, & J. I. Lacey (Eds.), *Psychology and the problems of society*. Washington, DC: American Psychological Association.

Beattie, J. (1964). *Other cultures: Aims, methods and achievements in social anthropology*. London: Routledge & Kegan Paul.

Beatty, J. (2001). Language and communication. In Leonore Leob Adler & Uwe P. Gielen (Eds.), *Cross-cultural topics in psychology* (pp. 47–62). Westport, CT: Praeger.

Beauchamp, T. L., & Childress, J. F. (1994). *Principles of biomedical ethics* (4th ed.). Oxford: Oxford University Press.

Becker, E. (1973). *The denial of death*. New York: Free Press.

Bellah, R. N. (1985). *Habits of the heart: Individuation and commitment in American life*, Berkeley, CA: University of California Press.

Benedict, R. (1934/1946). *Patterns of culture*. New York: Mentor.

Berreman, G. D. (1969). Academic colonialism: Not so innocent abroad. *Nation, 209*, 505–508.

Berreman, G. D. (1972). *Hindus of the Himalayas: Ethnography and Change* (2nd ed.). CA: University of California Press.

Berreman, G. D. (1973). Anthropology and moral responsibility. In T. Weaver (Ed.), *To see ourselves: Anthropology and modern social issues* (pp. 178–179). Glenview: Scott Foresman.

Berry, J. W. (1969). On cross-cultural comparability. *International Journal of Psychology, 4*, 119–128.

Berry, J. W. (1976). *Human ecology and cognitive style: Comparative studies in cultural and psychological adaptation*. New York: Sage/Halsted.

Berry, J. W., Poortinga, Y. H., & Pandey, J. (Eds.). (1996). *Handbook of cross-cultural psychology*. Vol. 1 Theory and Method (pp. 85–128). Boston, MA: Allyn & Bacon.

Berry, J. W., Poortinga, Y. H., Segall, M. H., & Dasen, P. R. (1992). *Cross-cultural psychology: Research and applications*. New York: Cambridge University Press.

Berry, J. W., & Sam, D. (1997). Acculturation and adaptation. In J. W. Berry, M. H. Segall, & C. Kagitcibasi (Eds.), *Handbook of cross-cultural psychology*, Vol. 3, Social behaviour and applications. Boston, MD: Allyn & Bacon.

Bettleheim, B. (1986). *The informed heart*. London: Paladin.

Bhattacharyya, N. N. (1975). *Ancient Indian rituals and their social contents*. Delhi: Manohar Book Service.

Biesheuvel, S. (Ed.). (1969). *Methods for the measurement of psychological performance*. International Biological Programme, No. 10. Oxford: Blackwell Scientific.

Billig, M. (1976). *Social psychology and intergroup relations*. London: Academic Press.

Bloom, L. (1971). *The social psychology of race relations*. London: Allen & Unwin.

Boaz, F. (1911). *The mind of primitive man*. New York: Macmillan.

Bochner, S. (1986). Observational methods. In W. L. Lonner & J. W. Berry (Eds.), *Field methods in cross-cultural research* (pp. 165–201). Newbury Park, CA: Sage.

Bock, P. K. (1980). *Continuities in psychological anthropology A historical introduction*. San Francisco, CA: Freeman.

Bock, P. K. (Ed.) (1994). *Handbook of psychological anthropology*. Westport, CT: Greenwood.

Bok, S. (1978). *Lying: Moral choice in public and private life*. New York: Vintage.

Boring, E. G. (1929/1950). *A history of experimental psychology* (2nd ed.). New York: Appleton-Century-Crofts.

Borman, W. A. (1990). *The other side of death: Upanishadic eschatology*. Delhi: India Book Centre.

Bougle, C. (1992). The essence and reality of the caste system. In Dipankar Gupta (Ed.), *Social stratification*. Delhi: Oxford University Press.

Bowling, A. (1992). *Measuring health: A review of quality life measurement scales*. Buckingham: Open University Press.

BPS (British Psychological Society) (1993). *The BPS code of conduct, ethical principles and guidelines*. Leicester: The British Psychological Society.

Brislin, R. W. (1981). *Cross-cultural encounters: Face-to-face interaction*. New York: Pergamon.

Brislin, R. W. (1983). Cross-cultural research in psychology. *Annual Review of Psychology, 34*, 363–400.

Brislin, R. (1990). Applied cross-cultural psychology: An introduction. In Richard Brislin (Ed.), *Applied cross-cultural psychology. Cross-cultural research and methodology* series, Vol. 14 (pp. 9–33). Newbury Park, CA: Sage.

Brislin, R. W. (1993). *Understanding culture's influence on behaviour*. Fort Worth, TX: Harcourt Brace.

Brislin, R. W. (2001). Intercultural contact and communication. In Leonore Leob Adler & Uwe P. Gielen (Eds.), *Cross-cultural topics in psychology* (pp. 213–228). Westport, CT: Praeger.

Brown, R. (1965). *Social psychology*. London: Collier-Macmillan.

Brunswick, E. (1956). *Perception and the representative design of psychological experiments*. Berkeley, CA: University of California Press.

Bullough, V. L., & Bullough, B (1993). *Crossdressing, sex, and gender*. Philadelphia, PA: University of Pennsylvania Press.

Bumpass, L., Raley, R. K., & Sweet, J. A. (1995). The changing nature of stepfamilies: Implications of cohabitation and nonmarital childbearing. *Demography, 32*, 425–436.

Camilleri, C., (1989). La communication dans la perspective interculturelle. In Carmel Camilleri, & Marguelit Cohen-Emerique (Eds.), *Chocs de cultures: Concepts et enjeux pratiques de l'interculturel*: Paris. L'Harmattan.

Camilleri, C. (1990). *Stratégies identitaires*. Paris: PUF.

Campbell, D. T. (1965). Ethnocentric and other altruistic motives. In D. Levine (Ed.), *Nebraska symposium on motivation* (pp. 283–311). Lincoln, NE: University of Nebraska Press.

Camus, A. (1955). *The myth of Sisyphus*. New York: Knopf.

Capron, A. M., & Cass, L. R. (1980). A statutory definition of the standards for determining human death. In Dennis J. Horan & David Mall (Eds.), *Death, dying and euthanasia: An appraisal and a proposal* (pp. 40–71). Frederick, MD: University Publications of America.

Channabasavanna, S. M., & Bhatti, R. S. (1982). A study on interactional patterns of family typologies in families of mental patients. In A. Kiev & V. Rao (Eds.), *Readings in transcultural psychiatry* (pp. 149–161). Madras: Higginsbothams.

Char, S. V. D. (1997). *Hinduism and Islam in India: Caste, religion, and society from antiquity to early modern times*. Princeton, NJ: Markus Wiener.

Chopra, D. (1991). *Perfect health: The complete mind/body guide*. New York: Harmony Books.

Christensen, L. B. (1980). *Experimental methodology* (2nd ed.). Boston, MD: Allyn & Bacon.

Condominas, G. (1973). Ethics and comfort: An ethnographer's view of his profession. *Annual Report of the American Anthropological Association*, pp. 1–17.

Condominas, G. (1977). *We have eaten the forest: The story of a Montagnard village in the central highlands of Vietnam*. London: Allen Lane.

Cooley, C. H. (1902/1968). The social self: On the meaning of 'I'. In C. Gordon & K. J. Gergen (Eds.), *Self in social interaction* (pp. 87–91). New York: Wiley.

Cooper, D. E. (1996). *World philosophies: An historical introduction*. Oxford: Blackwell.

Darwin, C. (1872/1965). *The expression of emotions in man and animals*. Chicago, IL: University of Chicago Press.

Das, G. (2002). *The elephant paradigm: India wrestles with change*. New Delhi: Penguin.

Das, V. (1995). *Critical events: An anthropological perspective on contemporary India*. Delhi: Oxford University Press.

Davidson, A. R., Jaccard, J. J., Triandis, H. C., Morales, M. L., & Diaz-Guerrero, R. (1976). Cross-cultural model testing: Toward a solution of the etic-emic dilemma. *International Journal of Psychology, 11*, 1–13.

Davies, P. (1990). *God and the New Physics*. London: Penguin.

de Riencourt, A. (1980). *Sex and power in history*. New York: Dell.

Deitchman, S. J. (1976). *The best-laid schemes: A tale of social research and bureaucracy*. Cambridge, MA: MIT Press.

Devor, H. (1999). *Female-to-male transsexuals in society*. Bloomington, IN: Indiana University Press.

Dharmakeerti, U. S. (1982). Review of 'Yoga and cardiovascular management'. *Yoga, 20*(6), 15–16.

Dilman, I. (1999). *Free will: A historical and philosophical introduction*. London: Routledge.

Draguns, J. G. (1981). Psychological disorders of clinicial severity. In H. C. Triandis, & R. W. Brislin (Eds.), *Handbook of cross-cultural psychology*, Vol. 5. Boston, MA: Allyn & Bacon.

Draguns, J. (2001). Psychopathological and clinical aspects of personal experience: from selves and values to deficits and symptoms. In L. L. Adler & U. P. Gielen (Eds.), *Cross-cultural topics in psychology* (pp. 247–262). Westport, CT: Praeger.

Dumon, W. (Ed.) (1992). *National family policies in EC-countries in 1991*. Luxembourg: Commission of European Countries.

Eckel, M D. (2003). *Understanding Buddhism*. London: Duncan Baird.

Edgar, S. (1992). *Organizational culture and leadership* (2nd ed.). San Francisco, CA: Jossey-Bass.

Ehrlich, P. (2000). *Human natures: Genes, cultures, and human prospect*. Washington, DC/ Covelo, CA: Island Press/Shearwater Books.

Eisenberg, L. (1972). The human nature of human nature. *Science, 176*, 123–128.

Ekman, P. (1972). Universals and cultural differences in facial expressions of emotion. In J. Cole (Ed.), *Nebraska symposium of motivation,* Vol. 19. Lincoln, NE: University of Nebraska Press.

Ekman, P. (1973). *Darwin and facial expression.* New York: Academic Press.

Ekman, P. (1985). *Telling lies: Clues to deceit in the marketplace, marriage, and politics.* New York: Norton.

Ekman, P. (1994). Strong evidence for universals in facial expressions: A reply to Russell's mistaken critique. *Psychological Bulletin, 115,* 268–287.

Ekman, P., & Freisen, W. V. (1975). *Unmasking the face.* Englewood Cliffs, NJ: Prentice-Hall.

Ekman, P., & Heider, K. (1988). The universality of a contempt expression: A replication. *Motivation and Emotion, 12,* 303–308.

Eliot, T. S. (1948). *Notes towards the definition of culture.* London: Faber & Faber.

Ellenberger, H. (1970). *The discovery of the unconscious.* New York: Basic Books.

Ellison, R. (1952). *Invisible man.* New York: Random House.

Embree, A. T. (1988). *The encyclopedia of Asian history, sources of Indian tradition.* New York: Scribner.

Encyclopaedia Britannica. (2003). *India: Book of the year 2003.* New Delhi: The Hindu.

Enriquez, V.G. (1993). Developing a Filipno psychology. In U. Kim & John W. Berry (Eds.), *Indigenous psychologies: Research and experience in cultural context,* Vol. 17, Cross-cultural research and methodology series. Thousand Oaks, CA: Sage.

Erikson, E. (1963). *Childhood and society.* London: Penguin.

Erikson, E. H. (1968). *Identity, youth and crisis.* New York: Norton.

Erikson, E. H. (1982). *The life cycle completed.* New York: Norton.

Esposito, J. L. (1998). *Islam: The straight path* (3rd ed.). New York: Oxford University Press.

Eysenck, H. J. (1952). *The scientific study of personality.* London: Routledge & Kegan Paul.

Eysenck, H. J. (1960). *The structure of human personnality.* London: Methuen.

Eysenck, H. J. (1963). Biological basis of personality. *Nature, 99, 1031–1034.*

Eysenck, H. J. (1964). *Crime and personality.* London: Routledge & Kegan Paul.

Eysenck, H. J. (1967). *The biological basis of personality.* Springfield, IL: Thomas.

Eysenck, H. J. (1985). *Decline and fall of the Freudian empire.* Harmondsworth: Viking.

Eysenck, H. J., & Eysenck, S. B. G. (1969). *Personality structure and measurement.* London: Routledge & Kegan Paul.

Eysenck, H. J., & Eysenck, S. B. G. (1983). Recent advances in the cross-cultural study of personality. In J. N. Butcher & C. D. Spielberger (Eds.), *Advances in personality assessment.* Vol. 2 (pp. 41–69). Hillsdale, NJ. Erlbaum.

Farah, C. E. (1994). *Islam* (5th ed.). New York: Barron's Educational Series.

Faulkner, W. (1948/1968). *Intruder in the dust.* London: Penguin Books.

Festinger, L. (1954). A theory of social comparison processes. *Human Relations, 7,* 117–140.

Filippi, S. G. (1996). *Mrtyu: Concept of death in Indian traditions.* Reconstructing Indian History & Culture No. 11. New Delhi: Printworld.

Fingarette, H. (1972). *Confucius: The sacred as secular.* New York: Harper & Row.

Finifter, B. M. (1977). The robustness of cross-cultural findings. In L. L. Adler (Ed.), *Issues in cross-cultural research. Annals of the New York Academy of Sciences, 285,* 151–184.

Firth, S. (1993). Approaches to death in Hindu and Sikh communities in Britain, and cross-cultural perspectives on bereavement. In D. Dickenson & M. Johnson (Eds.), *Death, dying and bereavement.* London: Sage.

Fisher, C. B., & Fyrberg, D. (1994). Participant partners. *American Psychologist, 49(5),* 417–427.

Fitzgerald, E. (1859/1972). *Rubaiyat of Omar Khayyam.* London: Book Club Associates.

Flew, A. (1989). *An introduction to western philosophy.* London: Thames and Hudson.

Flood, G. (1996). *An introduction to Hinduism*. Cambridge: Cambridge University Press.

Frankfurt, H. G. (1988). *The importance of what we care about*. Cambridge: Cambridge University Press.

Fraser, J. (1932/1954). *The golden bough: A study in magic and religion* (abridged edition). London: Macmillan.

Freilich, M., Raybeek, D., & Suvishinsky, J. (1991). *Deviance: Anthropological perspectives*. New York: Greenwood.

Freud, S. (1955/1974). Studies on hysteria: Joseph Breuer & Sigmund Freud. *The Pelican Freud Library,* Vol. 3. London: Penguin.

Friedman, T. (2000). *The lexus and the olive tree*. London: HarperCollins.

Frijda, N., & Jahoda, G. (1966). On the scope and methods of cross-cultural research. *International Journal of Psychology, 1,* 109–127.

Fukuyama, F. (2002). *Our posthuman future: Consequences of the biotechnology revolution*. London: Profile.

Fuller, C. J. (1992). *The camphor fame: Popular Hinduism and society in India*. Princeton, NJ: Princeton University Press.

Gallup, G. (1982). *Adventures in immortality*. New York: McGraw-Hill.

Geertz, C. (1973). *The interpretation of culture*. New York: Basic Books.

Gellner, E. (1985). *Relativism and the social sciences*. Cambridge: Cambridge University Press.

Gergen, K. J., Gulerce, A., Lock, A., & Misra, G. (1996). Psychological science in cultural context. *American Psychologist, 51,* 496–503.

Ghosh, S. (1989). *Hindu concept of life and death*. Delhi: Munshram Motilal.

Gielen, U. P. (Ed.). (2004). Pittu Launguani in conversation with William West. In *Conservations with international psychologists* available online at www.iiccp.freeservers.com

Gielen, U. P., & Markoulis, D. C., (2001). Preference for principled moral reasoning: A developmental and cross-cultural perspective. In Leonore Leob Adler & Uwe P. Gielen (Eds.), *Cross-cultural topics in psychology* (pp. 81–102). Westport, CT: Praeger.

Gjertsen, D. (1989). *Science and philosophy: Past and present*. London: Penguin.

Goldschmidt, W. (1966). *Comparative functionalism*. Berkeley, CA: University of California Press.

Gombrich, E. H. (1979). *Ideals and idols: Essays on values in history and in art*. Oxford: Phaidon.

Gorer. G. (1965). *Death, grief, and mourning in contemporary Britain*. London: Cresset Press.

Gray, B. H., Cooke, R. A., & Tannenbaum, A. S. (1978). Research involving human subjects. *Science, 201,* 1094–1101.

Grayling, A. C. (2003). *What is good? The search for the best way to live*. London: Weidenfield & Nicolson.

Greenberg, C. I., & Firestone, J. J. (1977). Compensatory response to crowding: Effects of personal space and privacy reduction. *Journal of Personality and Social Psychology, 35,* 637–644.

Grondona, M. (2000). A cultural typology of economic development. In Lawrence E. Harrison & Samuel P. Huntington (Eds.), *Culture matters: How values shape human progress* (pp. 44–55). New York: Basic Books.

Gudykunst, W. B., & Bond, M. H. (1997). Intergroup relations across cultures. In J. W. Berry, M. H. Segall, & C. Kagitcibasi (Eds.), *Handbook of cross-cultural psychology,* Vol. 3, *Social behaviour and applications* (pp. 119–161). Boston, MA: Allyn & Bacon.

Halbfass, W. (1981/1988). *India and Europe: An essay in understanding*. New York: State University of New York Press.

Hamilton, W. D. (1964). The genetical evolution of social behaviour I, II. *Journal of Theoretical Biology, 7,* 1–52.

Harris, M. (1968). *The rise of anthropological theory: A history of theories of culture*. London: Routledge & Kegan Paul.

Harrison, L. E. (2000). Promoting progressive cultural change. In Lawrence E. Harrison & Samuel P. Huntington (Eds.), *Culture matters: How values shape human progress* (pp. 296–307). New York: Basic Books.

Hatchett, M. J. (1995). *Commentary on the American prayer book.* New York: HarperCollins.

Haviland, W. A. (1975). *Cultural anthropology* (8th ed.). Austin, TX: Holt, Rinchart & Winston.

Hayakawa, S. I. (1965). *Language in thought and action* (2nd ed.). London: George Allen & Unwin.

Heisenberg, W. (1930). *The physical principles of the quantum theory.* Berkeley, CA: University of California Press.

Helman, C. G. (1994). *Culture, health and illness: An introduction for health professionals* (3rd ed.). Oxford: Butterworth-Heinemann.

Herman, A. (1976). *The problem of evil and Indian though.* New Delhi: Motilal Banarasidass.

Hiriyanna, M. (1949). *The essentials of Indian philosophy.* London: Allen and Unwin.

Hoch, E. M. (1974). Pir, Fakir, and psychotherapist. *The Human Context, 6*(3), 668–676.

Hockey, J. (1993). The acceptable face of human grieving? The clergy's role in managing emotional expression during funerals. In D. Clark (Ed.), *The sociology of death* (pp. 129–148). Oxford: Blackwell.

Hofstede, G. (1976). *Nationality and organizational stress.* Brussels: European Institute for Advanced Studies in Management.

Hofstede, G. H. (1980). *Culture's consequences: International differences in work-related values.* London: Sage.

Hofstede, G. H. (1991). *Cultures and organizations: Software of the mind.* New York: McGraw-Hill.

Hofstede, G. H. (2001). *Culture's consequences: Comparing values, behaviors, institutions and organizations across nations.* Thousand Oaks, CA: Sage.

Honderich, T. (1999). *The philosophers – introducing great western thinkers.* London: University College.

Horan, D. J., & Mall, D. (Eds.). (1980). *Death, dying and euthanasia.* Frederick, MD: University Publications of America.

Horowitz, I. L. (1973). Transaction magazine: A decade of critical social science journalism. *International Social Science Journal, 25,* 169–189.

Hui, C. H., & Triandis, H. C. (1986). Individualism-collectivism: A study of cross-cultural researchers. *Journal of Cross-Cultural Psychology, 17,* 222–248.

Hull, D. L. (1998). On human nature. In Donald L. Hull & Michael Ruse (Eds.), *The philosophy of biology.* New York: Oxford University Press.

Huxley, A. (1939). *Brave new world.* New York: Harper & Brothers.

Jaffrey, Z. (1996). *The invisibles: A tale of the eunuchs in India.* New York: Pantheon.

Jahoda, G. (1958). Child animisim I: A critical survey of cross-cultural research; Child animism II: A study in West Africa. *The Journal of Social Psychology, 47,* 197–212 and 213–222.

Jahoda, G. (1970). A cross-cultural perspective in psychology. *The Advancement of Science, 27*(31), 57–70.

Jahoda, G. (1977). In pursuit of the emic–etic division: Can we ever capture it? In Y. H. Poortinga (Ed.), *Basic problems in cross-cultural psychology* (pp. 55–62). Amsterdam: Swets & Zeitlinger.

Jahoda, G. (1982). *Psychology and anthropology.* London: Academic Press.

Jahoda, G. (1983). The cross-cultural emperor's conceptual clothes: The emic–etic issue revisited. In J. B. Deregowski, S. Dziurawiec, & R. C. Annis (Eds.), *Explications in cross-cultural psychology* (pp. 19–37). Lisse: Swets & Zeitlinger.

Jahoda, G. (1990). Variables, systems and the problem of explanation. In F. J. R. Van der Vijver & G. J. M. Hutschemaekers (Eds.), *The investigation of culture* (pp. 115–130). Tilburg: Tilburg University Press.

Jahoda, G. (1992). *Crossroads between culture and mind.* London: Harvester Wheatsheaf.

Jahoda, G., & Krewer, B. (1997). History of cross-cultural psychology and cultural psychology. In J. W. Berry, Y. H. Poortinga, & J. Pandey (Eds.), *Handbook of cross-cultural psychology,* Vol. 1, Theory and Method (pp. 1–42). Boston, MA: Allyn & Bacon.

James, W. (1890/1983). *Principles of psychology.* Cambridge, MA: Harvard University Press.

James, W. (1902/1958). *The will to believe and other essays in popular philosophy and human immortality.* New York: Dover.

James, W. (1910). *Psychology.* New York: Holt.

Jensen, A. R. (1969). How much can we boost IQ and scholastic achievement? *Harvard Educational Review, 39,* 1–123.

Johnson, P. (2000). *The Renaissance.* London: Phoenix.

Judd, C. M., Smith, E. R., & Kidder, L. H. (1991). *Research methods in social relations* (6th ed.). Philadelphia, PA: Harcourt Brace, Jovanovich College.

Justice, C. (1997). *Dying the good death: The pilgrimage to die in India's holy city.* New York: State University of New York Press.

Kagitcibasi, C. (1997). Individualism and collectivism. In J. W. Berry, M. H. Segall, & C. Kagitcibasi (Eds.), *Handbook of cross-cultural psychology: Social behavior and applications* (pp. 1–49). Boston, MA: Allyn & Bacon.

Kakar, S. (1979/1992). *Identity and adulthood.* Delhi: Oxford University Press.

Kakar, S. (1981). *The inner world – a psychoanalytic study of children and society in India.* Delhi: Oxford University Press.

Kakar, S. (1982). *Shamans, mystics and doctors.* London: Unwin.

Kakar, S. (1997). *Culture and psyche: Selected essays.* Delhi: Oxford University Press.

Kastenbaum, R. (2000). *The psychology of death* (3rd ed.). London: Free Association.

Kastenbaum, R., & Kastenbaum, B. (1989). *Encyclopaedia of death.* Phoenix, AZ: Oryx.

Katz, P. A., & Taylor, D. A. (1988). *Eliminating racism.* New York: Plenum.

Kelman, H. C. (1968). *A time to speak: On human values and social research.* San Francisco, CA: Jossey-Bass.

Kelman, H. C. (1972). The rights of the subjects in social research: An analysis in terms of relative power and legitimacy. *American Psychologist, 27,* 989–1016.

Kenny, A. (1994). *The Oxford illustrated history of western philosophy.* New York: Oxford University Press.

Khilnani, S. (1997). *The idea of India.* London: Penguin.

Kierkegaard, S. (1940). *The concept of dread.* Princeton, NJ: Princeton University Press.

Kim, U., & Berry, J. W. (Eds.). (1993). *Indigenous psychologies: Research and experience in cultural context,* Vol. 17 Cross-Cultural Research and Methodology Series. Newbury Park, CA: Sage.

Kim, U., Triandis, H.C. Kagitcibasi, C., Choi, S-C., & Yoon, G. (1994). *Individualism and collectivism: Theory, method, and applications.* Thousand Oaks, CA: Sage.

Kim, U., Triandis, H. C., & Yoon, G. (Eds.). (1992). *Individualism and collectivisim: Theoretical and methodological issues.* Newbury Park, CA: Sage.

Kirk, G. S. (1974). *The nature of Greek myths.* Harmondsworth: Penguin.

Klineberg, O. (1980). Historical perspectives: Cross-cultural psychology before 1960. In H. C. Triandis & W. W. Lambert (Eds.), *Handbook of cross-cultural psychology,* Vol. 1 (pp. 1–14, 31–67). Boston, MA: Allyn & Bacon.

Klostermaier, K. K. (1998). *A short introduction to Hinduism*. Oxford: Oneworld.

Klostermaier, K. K. (1999). *Buddhism: A short introduction*. Oxford: Oneworld.

Koestler, A. (1967). *The ghost in the machine*. London: Hutchinson.

Koestler, A. (1966). *The lotus and the robot*. New York: Harper.

Kohlberg, L. (1984). *Essays on moral development*, Vol. 2 The psychology of moral development. New York: Harper & Row.

Koller, J. M. (1982). *The Indian way: Perspectives*. London: Collier Macmillan.

Kroeber, A. L., & Kluckhohn, C. (1952). *Culture: A critical review of concepts and definitions*. Cambridge, MA: Peabody Museum.

Kubler-Ross, E. (1969). *On death and dying*. London: Tavistock.

Kuhn, T. (1970). *The structure of scientific revolutions*. Chicago, IL: The University of Chicago Press.

Kuhn, T. S. (1996). *The structure of scientific revolutions* (3rd ed.). Chicago, IL: University of Chicago Press.

Kuhn, T. (1998). The nature and necessity of scientific revolutions. In Martin Curd & J. A. Cover (Eds.), *Philosophy of science: The central issues* (pp. 86–101). New York: Norton.

Kurtz. P. (1983). *In defence of secular humanism*. New York: Prometheus.

Lakatos, I., (1978). The methodology of scientific research programmes. In J. Worrall & G. Currie (Eds.), *Philosophical papers*. Vol. 1. Cambridge: Cambridge University Press.

Lakatos, I., & Musgrave, A. (Eds.). (1970). *Criticism and the growth of knowledge*. Cambridge: Cambridge University Press.

Lambert, W. (1972). *Language, psychology and culture*. Stanford, CA: Stanford University Press.

Lannoy, R. (1975). *The speaking tree: A study of Indian culture and society*. London: Routledge.

Lannoy, R. (1976). *The speaking tree*. Oxford: Oxford University Press.

Laungani, P. (1988). Accidents in children – an Asian perspective. *Public Health, 103,* 171–176.

Laungani, P. (1990). Turning eastward – an Asian view on child abuse. *Health & Hygiene, 11*(1), 26–29.

Laungani, P. (1992a). Assessing child abuse through interviews of children and parents of children at risk. *Children and Society, 6*(1), 3–11.

Laungani, P. (1992b). Cultural variations in the understanding and treatment of psychiatric disorders: India and England. *Counselling Psychology Quarterly, 5*(3), 231–244.

Laungani, P. (1992c). *It shouldn't happen to a patient*. London: Whiting & Birch.

Laungani, P. (1993). Cultural differences in stress and its management. *Stress Medicine, 9*(1), 37–43.

Laungani, P. (1994). Cultural differences in stress: India and England. *Counselling Psychology Review, 9*(4), 25–37.

Laungani, P. (1995a). Can psychotherapies seriously damage your health? *Counselling, Journal of the British Association for Counselling, 6*(2), 110–115.

Laungani, P. (1995b). Patterns of bereavement in Indian and English societies. *Bereavement Care, 14*(1), 5–7.

Laungani, P. (1995c). Stress in eastern and western cultures. In John Brebner, Esther Greenglass, Pittu Laungani, & Ann O'Roark (Eds.). (Series Editors: Charles D. Spielberger and Irwin G. Sarason), *Stress and emotion*, Vol. 15, (pp. 265–280). Washington, DC: Taylor and Francis.

Laungani, P. (1996a). Death and bereavement in India and England: A comparative analysis. *Mortality, 1*(2), 191–212.

Laungani, P. (1996b). Death in a Hindu Family. In C. M. Parkes, P. Laungani, & W. Young, (Eds.), *Death and bereavement across cultures*. London: Routledge.

Laungani, P. (1996c). Research in cross-cultural settings: Ethical considerations. In E. Miao (Ed.), *Cross-cultural encounters*. Proceedings of the 53rd Annual Convention of International Council of Psychologists (pp. 107–136). Taipei: General Innovation Service (GIS).

Laungani, P. (1996d). Cross-cultural investigations of stress: Conceptual and methodological considerations. *International Journal of Stress Management, 3*(1), 25–35.

Laungani, P. (1997a). *The strange afflicition of Hamlet, Prince of Denmark*. Leicester: British Psychological Society.

Laungani, P. (1997b). Patterns of bereavement in Indian and English Society. In J. D. Morgan (Ed.), *Readings in thanatology* (pp. 67–76). Amityville, NY: Baywood.

Laungani, P. (1997c). Replacing client-centred counselling with culture-centred counselling. *Counselling Psychology Quarterly, 10*(4), 343–351.

Laungani, P. (1998). The changing patterns of Hindu funerals in Britain. *Pharos International, 64*(4), 4–10.

Laungani, P. (1999a). Culture and identity. In S. Palmer & P. Laungani (Eds.), *Counselling in a multi-cultural society* (pp. 35–70). London: Sage.

Laungani, P. (1999b). Death among Hindus in India and England. *International Journal of Group Tensions, 28*(1–2), 85–114.

Laungani, P. (1999c). Stress in India and England. In D. M. Pestonjee, Udai Pareek, & Rita Agarwal (Eds.), *Studies in stress and its management*. New Delhi: Oxford/India Book House.

Laungani, P. (2000a). The changing patterns of Hindu funerals in Britain: Cultural and psychological implications. *Asian Journal of Psychology and Education, 33*(1–2), 2–14.

Laungani, P. (2000b). Cultural influences on the development of identity: India and England. In Jitendra Mohan (Ed.), *Personality across cultures: Recent developments and debates*. (pp. 284–312). New Delhi: Oxford University Press.

Laungani, P. (2001a). Hindu deaths in India – I. *International Journal of Health Promotion and Education, 39*(3), 88–96.

Laungani, P. (2001b). Hindu Deaths in England – II. *International Journal of Health Promotion and Education, 39*(4), 114–120.

Laungani, P. (2001c). Terrorism: A world health hazard. *International Journal of Health Promotion and Education, 39*(4), 99.

Laungani, P. (2001d). The influence of culture on stress: India and England. In L. L. Adler, & U. P. Gielen (Eds.), *Cross-cultural topics in Psychology* (2nd ed.) (pp. 149–170). Westport, CT: Prager.

Laungani, P. (2002a). The Hindu caste system. In G. Howarth & O. Leman (Eds.), *The encyclopaedia of death and dying*. London: Routledge.

Laungani, P. (2002b). Hindu Spirituality in life, death, and bereavement. In J. Morgan & P. Laungani (Eds.), *Death and bereavement around the world,* Vol. 1 Major religious traditions. Amityville, NY: Baywood.

Laungani, P. (2002c). Cross-cultural psychology: A handmaiden to mainstream western psychology. *Counselling Psychology Quarterly, 15*(4), 385–397.

Laungani, P. (2003). Family life in India. In Roopnarine Uwe Gielen (Ed.), *Families in global perspective*. Boston: MA: Allyn & Bacon.

Laungani, P. (2004a). *Asian perspectives in counselling and psychotherapy*. London: Routledge.

Laungani, P. (2004b). Counselling and therapy in a multicultural setting. *Counselling Psychology Quarterly, 17*(2), 1–13.

Laungani, P. (2004c). Culture and psychotherapy. *Forum – IGAP Textbook No. 0–2004. Special Edition., The Intercultural Group Work* (pp. 9–21).

Laungani, P. (2005a). Family life in India. In Roopnarine Uwe Gielen (Ed.), *Families in global perspective*. Boston, MA: Allyn & Bacon.

Laungani, P. (2005b). Stress, culture, and personality. In C. Cooper (Ed.), *Handbook of stress medicine and health* (2nd ed.) (pp. 209–227). Boca Raton, FL: CRC Press, LLC.

Laungani, P. (2005c, June). *Building multicultural counselling bridges: The holy grail or a poisoned chalice?* Keynote paper presented at the Lifetime Achievement Award Conference in honour of Dr Pittu Laungani, University of Toronto, Canada.

Laungani, P. (2005d). Stress in a life-threatening illness. In Charles D. Spielberger & Irvin Sarason (Eds.), *Stress and emotion*, Vol. 17 (pp. 3–30). Washington, DC: Taylor and Francis.

Laungani, P. (2005e). Hindu spirituality and healing practices. In R., Moodley, & W. West, (Eds.), *Healing practices into counselling and psychotherapy* (pp. 138–147). Thousand Oaks, CA: Sage.

Laungani, P. (2005f). Caste, class and culture: A case study. *Counselling Psychology Quarterly, 18*(1), 61–71.

Laungani, P., & Roach, F. (1997). Counselling, death and bereavement. In S. Palmer (Ed.), *Handbook of counselling*. London: Sage.

Laungani, P., & Sookhoo, D. (1995, July). *Myocardial infraction in British white and Asian adults: Their health beliefs and health practices*. Paper read at the 4th European Congress of Psychology, Athens, Greece.

Lavine, T. Z. (1989). *From Socrates to Sartre: The philosophic quest*. New York: Bantom.

Leach, E. (1964). Comment on Naroll's 'On ethnic unit classification'. *Current Anthropology, 5*(4), 299.

Leahey, T. H. (1997). *A history of psychology: Main currents in psychological thought* (4th ed.). Englewood Cliffs, NJ: Prentice-Hall.

Lee, H. (1960/2002). *To kill a mockingbird*. New York: HarperCollins.

Leridon, H., & Toulemon, L. (1995). Trends in family formation: France. In H. P. Blossfeld (Ed.), *The new role of women: Family formation in modern societies* (pp. 77–101). Boulder, CO: Westview.

Levine, C. (1991). *Sexuality and politics in Renaissance drama* (Co-edited with Karen Robertson). Lewiston, NY: Edwin Mellen.

Levine, R. A. (1973). *Culture, behaviour and personality*. Chicago, IL: Aldine.

Lewis, O. D. (1973). Anthropology and colonialism. *Current Anthropology, 14*, 581–591.

Lifton, R. (1986). *The nazi doctors: Medical killing and the psychology of genocide*. New York: Basic Books.

Lindgren, H. C., & Tebcherani, A. (1971). Arab and American auto-heterostereotypes: A cross-cultural study of empathy. *Journal of Cross-cultural Psychology, 2*, 173–180.

Lipner, J. (1994). *Hindus: Their religious beliefs and practices*. London: Routledge.

Loffland, L. (1978). *The craft of dying*. Beverly Hills, CA: Sage.

Lonner, W. J. (1980). The search for psychological universals. In H. C. Triandis & W. W. Lambert (Eds.), *Handbook of cross-cultural psychology*, Vol. 1, (pp. 143–204). Boston, MA: Allyn & Bacon.

Lonner, W. J., & Berry, J. W. (1986). *Field methods in cross-cultural research*. Boston, MA: Allyn & Bacon.

Low, B. S. (2005). Families: An evolutionary anthropological perspective. In Jaipaul L. Roopnarine & Uwe P. Gielen (Eds.), *Families in global perspective* (pp. 14–32). Boston, MA: Allyn & Bacon.

Luker, K. (1996). *Dubious conceptions: The politics of teenage pregnancy*. Cambridge, MA: Harvard University Press.

Lukes, S. (1973). *Individualism*. Oxford: Blackwell.

Lynn, J., & Childress, J. F. (1986). Must patients be always given food and water? In R. F. Weir (Ed.), *Ethical issues in death and dying*. New York: Columbia University Press.

Madan, T. N. (1987). *Non-renunciation: Themes and interpretations of Hindu culture*. Delhi: Oxford University Press.

Magee, B. (1997). *Confessions of a philosopher*. London: Weidenfeld & Nicolson.

Magee, B. (2002). *Confessions of a philosopher: A journey through western philosophy*. London: Phoenix.

Malinowski, B. (1927). *Sex and repression in savage society*. London: Routledge.

Mandelbaum, D. G. (1972). *Society in India*, Vol. 2. Berkeley, CA: University of California Press.

Manorama (2003). *Manorama yearbook 2003*. Malayala Manorama.

Marglin, S. M., & Marglin, F. A. (Eds.). (1993). *Dominating knowledge*. Oxford: Clarendon.

Markus, H. R., & Kitayana, S. (1991). Culture and the self: Implications for cognition, motivation, and emotion. *Psychological Review, 98*, 224–253.

Marsella, A. J. (1982). Depressive experience and disorder across cultures. In H. C. Triandis & R. W. Brislin (Eds.), *Handbook of cross-cultural psychology*. Boston, MA: Allyn and Bacon.

Maslow, A. (1970). *Motivation and personality* (2nd ed.). New York: Harper & Row.

Maslow, A. (1971*). The farther reaches of human nature*. New York: McGraw-Hill.

Matsumoto, D. (1989). Cultural influences on the perception of emotion. *Journal of Cross-Cultural Psychology, 20*, 92–105.

Matsumoto, D. (1992). American–Japanese cultural differences in the recognition of universal facial expresssions. *Journal of Cross-Cultural Psychology, 23*, 72–84.

Matsumoto, D. (1996a). *Culture and psychology*. Belmont, CA: Brooks/Cole.

Matsumoto, D. (1996b). *Unmasking Japan: Myths and realities about the emotions of the Japanese*. Stanford, CA. Stanford University Press.

McClelland, D. C. (1961). *The achieving society*. Princeton, NJ: Van Nostrand.

McCormick, R. (1976). Proxy consent in the experimental situation. *Perspectives in Biology and Medicine, 18*, 2–20.

McCormick, R., & Ramsey, P. (Eds.). (1978). *Doing evil to achieve good: Moral choices in conflict situations*. Chicago, IL: Loyola University Press.

McNamara, J. R., & Woods, K. M. (1977). Ethical considerations in psychological research: A comparative review. *Behaviour Therapy, 8*, 703–708.

Mead, G. H. (1934). *Mind, self and society from the point of view of a social behaviourist*. Chicago, IL: University of Chicago Press.

Mead, M. (1928). *Coming of age in Samoa*. New York: Morrow.

Mead, M. (1930). *Growing up in New Guinea*. New York: Morrow.

Mead, M. (1932). An investigation of the thought of primitive children, with special reference to animism. *Journal of the Royal Anthropological Institute, 62*, 173–90.

Mead, M. (1935). *Sex and temperament in three primitive societies*. New York: Morrow.

Milgram, S. (1974). *Obedience to authority*. London: Tavistock.

Mill, J. (1817). *History of British India*. London: Baldwin, Cradock and Joy.

Miller, G. A. (1969). Psychology as a means of promoting human welfare. *American Psychologist, 24*, 1063–75.

Miller, J. G. (1997). Theoretical issues in cultural psychology. In J. W. Berry, Y. P. Poortinga, & J. Pandey (Eds.), *Handbook of cross-cultural psychology* (2nd ed.) (pp. 85–128). Boston, MA: Allyn & Bacon.

Mishra, R. (1997). Cognition and cognitive development. In J. W. Berry, P. R. Dasen, & T. S. Saraswathi (Eds.), *Handbook of cross-cultural psychology*, Vol. 2 Basic processes and human development (pp. 143–175). Boston, MA: Allyn & Bacon.

Mishra, R. C., Sinha, D., & Berry, J. W. (1996). *Ecology, acculturation and psychological adaptation*. Newbury Park, CA: Sage.

Mixon, D. (1977). Temporary false belief. *Personality and Social Psychology Bulletin, 3*, 479–488.

Moller, D. W. (1996). *Confronting death: Values, institutions and human mortality*. New York: Oxford University Press.

Moodley, R. (2005). Shamanic performance: Healing through magic and supernatural. In R. Moodley & W. West (Eds.). *Healing practices into counselling and psychotherapy* (pp. 2–14). Thousand Oaks, CA: Sage.

Moody, R. A., Jr. (1975). *A life after life*. St Simon Island, GA: Mockingbird.

Moody, R. A., Jr. (1977). *Reflections on after-life*. St Simon Island, GA: Mockingbird.

Moody, R. A., Jr. (1989). *The light beyond*. New York: Bantam.

Moore, B. N. (1981). *The philosophical possibilities beyond death*. Springfield, IL: Thomas.

Morgan, J., & Laungani, P. (Eds.). (2002). *Death and bereavement around the world*, Vol. 1. Amityville, NY: Baywood.

Morgan, J., & Laungani, P. (Eds.). (2003). *Death and bereavement around the world*, Vol. 2. Amityville, NY: Baywood.

Morgan, J., & Laungani, P. (Eds.). (2004). *Death and bereavement around the world*, Vol. 3. Amityville, NY: Baywood.

Morgan, J., & Laungani, P. (Eds.). (2005). *Death and bereavement around the world*, Vol. 4. Amityville, NY: Baywood.

Morgan, J., & Laungani, P. (Eds.) (in press). *Death and bereavement around the world*, Vol. 5. Amityville, NY: Baywood.

Mosca, Alexandria K. (2002).The funeral of John Gotti. *The American Funeral Director, Dec.*, 64–65.

Munroe, R. L., & Munroe, R. H. (1980). Perspectives suggested by anthropological data. In *Handbook of cross-cutural psychology,* Vol. 1 (pp. 253–317). Boston, MA: Allyn & Bacon.

Munroe, R. L., & Munroe, R. H. (1994). *Cross-cultural human development*. New York: Garland.

Munroe, R. L., & Munroe, R. H. (1997). A comparative anthropological perspective. In J. W. Berry, Y. P. Poortinga, & J. Pandey (Eds.), *Handbook of cross-cultural psychology* (2nd ed.) (pp. 171–214). Boston, MA: Allyn & Bacon.

Murdock, G. P. (1945). The common denominator of cultures. In R. Linton (Ed.), *The science of man in world crisis*. New York: Columbia University Press.

Murdock, G. P. (1964). Comment on Naroll's 'On ethnic unit classification'. *Current Anthropology, 5*(4), 301–302.

Murdock, G. P. (1967). *Ethnographic atlas*. Pittsburgh, PA: University of Pittsburgh Press.

Murdock, G. P. (1981). *Atlas of world cultures*. Pittsburgh, PA: University of Pittsburgh Press.

Murdock, G. P., & Provost, C. (1973). Factors in the division of labour by sex. *Ethnology, 12*, 203–225.

Murdock, G. P., & Provost, C. (1979). Measurement of cultural complexity. *Ethnology, 12*, 379–392.

Musgrove, F. (1982). *Education and anthropology: Other cultures and the teacher*. Chichester: Wiley.

Nagel, E. (1965). Psychology and the philosophy of science. In Ernest Nagel (Ed.), *Scientific psychology: Principles and approaches* (pp. 24–27). New York: Basic Books.

Naito, T., & Gielen, U. P. (1992). *Tatemae* and *Honne*: A study of moral relativism in Japanese culture. In U. P. Gielen, L. L. Adler, & N. A. Milgram (Eds.), *Psychology in the international perspective* (pp. 161–162). Amsterdam: Swets & Zeitlinger.

Nanda, S. (1998). *Neither man nor woman: The Hijras of India*. Belmont, CA: Wadsworth.

Nandy, A. (1974). The non-paradigmatic crisis in Indian psychology: Reflections on a recipient culture of science. *Indian Journal of Psychology, 49*, 1–20.

Nichols, K. R., & McAndrew, F. T. (1984). Stereotyping and autostereotyping in Spanish, Malaysian, and American college students. *Journal of Social Psychology, 124*, 179–189.

O'Flaherty, W. D. (1976). *The origins of evil in Hindu mythology*. Berkeley, CA: University of California Press.

O'Flaherty, W. D. (1980). *Karma and rebirth in classical Indian traditions*. Berekely, CA: University of California Press.

Oldstone-Moore, J. (2003). *Understanding Confucianism*. London: Duncan Baird.

Onians, R. B. (1951). *The origins of European thought*. Cambridge: Cambridge University Press.

Osgood, C. E., Suci, G. J., & Tannenbaum, P. H. (1957). *The measurement of meaning*. Urbana, IL: University of Illinois Press.

Pande, S. (1968). The mystique of 'western' psychotherapy: An eastern interpretation. *The Journal of Nervous and Mental Disease, 146*, 425–432.

Pandey, R. (1948/1969). *Hindu Samskaras: Socio-religious study of the Hindu sacraments*. Delhi: Motilal Banarasidass.

Pandey, R. S., Srinivas, K. N., & Muralidhar, D. (1980). Socio-cultural beliefs and treatment acceptance. *Indian Journal of Psychiatry, 22*, 161–166.

Pankhania, J. (2005). Yoga and its practice in psychological healing. In R. Moodley & W. West (Eds.), *Healing practices into counselling and psychotherapy* (pp. 246–256). Thousand Oaks, CA: Sage.

Paranjpe, A. C. (1998). *Self and identity in modern psychology and Indian thought*. New York: Plenum.

Parekh, B. (2000). *Rethinking multiculturalism: Cultural diversity and political theory*. Basingstoke: Macmillan/Palgrave.

Park, J. E., & Park, K. (1991). *Park's textbook of preventive and social medicine* (13th ed.). Jabalpur: Banarasidas Bhanot.

Parkes, C. M., Laungani, P., & Young, W. (Eds.). (1997). *Death and bereavement across cultures*. London: Routledge.

Parry, J. P. (1994). *Death in Banaras*. Cambridge: Cambridge University Press.

Pater, W. (1986). *The Renaissance: Studies in art and poetry* (First published 1873). Oxford: Oxford University Press.

Patterson, C. J., & Freil, L. V. (2000). Sexual orientation and fertility. In G. Bentley & N. Mascie-Taylor (Eds.), *Infertility in the modern world: Biosocial perspectives* (pp. 238–261). Cambridge: Cambridge University Press.

Paxman, J. (1998). *The English: A portrait of a people*. London: Michael Joseph.

Pelikan, J. (1974). *The spirit of eastern christiandom: 1600–1700*. Chicago, IL: University of Chicago Press.

Pettigrew, T. F. (1978). Three issues in ethnicity: Boundaries, deprivations, and perceptions. In J. M. Yinger & S. J. Cutler (Eds.), *Major social issues: A multidisciplinary view* (pp. 25–49). New York: Free Press.

Piaget, J. (1948). *The moral judgment of the child*. New York: Free Press.

Pike, K. L. (1966). *Language in relation to a unified theory of the structure of human behaviour*. The Hague: Mouton.

Popper, K. (1963). *Conjectures and refutations*. London: Routledge & Kegan Paul.

Popper, K. (1966). *The open society and its enemies*: Vol. 1, The spell of Plato. Princeton, NJ: Princeton University Press.

Popper, K. (1972). *Objective knowledge: An evolutionary approach*. Oxford: Clarendon.

Popper, K. (1988). *The open universe: An argument for indeterminism*. London: Hutchinson.

Prasad, R. (1989). *Karma causation and retributive morality. Conceptual essays in ethics and metaethics*. Indian Council of Philosophical Research. New Delhi: Munshiram Manoharlal.

Prince, R. (2004). Western psychotherapy and the Yoruba: Problems of insight and non-directive technique. In U. P. Gielen, J. M. Fish, & J. G. Draguns (Eds.), *Handbook of culture, therapy, and healing* (pp. 311–319). Mahwah, NJ: Erlbaum.

Pryzwansky, W. B., & Wendt, R. N., (1999). *Professional and ethical issues in psychology: Foundations of practice*. New York: Norton.

Quindlen, A. (1994). Death carves a chasm of loss deep in the centre of life. *The Kansas City Star, C-5*.

Radhakrishnan, S. (1927/1948). *Indian philosophy*, Vol. 1. London: Allen & Unwin.

Radhakrishnan, S. (1923/1989). *Indian philosophy*, Vol. 2. Delhi: Oxford University Press.

Radhakrishnan, S. (1939). *Eastern religions and Western thought*. Oxford: Clarendon Press.

Rahula, W. (1997). *What the Buddha taught*. Oxford: Oneworld.

Rando, Therese A. (1984). *Grief, dying and death: Clinical interventions for caregivers*, Champaign, IL: Research Press.

Ratner, C., & Hui, L. (2003). Theoretical and methodological problems in cross-cultural psychology. *Journal for the Theory of Social Behaviour, 3*, 67–94.

Reichenbach, B. R. (1990). *The law of karma: A philosophical study*. Honolulu, HI: University of Hawaii Press.

Reyes, B. (1986). *Conscious dying: Psychology of death and guidebook to liberation*. Ojal, CA: World University of America.

Riesman, D. (1954). *Individualism reconsidered*. New York: Doubleday Anchor.

Ring, K., Wallston, K., & Corey, M. (1970). Mode of debriefing as a factor affecting reaction to a Milgram-type obedience experiment: An ethical inquiry. *Representative Research in Social Psychology, 1*, 67–88.

Rivers, W. H. R. (1901). Part I, Introduction and vision. In A. C. Haddon (Ed.), *Reports of the Cambridge anthropological expedition to Torres Straits*, Vol. 2. Cambridge: Cambridge University Press.

Rivers, W. H. R. (1905). Observations on the sense of the Todas. *British Journal of Psychology, 1*, 321–396.

Robinson, D. N. (2001). Sigmund Koch – philosophically speaking. *American Psychologist, 56*(5), 420–424.

Rogers, C. (1961). *On becoming a person*. Boston, MA: Houghton Mifflin.

Rogers, C. (1980). *A way of being*. Boston, MA: Houghton Mifflin.

Rohner, R. P. (1974). Proxemics and stress: An empirical study of the relationship between space and roommate turnover. *Human Relations, 27*, 697–702.

Roland, A. (1988). *In search of self in India and Japan*. Princeton, NJ: Princeton University Press.

Roland, A. (1996). *Cultural pluralism and psychoanalysis: The Asian and North American experience*. New York: Routledge.

Roopnarine, J. L., & Gielen, U. (Eds.). (2005). *Families in global perspectives*. Boston, MA: Allyn & Bacon.

Rorschach, H. (1921). *Psychodiagnostik* (2nd ed.). Berlin and Leipzig: Huber.

Rosenblatt, P. C. (1997/2003). Grief in small societies. In C. M. Parkes, P. Laungani, & B. Young (Eds.), *Death and bereavement across cultures* (pp. 27–51). London: Routledge.

Rosenthal, R., & Jacobson, L. (1968). *Pygmalion in the classroom: Teacher expectation and pupils intellectual development*. New York: Rinehart and Winston.

Rosenthal, R., & Rosnow, R. L. (1974). *The volunteer subject*. New York: Wiley.

Roy, A. (2001). *The algebra of infinite justice*. New Delhi: Penguin.

Rubin, J. B. (2004). Psychoanalysis and Buddhism. In Uwe P. Gielen, Jefferson M. Fish, & Juris G. Draguns (Eds.), *Handbook of culture, therapy, and healing* (pp. 253–276). Mahwah, NJ: Erlbaum.

Russell, B. (1912). *Problems of philosophy.* London: Oxford University Press.

Russell, B. (1946/1961). *History of western philosophy.* London: Allen & Unwin.

Russell, B. (1961). *Religion and science.* Oxford: Oxford University Press.

Sachdev, D. (1992). *Effects of psychocultural factors on the socialisation of British-born Indian children and indigenous British children living in England.* Unpublished doctoral dissertation, South Bank University, London.

Sampson, E. E. (1977). Psychology and the American ideal. *Journal of Personality and Social Psychology, 15,* 189–194.

Sarbin, T. R. (1986). Emotion and act: Roles and rhetoric. In R. Harre (Ed.), *The social construction of emotions.* Oxford: Blackwell.

Sartre, J. P. (1956). *Being and nothingness.* New York: Philosophical Library.

Sartre, J. P. (1966). *Being and nothingness: A phenomenological essay on ontology.* New York: Washington Square.

Satyavathi, K. (1988). Mental health. In J. Pamdey (Ed.), *Psychology in India: The state-of-the-art,* Vol. III Organizational behaviour and mental health (pp. 217–288). New Delhi: Sage.

Schachter, S. (1959). *The psychology of affiliation.* Stanford, CA: Stanford University Press.

Schwartz, S. H. (1990). Individualism–collectivism: Critique and proposed refinements. *Journal of Cross-cultural Psychology, 21*(2), 139–157.

Sechrest, L. (1977). On the need for experimentation in cross-cultural research. In L. L. Adler (Ed.), *Issues in cross-cultural research* (pp. 104–118). New York: Annals of the New York Academy of Sciences.

Segall, M. H. (1979). *Cross-cultural psychology: Human behaviour in global perspective.* Belmont, CA: Wadsworth.

Segall, M. H., Dasen, P. R., Berry, J. W., & Poortinga, Y. H. (1999). *Human behaviour in global perspective: An introduction to cross-cultural psychology* (2nd ed.). Boston, MA: Allyn & Bacon.

Segall, M. H., Lonner, W. J., & Berry, J. W. (1998). Cross-cultural psychology as a scholarly discipline: On the flowering of culture in behavioural research. *American Psychologist, 53,* 1101–1110.

Seligman, M. (1975). *Helplessness: On depression, development, and death.* San Francisco, CA: Freeman.

Seligman, M. (1991). *Learned optimism.* New York: Knopf.

Seligman, M. (1993). *What you can change and what you can't: The complete guide to successful self-improvement.* New York: Knopf.

Seligman, M. E. P., Klein, D. C., & Miller, W. (1974). Depression. In H. Leitenberg (Ed.), *Handbook of behaviour therapy.* Englewood Cliffs, NJ: Prentice Hall.

Semin, G. R. (1995). Interfacing language and social cognition. *Journal of Language and Social psychology, 14,* 182–194.

Sen, A. (2000). *Development as freedom.* New Delhi: Oxford University Press.

Sethi, B. B., & Manchanda, R. (1978). Family structure and psychiatric disorders. *Indian Journal of Psychiatry, 20,* 283–288.

Shallice, T. (1972). The Ulster depth interrogation techniques and their relation to sensory deprivation research. *Cognition, 1,* 385–405.

Sharma, A. (2001). *Classical Hindu thought: An introduction.* New Delhi: Oxford University Press.

Shweder, R. A. (1991a). Cultural psychology: What is it? In R. A. Shweder (Ed.), *Thinking through cultures* (pp. 73–110). Cambridge, MA: Harvard University Press.

Shweder, R. A. (1991b). *Thinking through cultures: Expeditions in cultural psychology.* Cambridge, MA: Harvard University Press.

Shweder, R. A. (2000). Moral maps, 'first world' conceits, and the new evangelists. In Lawrence E. Harrison & Samuel P. Huntington (Eds.), *Culture matters: How values shape human progress* (pp. 158–176). New York: Basic Books.

Shweder, R. A., & Sullivan, M. A. (1993). Cultural psychology: Who needs it? *Annual Review of Psychology, 44,* 497–527.

Silverman, I. (1977). *The human subject in the psychological laboratory.* New York: Pergamon.

Silverstein, L. B., & Aurbach, C. F. (2005). (Post) modern families. In J. L. Roopnarine & U. P. Gielen (Eds.), *Families in global perspective* (pp. 33–48). Boston, MA: Pearson Education.

Simonton, D. K. (1999). *Origins of genius: Darwinian perspectives on creativity.* New York: Oxford University Press.

Sinari, R. A. (1984). *The structure of Indian thought.* Delhi: Oxford University Press.

Singer, M. A. (1961). A survey of personality theory and research. In B. Kaplan (Ed.), *Studying personality cross-culturally.* Evanston, IL: Row, Peterson.

Sinha, D. (1993). Indigenization of psychology in India and its relevance. In U. Kim & J. W. Berry (Eds.), *Indigenous psychologies: Research and experience in cultural context* (pp. 30–43). Thousand Oaks, CA: Sage.

Sinha, D., & Kao, H. S. R. (1997). The journey to the East: An introduction. In H. S. R. Kao & D. Sinha (Eds.), *Asian perspectives on psychology,* Vol. 19 Cross-cultural research and methodology series (pp. 9–22). New Delhi: Sage.

Sinha, D., Mishra, R. C., & Berry, J. W. (1996). Some eco-cultural and acculturational factors in intermodal perception. In J. Pandey, D. Sinha, & D. P. S. Bhawuk (Eds.), *Asian contributions to cross-cultural psychology* (pp. 151–164). New Delhi: Sage.

Sjoberg, G. (1967). *Ethics, politics and social research.* Cambridge, MA: Schenman.

Sklar, F. (1991/1992). Grief as a family affair: Property rights, grief rights, and the exclusion of close friends as survivors. *Omega, 24*(2), 109–121.

Smart, N. (1996). *World philosophies.* London/New York: Routledge.

Smith, D. P. (2005). The sweat lodge as psychotherapy: Congruence between traditional and modern healing. In R., Moodley & W. S. West (Eds.), *Integrating traditional healing practices into counselling and psychotherapy* (pp. 196–209). Thousand Oaks, CA: Sage.

Smith, H. I. (in press). Ritual: Making special – the right of every griever. In John D. Morgan & Pittu Laungani (Eds.), *Death and bereavement around the world,* Vol. 5. New York: Baywood.

Smith, P. B., & Bond, M. H. (1993). *Social psychology across cultures: Analysis and perspectives.* Hemel Hempstead: Harvester Wheatsheaf.

Sookhoo, D. (1995, August). *A comparative study of the health beliefs and health practices of British whites and Asian adults with and without mycardial infarction.* Paper read at the 53rd Annual Convention of the International Council of Psychologists, Taipei, Taiwan.

Spence, J. T. (1985). Achievement American style: The rewards and costs of individualism. *American Psychologist, 40,* 1285–1295.

Squadrito, K. (2002). Locke and the dispossession of the American Indian. In Julie K. Ward & Tommy L. Lott (Eds.), *Philosophers on race: Critical essays* (pp. 101–124). London: Blackwell.

Srinivasa, D. K., & Trivedi, S. (1982). Knowledge and attitude of mental diseases in a rural community of South India. *Social Science and Medicine, 16,* 1635–1639.

Stiglitz, J. (2002). *Globalisation and its discontents.* London: Allen Lane.

Sullivan, D. S., & Deiker, T. E. (1973). Subject–experimenter perceptions of ethical issues in human research. *American Psychologist, 28,* 587–591.

Tanaka-Matsumi, J., & Draguns, J. G. (1997). Culture and psychopathology. In John W. Berry, Marshall H. Segall, & Cigdem Kagitcibasi (Eds.), *Handbook of cross-cultural psychology,* Vol. 3 (pp. 449–441). Needham Heights, MA: Allyn & Bacon.

Tapp, J. L., Kelman, H. C., Triandis, H. C., Wrightsman, L. S., & Coelho, G. V. (1974). Continuing concerns in cross-cultural ethics: A report. *International Journal of Psychology, 9*, 231–249.

Taylor, D. M., & Moghaddam, F. M. (1987). *Theories of intergroup relations: International social psychological perspectives.* New York: Praeger.

Taylor, S. E. (1989). *Positive illusions: Creative self-deception and the healthy mind.* New York: Basic Books.

Thomson (2005). *The watch on the heath: Science and religion before Darwin.* London: HarperCollins.

Tillich, P. (1961). The meaning of health. *Perspectives in Biological Medicine, 5*(1), 92–100.

Trefil, J. (1980). *From atoms to quarks: An introduction to the strange world of particle physics.* London: Althone.

Triandis, H. C. (1972). *The analysis of subjective cultures.* New York: Wiley.

Triandis, H. C. (1980). Introduction. In H. C. Triandis & J. W. Berry (Eds.), *Handbook of Cross-cultural Psychology,* Vol. 2. Boston, MA: Allyn & Bacon.

Triandis, H. C. (1986). Collectivism vs. individualism: A reconceptualization of a basic concept in cross-cultural psychology. In C. Bagley & G. Verma (Eds.), *Personality, cognition, and values* (pp. 57–89) New York: Macmillan.

Triandis, H. C. (1994). *Culture and social behavior.* New York: McGraw-Hill.

Triandis, H. C., & Vassiliou, V. (1967). Frequency of contact and stereotyping. *Journal of Personality and Social Psychology, 7,* 316–328.

Trost, J. (1996). Family structure and relationships: The dyadic approach. *Journal of Comparative Family Studies, 27*(2), 395–408.

Tully, M. (1995). *The heart of India.* London: Viking.

Tyler, S. A. (1969). *Cognitive anthropology.* New York: Holt, Rinehart & Winston.

United Nations. (1992). *Family: challenges for the future.* New York: Author.

United Nations. (1996). *Families: Victims of poverty and homelessness.* New York: Author.

Vahia, N. S. (1982). Yoga in psychiatry. In A. Kiev & A. V. Rao (Eds.), *Readings in transcultural psychiatry* (pp. 11–19). Madras: Higginbothams.

Valsiner, J. (1989). *Human development and culture.* Toronto: Lexington.

Valsiner, J. (2000). *Culture and human development.* Thousand Oaks, CA: Sage.

Vassiliou, V. G., & Vassiliou, G. (1973). The implicative meaning of the Greek concept of philotimo. *Journal of Cross-cultural Psychology, 4,* 326–341.

Vijver, F. V. D., & Leung, K. (1997). Methods and data analysis of comparative research. In J. W. Berry, Y. H. Poortinga, & J. Pandey (Eds.), *Handbook of cross-cultural psychology,* Vol. 1 *Theory and method* (pp. 257–300). Boston, MA: Allyn & Bacon.

Vine, I. (1982). Crowding and stress: A personal space approach. *Psychological Review, 2*(1), 1–18.

von Furer-Haimendorf, C. (1974). The sense of sin in cross-cultural perspective. *Man, 9,* 539–556.

Walter, T. (1997). Secularization. In C. M. Parkes, P. Laungani, & W. Young (Eds.), *Death and bereavement across cultures* (pp. 166–190). London: Routledge.

Wambach, H. (1978). *Reliving past lives.* New York: HarperCollins.

Ward, C. A., & Kennedy, A. (1996a). Crossing cultures: The relationship between psychological and socio-cultural dimensions of cross-cultural adjustment. In J. Pandey, D. Sinha, & D. P. S. Bhawuk (Eds.), *Asian contributions to cross-cultural psychology* (pp. 289–306). New Delhi: Sage.

Ward, C. A., & Kennedy, A. (1996b). Psychological and socio-cultural adjustment during cross-cultural transitions: A comparison of secondary students overseas and at home. *International Journal of Psychology, 28,* 129–147.

Ward, J. K., & Lott, T. L. (Eds.). (2002). *Philosophers on race: Critical essays.* London: Blackwell.

Warwick, D. P. (1980). The politics and ethics of cross-cultural research. In H. C. Triandis (Ed.), *Handbook of cross-cultural psychology,* Vol. 1. New York: Allyn & Bacon.

Waterman, A. A. (1981). Individualism and interdependence. *American Psychologist, 36,* 762–773.

Webb, S. D. (1978). Privacy and psychosomatic stress: An empirical analysis. *Social Behaviour and Personality, 6,* 227–234.

Wei-Ming T. (1985). *Confucian thought: Selfhood as creative transformation.* Albany, NY: State University of New York Press.

Wescott, R. W. (1970). Of guilt and gratitude: Further reflections on human uniqueness. *The Dialogist: A Journal of Dialogue in Theory and Practice, 2*(3), 69–85.

West, W. (2004). Pittu Laungani in conversation with William West. *British Journal of Guidance and Counselling, 32*(3), 419–435. Reprinted in U.P. Gielen (Ed.), *Conversations with international psychologists* available online at www.iiccp.freeservers.com.

White, L. A. (1947). Cultural versus psychological interpretations of human behaviour. *American Sociological Review, 12,* 686–689.

Whiting, B. B. (1963). *Six cultures: Studies of child rearing.* Cambridge, MA: Harvard University Press.

Whiting, J. W. M. (1968). Methods and problems in cross-cultural research. In G. Lindzey, & E. Aronson (Eds.), *Handbook of social psychology,* Vol. 2 (pp. 693–728). Cambridge, MA: Addison-Wesley.

WHO (1984). *World Health,* July.

Williams, B. (1985). *Ethics and the limits of philosophy.* Cambridge, MA: Harvard University Press.

Wolman, B. (Ed.) (1977). *Handbook of parapsychology.* New York: Van Nostrand.

Woodworth, R. S. (1910). Racial differences in mental traits. *Science, 31,* 171–186.

World Bank. (2000). *Global economic prospects and the developing countries.* Washington, DC: Author.

Wright, R. (1940/1972). *Native Son.* Harmondsworth: Penguin.

Yang, K-S. (1997). Theories and research in Chinese personality: An indigenous approach. In H. S. R. Kao & D. Sinha (Eds.), *Asian perspectives on psychology* (pp. 236–262). New Delhi: Sage.

Zaehner, R. C. (1962). *Hinduism.* Toronto: Oxford University Press.

Zaehner, R. C. (1966a). *Hinduism.* New Delhi: Oxford University Press.

Zaehner, R. C. (1966b). *Hindu scriptures.* London: Dent.

Zaman, R. M. (1992). Psychotherapy in the third world: Some impressions from Pakistan. In Uwe P. Gielen, Leonore Loeb Adler, & Noorman A. Mulgram (Eds.), *Psychology in international perspective.* Amsterdam: Swets and Zeitlinger.

Zilbergeld, B. (1983). *The shrinking of America: Myths of psychological change.* Boston, MA: Little, Brown.

Zimbardo, P. C., Haney, C., & Banks, W. C. (1973). A Pirandellian prison. *The New York Times Magazine,* 8 April.

Zimmer, H. (1951/1989). *Philosophies of India.* Bollinger Series XXVI. Princeton, NJ: Princeton University Press.

Author Index

Subject Index

NOTE: page numbers in *italic type* refer to tables.